Presence

Presence

The
Strange Science
and
True Stories of
the Unseen Other

Ben Alderson-Day

ST. MARTIN'S PRESS
NEW YORK

First published in the United States by St. Martin's Press, an imprint of St. Martin's Publishing Group

www.stmartins.com

The Library of Congress Cataloging-in-Publication Data is available upon request.

ISBN 978-1-250-27825-8 (hardcover)
ISBN 978-1-250-27826-5 (ebook)

First Edition: 2023

10 9 8 7 6 5 4 3 2 1

For Annabelle

CONTENTS

Contents

A young man steps through a gate. He feels a shiver pass down his spine.

The hairs on his skin stand up, all the way from his hand, past his shoulder, to under his chin. He dare not look back.

A woman wakes from a dream, and peers toward the bedroom curtain.

A door creaks somewhere in the house.

She feels it. There is something in the corner.

It is waiting for her, watching.

In a small, terraced house, an old man waits for the kettle. Two cups in front of him. The visitor is here again, he doesn't know why or what for.

He can't remember how he takes his tea, or how long he will be here.

Preface

What is there?

Most of us are used to the idea of having five senses. Five ways of encountering the world around us, five ways of perceiving, learning, and discovering. Some people's senses may change gradually over time, and for others they might change overnight. Some may be born without hearing or vision, while others may experience their senses in unusual combinations—for a person with synesthesia, words might have colors, or sounds might have smells. But for most of us, most of the time, the five senses define our world.

Our perception of the world has a close ally in imagination. Some people can imagine pictures and sounds so vivid that it feels as if they are really happening. A friend's laugh could ring out just like they were standing in front of you. Mountains might spring from the sands of the mind before scattering away just as quickly in the wind. But the inner land of imagery feels quite different from the world of sensation and perception. Usually we get to choose what we experience in the mind's eye; we are the director, the sculptor, the architect. In contrast, the world is just there, present to us, whatever we might imagine it to be. It has immediacy, concreteness—a reliability, even. We feel it and know it immediately; we can hear it, see it, and touch it. And when we look away, it will still be there.

The senses rely on stimulation, although the connection between the outside world and what we experience is not always straightforward. When we encounter illusions, something is out there in the world, but our perception is of something else. In the case of hallucinations, we have a sensory experience, but without that original prompt—without there being something out there for us to even misperceive.

What happens, though, when we get that feeling *without* the five senses? What happens when we feel that something—or someone—is present to us, and yet we can't say how? A silent figure. A visitor. An indefinable change in the feeling of a room. Something is there, unmistakably so. And try as we might, if someone asks how we know, we cannot explain it.

We just know it. We just feel it.

This is a felt presence.

A voice without sound, a vision that cannot be seen. Just the direct apprehension of something in the space around you. It is often a person, but it might not be. It could be an animal, it could be a spirit. It could be something altogether more unnerving. Its presence is the only thing you can know about it.

The concept of presence has fascinated scholars of philosophy, history, anthropology, and religion for hundreds of years. But my own discipline—psychology—has presence in its bones. What we can sense beyond ourselves was a question that occupied some of the very first theorists and scientists seeking to build a science of the mind. Writing in 1904, the American psychologist and philosopher William James described the experience like this:

It is as if there were in the human consciousness a *sense of reality, a feeling of objective presence, a perception* of what we may call "*something there*," more deep and more general than any of the special and particular "senses" by which the current psychology supposes existent realities to be originally revealed. . . . It often happens that an hallucination is imperfectly developed: the person affected will feel a "presence" in the room, definitely localized, facing in one particular way, real in the most emphatic sense of the word, often coming suddenly, and as suddenly gone; and yet neither seen, heard, touched, nor cognized in any of the usual "sensible" ways.[1]

James was writing about a feeling that had been described to him on more than one occasion, including by a friend who had had several experiences:

It was about September, 1884, when I had the first experience. On the previous night I had had, after getting into bed at my rooms in College, a vivid tactile hallucination of being grasped by the arm, which made me get up and search the room for an intruder; but the sense of presence properly so called came on the next night. After I had got into bed and blown out the candle, I lay awake awhile thinking on the previous night's experience, when suddenly I *felt* something come into the room and stay close to my bed. It remained only a minute or two. I did not recognize it by any ordinary sense and yet there was a horribly unpleasant "sensation" connected with it. It stirred something more at the roots of my being than any ordinary perception.[2]

The kinds of sensations that James's friend described are vividly representative of many accounts of felt presence. This is an experience that goes beyond the senses, bringing forth strong and unusual emotions. When it happens to people, it seems to challenge many of their assumptions about how minds, bodies, and the world are supposed to work.

This book is an attempt to understand what presence is. It begins with a conversation about psychosis, and a voice that can be there without speaking. From there, we will encounter epilepsy, sleepwalking, and imaginary friends, and meet robots, psychics, and ethereal spirits. We will hear of playwrights sent mad by mercury, nighttime visitors who can literally scare people to death, and a figure who could stop your heart with a touch.

If there is a central thesis to the book, it is this. Understanding an experience like felt presence—what it is, why it happens, and who it happens to—requires us to cast the net wide, comparing stories of presence from close to home and further afield, across oceans and mountains, and from early life to old age. Faced with little more than a shadow—a mirage of mind and body—we have to approach our subject from as many angles as possible. In doing so, we will find out more about ourselves than anything else. Presences tell us who we are, what we value, and how we respond to adversity. The story of presence is truly a story about the self.

* * *

I AM A psychologist, so I start from the perspective that experiences like felt presence are a product of mind and brain. Lots of books on the brain will promise an astonishing new theory or a revolutionary model that will tell you how the mind works. This is not that book. This is not that book because it cannot be. In my experience of working in psychology and neuroscience, the certainty of such astonishing theories is very, very hard to come by. Things move slowly, experiments give clues but rarely full answers. Explanations are offered tentatively, and they are always awaiting further evidence. The default position in research is not certainty but its opposite. Uncertainty, indeterminacy, and questions leading to more questions.

That kind of uncertainty is true for ordinary aspects of human experience—but it is especially the case for felt presence. It is no mistake that when people describe this phenomenon, they might talk of a "sixth sense," as if we are in the realm of something supernatural. Seeing apparitions, reading thoughts, having eyes in the back of your head—all these experiences are not presence, and yet they cannot be divorced from the uncanny encounters that people describe. Felt presence is a topic that tests the limits of what we can explain. And as we will see, it often appears to ride roughshod over scientific theories and evidence.

Because of that, the language of this book is a compromise. Everyone's subjective experience is unique to them, each person has their own explanation and interpretation, and they may never have shared it with anyone—indeed, many of the people in this book have never told their stories before. Felt presences are often transformative in the personal impact they have. Here I have aimed to listen to people and understand their experience while conveying it to others in language that makes sense.

However, doing so also involves using terms that some people may not recognize or find acceptable. Concepts like psychosis or schizophrenia can be problematic for some, and even using a term like *hallucination* has its pitfalls. Calling someone's experience a hallucination might feel undermining or pathologizing; it might seem to deny how real their experiences feel to them.

I do use that term here. It isn't used lightly, but it is necessary—because felt presence is an experience that almost defies description. When people have spoken to me about the feeling, they stumble, their words grinding to a halt in the face of something beyond their understanding. *Hallucination* is just one term that has been applied to the experience, and in some contexts, it is still the best term we have. The concept of hallucination offers us a way into the labyrinth, a first step toward the presence at its core.

It is time to see what is there.

In a hospital cubicle, the "family" sit and wait off to his side. He receives the news with little emotion, but he knows their reaction. It is little comfort, but at least they are here. The man, the woman, the girl, the boy—he wonders how far their line goes.

A winter lodge. A silver-haired woman sees the movement out of the corner of her eye. He is probably shifting to get closer to the fire.

    The room is warm all around—it always is when he is here.

At the bottom of the world, a bearded man stands up from his sledge, the skin on his face blistered and burnt.

    He listens and waits, then sets off again.

    One ahead, one behind. And him.

Part 1

Phantom Others

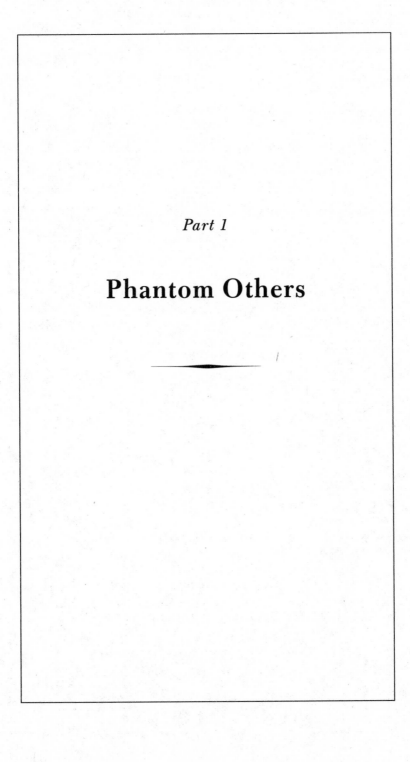

1

A Thickness in the Air

The interview is drawing to an end. We have been talking for over an hour. I look up from my notes at the young man across from me.

"Before we finish, is there anything you want to describe that we're missing? Anything we haven't talked about but should?" I ask.

"There's nothing, really, I don't think. I think we've covered it all," he replies. "I mean, apart from the presence thing."

"The presence thing . . ." I answer, looking back and down at my notes again. He takes a few seconds before continuing.

"Yeah, like when they are there, I can feel them there. The voices."

"What—even when they're not talking?" I ask.

"Yeah, just *there*, right next to you. Like someone is standing be-hind you, looking over your shoulder."

Alex hears four voices that other people cannot hear. He has heard voices for as long as he can remember. They talk to him every day. That's what our interview is about: how often he hears voices, what they sound like, and how they make him feel. Of all Alex's voices, one talks nearly constantly. It shouts, it cajoles, it criticizes, and it threatens; it is an in-cessant menace in his life. The first time I met Alex to do an interview—nearly three years prior—I asked him at one point what that voice was saying, right at that moment. It was telling him to throw some pens at me (he didn't). I think I got off lightly.

The voice Alex hears nearly constantly is positioned very close to him, he explains. Just off to the right, behind his ear. "You know when it feels like someone is watching you? Like that," he says. I try to imagine what that must be like. A set of voices with you all the time. Commenting on everything you do, questioning your actions, your decisions—even your thoughts themselves. The previous week, someone else had told me her voices were like "a proper little mackem[1] gang, talking about you all the time." She felt like they were constantly waiting near her house, plotting.

"If they are speaking most of the time, are you just getting used to them being there?" I suggest. "Like you expect them to say something, even when you aren't hearing them?"

"Well, yeah, but it's not just that," says Alex. He pauses, thinking of the best way to help me understand. "In the morning when I wake up, it's like I have a brief moment of peace, and then they make me jump, and I remember they are there," he says.

"And how does that make you feel?"

"It's horrible, really." He shudders. "I mean, I know some of them are OK. But you still don't want them around all the time. It's just . . . *creepy.*"

This is the third time I have interviewed Alex. He is taking part in a research study that we are running with the National Health Service (NHS), trying to understand more about "voices" and how they might change over time, for the people who hear them. By *voices*, I mean auditory verbal hallucinations—hearing things that no one else can hear, an experience that most people would usually associate with schizophrenia. Roughly 75 percent of people with a diagnosis of schizophrenia report auditory hallucinations, and between 5 and 15 percent of adults will also hear voices at some point in their lives.[2] The latter statistic can be a surprise, but once you start asking people about unusual experiences they might have had—a shout of their name, a vision in the night, a weird, premonition-like dream—many of them can describe at least something like that, and some have encountered these occurrences more than once. When people tell you about them, they often do so quietly and cautiously. Some are just pleased to know they aren't the only one.

Not everybody hears the kind of voices that Alex does. He's using early intervention in psychosis (EIP) services, the frontline NHS pathway that people access when they first start to show frequent signs of psychosis. Psychosis involves a break from reality. Distinguishing the real and unreal becomes challenging, even impossible, while feelings of distress and confusion spiral and multiply. People experiencing psychosis might have hallucinations involving sounds, smells, visions, or any of the senses. Their thinking might change as well: they might hole themselves up in their home or apartment for fear of a plot to kidnap them; they might think someone has implanted something in their brain, or they might think the world around them is transformed somehow. Strong unusual beliefs in this vein are often referred to as *delusions*, and it is very common to see them accompanying hallucinations when someone is in a state of psychosis. All the participants in the research study are using EIP to help them with their experiences. They don't all have a diagnosis of schizophrenia—and in fact, many don't at this stage. Psychosis can happen for lots of reasons. It can occur in people with conditions like bipolar disorder, depression, anxiety, and post-traumatic stress disorder, and it can be prompted by drugs or alcohol, or severe stress and sleep deprivation.

The first time I met Alex, he was still getting his head around the idea that he was hearing voices. Many people don't realize initially that others can't hear the voices; for young people in particular, if it has been happening for a while, it might take a long time before they realize that other people don't hear the voices too. Alex is in his early twenties, and when I ask him, he thinks this has been happening since at least primary school. He says it started with two voices—a man's and a woman's. Then it became four voices, but he finds it hard to remember specifically when that happened. He can't recall exactly when he realized he was hearing voices; it began to dawn on him the year before we first spoke, or the year before that. He then told his parents, and they were concerned. They got him to talk to his general practitioner (GP), then a crisis team, then the people from EIP services.

We meet in an old mental health hospital that looks alarmingly gothic and strange—literally the last place you would want to go if you were in distress. Many of the older NHS buildings have been sold off now for flats, but this one has survived for some reason. Inside, the surroundings are more modern and clinical, but unsettling in a different way. It is all cleaning fluid and rounded edges: no door handles in sight, with each room looking like the inside of a 1980s *Star Trek* spaceship but with unfinished furnishings. Alex isn't an inpatient here, it's just where we could get a room for the research study. This is true of most of our participants. Although their experiences are distressing, they generally manage them at home and in the community. They would only have been admitted to an inpatient ward if and when they were acutely unwell and couldn't manage outside.

There are a lot of stereotypes about what it's like to hear voices, and that can make people reluctant to talk. No one wants to be labeled as crazy or dangerous. The person most likely to ask about voices would usually be a clinician of some kind, who then decides what pathway the patient should proceed to (i.e., what services they are offered), what (if any) medication should be prescribed, or whether to start a process of therapy. It might be important to assess for the risk of things like self-harm or suicide. And if time is limited or the connection isn't there, some questions may get missed in favor of others.

Because our interviews are for research, I have the luxury of time when I see people like Alex. We let people talk as much or as little as they need to, and we tend to ask more questions about the immediate subjective experience of voices—what is sometimes referred to as their *phenomenology*. I'm not a clinician—I'm a researcher and a lecturer, trained in psychology, but not someone qualified to deliver therapy or prescribe drugs. I'm just there to try to understand more about what the experience is like.

The second time I talk to Alex, we discuss some of the differences between his voices. There are still four, but only two really speak. One is an angry, dominant male voice—this is the one that talks almost constantly, and he sounds middle-aged. The other is a woman, just a little older than Alex, who seems to be more supportive. She will often argue with the male voice, and she might defend Alex against taunts and accusations. But she can also be manipulative, he says—it's hard to know sometimes what she is after. For Alex, the voices can say one thing and mean another; they can be sarcastic, or disingenuous— despite the fact that their words are all they are, ultimately. When I ask if these voices remind him of anyone he knows, Alex shrugs. He's thought about this question a number of times with his therapist, tried out different people for size, tried to fit words to faces. But the voices don't track his past and the people in it, not quite. If they are people he knows, they have gone through a deep and elaborate trans- formation, as if they have passed through a hall of mirrors.

The other thing we talk about in our second interview is the bigger picture—what else might be going on for Alex. We've kept the focus on voices so far, but it's important to consider what other things might be occurring for someone in this situation. When people start hearing voices, they might reach for explanations about what is happening. How can voices come from walls or comment on thoughts? Neigh- bors, technology, spies, even spirits—all become plausible candidates. Voices change the lens through which people view reality; they (some- times literally) announce an essential shift in the universe. Each time they speak, they act as a reminder that they are here now, with you, and the world that you thought existed doesn't anymore. They might warn you against attempting to explain it to others; they say it will fall flat or cause alarm. Better keep this new world to yourself.

And that world has gaps; things you still can't explain. In those gaps—answering that uncertainty—develop new ideas that provide a better fit for the frame. You might become convinced that the voices might be right and they know things that you don't. Or some of your other suspicions might feel right, and you search the house for bugs and hidden cameras. Maybe neither of those things feels quite right—but *you* feel different somehow, you are special. Not necessarily in a big way (there are fewer messiahs in an EIP clinic than one might think), but in a quiet, subtle way, as if your center of mass is slightly off balance, pulling you forward, an uneasy suggestion of impulse and momentum. The voices are here for you—and you have been chosen.

The second time we meet, Alex tries to describe a feeling of that kind. It comes at the end of the interview, and it is clearly something he is hesitant about sharing. Even after all the talk of disembodied voices, this is somehow more personal—something that perhaps makes him more vulnerable to misinterpretation. Maybe he thinks it makes him sound even crazier.

What he describes is a feeling that, over and above everything else, someone or something is pulling the strings. Someone is organizing everything in his life, sending the voices to answer some sort of transgression. Their purpose is orchestrated, being part of some grand plan or design. And Alex is, if not quite at ease with it, accepting of the idea. It provides comfort: at least someone is in control.

When we talk for the third time, Alex's voices haven't changed that much, although the angry man is quieter now and further away. He used to "check in" with the female voice from time to time, but he doesn't much anymore. When I ask Alex, he is feeling much more in control of what is going on—something he puts down to working closely with his therapist, a clinical psychologist in the local NHS trust.

But it's the feeling of presence that we end up talking about. The end of his third and final interview in the study, the topic of a voice that can be felt but not heard comes up. He had mentioned it in passing earlier, but he didn't elaborate. Secretly I am relieved when he returns to it at the end of the interview—I wanted to understand it properly (or at least a little better). The exchange we have makes me more curious, though. A voice without sound; a presence alone.

"The best way I can describe it is goosebumps—you feel it up the back of your neck," says Alex. "I don't even try to describe it in therapy, it's just so weird. That was the bit that I thought no one had. Like, you learn about how lots of people hear voices, and that's helpful—but this just seemed bizarre. I don't even know really how to describe it."

He shakes his head as he says this. How do you describe a voice that isn't heard, a presence that is only felt? Alex had tried—but it was clear that he wasn't satisfied with his description.

This was not a comfortable familiarity for Alex; the voices being around was not like the welcome presence of a childhood friend or the regular appearance of a neighbor. It sounded more like a haunting of some kind; an unruly spirit that had latched on to Alex's person. I wondered whether Alex's presences would stay like that forever. If a voice just sticks around, even when it has mostly stopped speaking, will it always just feel like someone is there? As if someone is constantly reading over your shoulder, or standing too close?

This was where we ended up; this was the last thing he tried to talk about amid everything else going on. We had gone from voices to grand plans to presence. This last feeling was the hardest, weirdest, most unsettling thing. This, of all things, was where the words just stopped.

As it happens, I had heard someone describe it before.

Daniel

The seminar room is light and airy. People bustle in and say hello to one another; some people clearly know each other already, others are quieter and wait to be spoken to. I am one of the latter, and I take a seat with my back to the wall, near the door. Across from me sits a young man with a neat beard and spiky hair. His arms are powerful and toned, and he sits forward in his chair as if ready to spring, his balance already on the balls of his feet. Like me, he's not really talking to anyone yet, bar the odd smile and hello, and a question here and there.

I'm not talking much because I am new here. I am a postdoctoral researcher—the bit of an academic's career immediately following a

PhD but before moving on to a permanent role, like a lecturer. My PhD had been on autism, and I became interested in language and the mind—how we talk to ourselves, and how that might affect our thinking and our mental health. Through that I came to learn about a new project at Durham University—Hearing the Voice—an initiative funded by the Wellcome Trust to further the understanding of auditory hallucinations. The project caught my eye because it planned to do this research in an unconventional way, drawing upon ideas and study from lots of different areas—so not just psychologists or psychiatrists doing the work but also philosophy and religious studies scholars, for example. I had studied a bit of philosophy as a student, and I was keen to see how this would work in practice.

Once we sit down, the first thing I notice is the lack of mixing. Like on a school playground, the safety of a preexisting tribe is hard to ignore, and we cluster in that room in rough groupings of disciplines—a literary studies corner, a couple of philosophers, the historian sat next to the medievalist. And, on his own, the young man opposite me.

"Thank you and welcome, everyone," says the facilitator, standing at the front. "We won't go around to everyone, but I would just like to welcome Daniel to the session today. Daniel is joining us from the Recovery College. Welcome, Daniel."

The team acknowledges the visitor with a mixture of smiles, nods, and mumbled hellos. The Recovery College is an education center in a town nearby for people who are struggling with their mental health. Daniel is here with us because he's a voice-hearer, the term many people prefer to use when they hear voices for a long period of time. Daniel has been asked to take part in the seminar not as a speaker but as a participant; another academic is presenting that day. Daniel, though, is very engaging and open—chipping in with questions and observations from the start and fielding any number of awkward enquiries from us. Before long, the session has become a Q&A, with Daniel holding court.

The topic of voices is one that invites a number of interpretations. Across epochs and cultures, it is the kind of experience that wouldn't always have been considered a symptom of illness but maybe instead a sign of inspiration, or revelation. As recently as the early twentieth century, attitudes toward unusual and hallucinatory experience could be much more mixed than the largely pathological lens that we view things through today. How we think about unusual experiences is shaped by the times we live in, so we have to try to think about it from more than one point of view. Even the more recent history of hearing voices is a mishmash of psychiatry, psychotherapy, neuroscience, and philosophy.

For quite a few people in the seminar room that day, it is the first time they have met someone who hears voices. Everyone has different questions. Does Daniel know when the voices are about to speak? Surely there would be some sort of stirring or change in the world, something that marked their arrival? Does Daniel's voice feel like a character in a book? Can he picture him? What is his backstory?

I say "voice," singular, because Daniel is clear that he hears one main voice; a military-style male voice that comments on his daily thoughts and activities. Daniel is not long out of the forces himself, and his experiences have gotten worse following his time in the military. I would later learn that he always sits with a view of the door, like he had that day. Daniel can picture this voice in his mind's eye. He isn't sure if there has always been an image, or whether that is something he has come to know; a figure emerging from the commands and barks in his head. The voice looks out for him, he says; but it also criticizes and mocks him, sometimes mercilessly. He has been around so long that Daniel describes his own thoughts intertwining with the voice at times. It can be hard to know who has said and who has thought what.

Daniel's a natural talker. We have been going for half an hour, maybe longer, and I can see the facilitator is keen to move on. I wonder about whether Daniel needs a break, and whether we should be bombarding him in this way. Well-meaning curiosity can go too far, and Daniel's not here to be a subject of research. My thoughts are interrupted then by something Daniel has just said.

> You know, sometimes you don't even have to hear him—sometimes you just know he's there.

Just there. What does that mean? No sound, no vision—just there. Daniel can describe what he thinks his voice looks like—in full military garb—but he doesn't mean he pictures the voice there. He means something more basic, something indivisible. A voice that is there, and there alone.

The scholars around the room lean in for clarification. New questions come in, and Daniel fields each with politeness and patience, sometimes with just a shrug. It feels important—the shift in focus, the change of parameters. It feels as if our topic—voices—is a mere cardboard cutout, or a building front on a film set, with the real experience somewhere behind, in the shadows. It's one thing to hear a voice and imagine what the person looks like, or listen for a voice that you expect to speak. But a voice, or rather, an *identity*, that can just be felt—not heard, not imagined—seems like something very different entirely.

* * *

WHAT DID THEY mean, Alex and Daniel? Since that day in the seminar room, I have continued to wonder. I talked to more people who had heard voices and felt something similar. Some weren't quite as definitive: they might hear a voice and describe that as somehow having a real presence itself. It was as if the voice heralded the arrival of someone, in a way that felt almost impossible to ignore, as it would if a person actually arrived in your company. In a study we ran with over 150 voice-hearers, one participant wrote: "I have never encountered anyone with as powerful a presence as my voices. They are loud and feel enormous. . . . They feel very much here when I hear them."[3] For some, their voices had bodies, or made their own body feel different: their presence was in their physicality, a tangible reverberation that signified that someone was close.

But for others, they were adamant: the voices could be there without speaking, a cloud of pure identity, hovering and amassing, threatening to sweep across and rain down new words.

I searched for comparable experiences and read what I could, trying to understand more but not getting much further. A colleague of mine asked, "Is that a thing, then, in psychology? Felt presence—is it a concept that gets used?" I shrugged sheepishly—not that I was aware of. I'd heard of a few similar things in very different contexts: survival stories, brain damage, that sort of thing. Nothing quite like this, though. It felt altogether too hard to grasp, too experiential. You could try to describe that kind of feeling, but how would you ever investigate it? It's not even clear we know how to define what *it* is. It felt like trying to catch a ghost on camera.

What Daniel had been talking to us about sounded a bit more like a delusion than a hallucination—in other words, a matter of belief and facts, not senses and perceptions. Hallucinations and delusions carve up the world of psychosis into perception and belief. Hallucinations rely on sensory content; by definition they involve perceiving something without a corresponding stimulus in the outside world (a sound, a touch, or a smell, for example). Delusions, by contrast, are the stuff of thoughts. They are usually *about* something in the world (what philosophers sometimes call "intentionality"), but they don't involve sensation.

The presence of Daniel's voice didn't seem to have any sensation attached. It didn't speak, and he didn't describe it touching him or appearing in his sight. Its sensory content was bare. In contrast, he said he "knew" the voice was there—it was something he was aware of, that he expected, that he believed about the world. He held it to be true that this voice, or entity, or whatever it might be, was accompanying him. In psychiatric terms, this notion of presence was merely delusional; thinking, not feeling, that someone was there.

A few months after our meeting with Daniel, a senior professor visits us, a psychologist who has worked in the field for a long time. He's not having a great day—his train is late, his accommodation booking doesn't quite work, and he isn't sure how long he can stay. He presents some of his new work, on stigma and beliefs about voices.

Afterward, some of us accompany the visitor to the pub. We try to describe the concept of presence, alongside other ideas, like voices feeling like characters or imaginary people. It felt like a question that had been overlooked: What might be experienced beyond the immediate properties of a voice? Are we missing something?

"Well, people come to believe lots of strange things about their voices," he says with a shrug, finishing his pint.

As he gets up to leave, I wonder if that's all it is. Maybe we are looking for something that isn't there—conceptually, I mean. Maybe we are reading too much into something that's just peripheral to what people are experiencing. Maybe we're just academics looking for something to justify our musings, but little else.

It didn't feel like that, though. It felt like an itch that needed to be scratched, a question that would keep arising. What else was there, with the voice? It was as if the idea itself was looming over us, unwilling to leave us be.

Keira

It's 2018. I'm finishing another interview, this time with Keira. She has a poetic way of talking about her voices, but she's struggling a lot as well. A successful interview brings up loads of new ideas and questions, but it can also feel intrusive, one-sided. I want to ask about presence, but I can't—it's the sort of thing that if you describe it, you might end up leading people to give the kinds of answers you want instead of truthful answers. Fortunately, it comes up after the interview is over. As I'm packing up, Keira asks me if it's just voices that I'm interested in. I clumsily try to describe the presence feeling. She doesn't hesitate.

"I know exactly what you mean, yeah. It's like a thickness in the air."

Inside I curse that I'd already turned off the recorder following the conclusion of the interview. I desperately want to ask her more, ask what she could see or feel—but our time is up, and we had already run over. Still, I feel pleased that she has recognized what I suggested. It is the opposite of the feeling the psychologist left me with. There is something there—something not being talked about.

A little over a year later, we are finishing the coding of interviews for the first year of the study; forty voice-hearers, all from EIP services, all describing their experiences in detail, for us. Over half report felt presences.[4]

Mice on the walls

Accounts of hallucinations and delusions can be found in some of the earliest clinical descriptions of what would now be called schizophrenia, although their prominence (as clinically important "symptoms" of disorder) has changed considerably over the past century. The term *schizophrenia* was coined by the Swiss psychiatrist Eugen Bleuler in 1908, but histories of the concept tend to begin with the work of his contemporary Emil Kraepelin, who first described a different kind of madness affecting younger people than that typically observed in old age. Kraepelin's name for the condition was "dementia praecox," denoting a degenerative condition of the mind occurring prematurely (i.e., in young adulthood). For Kraepelin, this dire prognosis and chronicity was what made the disorder distinct from other kinds of insanity, such as manic depression (today's bipolar disorder). It was a biologically driven disorder of the mind and brain, but not something primarily characterized by hallucination or delusion.[5]

Hallucinations were given a more prominent and influential role—along with delusions—in the work of Karl Jaspers and Kurt Schneider, two psychiatrists who drew upon ideas from existential philosophy in their study of schizophrenia. One of Jaspers's main contributions is the claim that the form of psychiatric symptoms is more important than their content, with the latter often being so bizarre as to be "un-understandable."[6] It's debatable what that means, but the typical interpretation is that the kinds of things people experience in psychosis are so unusual, so far from the logic of everyday life, that we are pursuing a lost cause interrogating their meaning. Instead, efforts should be focused on identifying which hallucinations and delusions someone might have rather than trying to understand their content, and this in turn could help to indicate what treatment they might need or the specific diagnosis they should receive. It was Schneider who placed hallucinations and delusions right at the heart of diagnosing schizophrenia, with the claim that specific forms of each make up the "first-rank" symptoms of the disorder.[7]

The distinction between hallucinations and delusions, and their prominence in psychosis, has stuck in clinical practice and research to the present day. Different treatments are increasingly being developed to target aspects of hallucinations and delusions respectively, including therapies that slow down reasoning and thinking to avoid jumping to paranoid and suspicious conclusions.[8] In practice, though, experience is an unruly customer. This is true of anyone's lived experience, whether they are in distress or deemed as having a form of psychosis. As long as the concepts of hallucination and delusion have been deployed, they have also been challenged and queried. Can we really cleave apart what we believe and what we perceive?

Some things that we see or hear might be so strongly shaped by what we expect that it can be hard to know what was experienced and what was simply thought or imagined. If we take UFO sightings, for example, the desire to believe will shape how people interpret what they see in ambiguous situations—it will perhaps even directly determine what is seen. Conversely, some of our strongest beliefs aren't so far from sensations or feelings. Our core beliefs are not like rational propositions that we entertain, as if they were abstract debating motions that we can pick up and put down at will. They are felt, at a gut level, often to a degree that we just know couldn't be any other way. Political beliefs, moral convictions, and taboos are all ideas, but nevertheless we might feel them with our body, with the whole of our being. When someone says "they just know" something but can't offer any evidence for it, the distinction between knowing and feeling is almost impossible to define. And between those concepts, into the cracks and fissures in our categories, a lot of things can fall and get lost—particularly those experiences that are the hardest to put into words.

Despite this, presences do feature in some of the earliest descriptions of psychosis—but they can be hard to tease apart from other unusual phenomena. Bleuler, for example, also described unusual things like "soundless" voices, where people are convinced that they are being spoken to or are receiving messages of some kind, and yet they deny any experience of sound. One patient of Bleuler's explained that "I do not hear it in my ears. I have the feeling in my breast. Yet it seems as if I heard a sound." In the words of another, "I could be stone deaf and still hear the voices."[9] As the philosopher Sam Wilkinson and psychologist Vaughan Bell have noted, examples of soundless voices lead us to think about what kind of character might seem to linger "behind" a voice that is usually heard.[10]

Something closer to felt presence appears in the work of Karl Jaspers. Jaspers wrote of *leibhaftige Bewusstheit* (bodily awareness),[11] which he described as "a certain feeling (in the mental sense) or awareness that someone is close by, behind them or above them, someone that they can in no way actually perceive with the external senses, yet whose actual/concrete presence is directly/clearly experienced."[12]

Jaspers also described a number of examples of presence in people diagnosed with dementia praecox.[13] One patient reported "the feeling that someone was inside me and then stepped out, perhaps out of the side or somehow. . . . I felt as if someone constantly walked by my side." In other words, this was a following presence, tethered to the person somehow. A second felt "as if his father were in the room behind him," denoting that identity could be perceived as part of the experience—just as Alex knew which voices were where. Others described more mixed feelings: a sensation of being propelled by another—again from behind—or of having their movements matched as they traveled through space. The final case summed up the archetypal *leibhaftige Bewusstheit*: a presence "constantly felt, as though someone were present, whom [the subject] could not see and who was watching her."

A similar idea is seen in some of the experiences described by Bleuler as "extracampine" hallucinations—literally, hallucinations beyond the (sensory) field. In a review of Bleuler's work[14] in 1904 for the *Journal of Mental Science*, Conolly Norman provided the following examples of extracampine hallucinations:

(1) a patient sees things out of the window though his back is turned to the window

(2) a delirium tremens patient complains that jets of water play upon the back of his hand from a certain corner of the ceiling; he does not see them, but he feels with the skin of the back of his hand that they come from this particular spot . . .

and

(4) a patient is conscious of mice on the walls; she does not see them but feels their movement in her skin.[15]

Felt presence seems similar to this in some ways, but not in others. In feeling that something is there, but not via our normal senses, we are sensing something impossible—we are "going beyond" the ordinary sensory field. But at the same time, these experiences don't quite seem to fit the sensation of presence we have encountered already. They are beyond what someone could conceivably experience, but they don't pick out the social bit—the sense of some*one* being there. These extracampine experiences also include sensory content, even if transported and at impossible distances—things are still felt as a touch, or seen in impossible ways. In contrast, the confusing thing about presence is the lack of any clear content. How does Daniel or Alex know that their voices are there? They feel them there, but they don't mean by being touched or by catching a glimpse of them. They are purely there.

For these reasons, it has been suggested that applying the label *extracampine* leads us down the wrong path when it comes to presence.[16] It probably pushes us to assume too much sensory content and ignores the thorny question of what is really going on when literally nothing is being sensed. A whole swathe of other terms have been suggested along the way: "false proximate awareness," "vivid physical awareness," "concrete awareness," "idea of a presence," "false bodily awareness," and the German *Anwesenheit* (simply, "presence").[17] We may need aspects of all of these ideas to understand presence: proximity, vividness, physicality and the body, and the concrete stuff of things versus the abstract world of ideas. By these various names, presence can come to be defined—but only via a long and circuitous journey.

Presences, then, are not new. They have been there all along, with people trying to describe them but unable to pin them down or grasp why they come, why they are there. What Alex or Daniel described was not undiscovered territory; it was something that had been observed and documented since the beginnings of psychiatry.

But that doesn't mean it is old news. These kinds of early accounts are vital to how we approach the topic of presence today. Examples like these highlight the possibility that it *can* just be a feeling; it can be something that is more akin to a sensory experience than a belief, despite being divorced from normal perception.

I feel them closing in

If hallucinations can occur beyond the sense somehow, then where are they? If presences are just there—what does *there* mean? A precise spatial location? An impossible location, like Bleuler's mice? Or a position relative to ourselves?

When we turn back to Alex, we find that he was very clear where his voices were. They took up space and were anchored to him. This might make sense, given that they were his voices, in his mind, and no one else's, but there is no reason why that had to be the case. Some voices proliferate at walls, doors, or thresholds—in other words, the boundaries of our immediate space. Others might be strongly associated with specific rooms or situations. Alex's voices, whether speaking or not, took up consistent locations, relative to Alex's point of view.

Added to this was the feeling of the voices being just over his shoulder—as if someone was looking over it, paying attention to the same things as Alex was. When we realize people are doing this, we often react with annoyance, discomfort, or even alarm—we might wonder how long someone has been there and ask them to move away or explain themselves. When people, uninvited, stand that close, it feels intrusive, not only physically but mentally, as if they were a surreptitious passenger on one's train of attention or a backseat driver of the mind.

The colloquial term for that zone around us is *personal space*; an area that we protect and only open to those we know the best. People who don't respect our personal space are rude, clumsy, or even abusive. Another term used in psychological research on the body is *peripersonal space*; in other words, the area immediately around us in which we can extend our limbs, reach objects, and generally be active agents in the world. Think of this space like that which a large Hula-Hoop occupies that has swung so most of it is in front of you. We can't see what's behind us, and our arms and legs aren't designed to easily reach backward, so the zone of our possible actions extends out in front of us instead.

If someone is in that space, the things we can do are more limited. I might want to walk straight ahead, but I will need to change my path; you might want that apple, but I might pick it up first; you might step forward, and I need to step back. The unexpected whisper at my ear, or sudden feeling of something behind me, immediately prompts me to wheel around and establish space to determine who or what is there. By doing so, I change that zone again to allow for more effective action and reaction. The feeling of peripersonal space

changes when someone else is there; it's not just about the uneasy feeling of someone being too close but about how that closeness changes
my options, possibilities, even aspirations, as a person in the world.
If you are in my space, you change what I can do; by doing that, you
change my possible world.

Voices that do not speak are not inert. It might be unbearable
when voices threaten to harm or prey on one's worst fears, but when
silent even that persistence has an impact. By occupying space—
whether we call it personal or peripersonal—they affect how Alex,
Daniel, and Keira view and think about the world. The voices might
be literally disembodied, but by taking up space they affect the bodies
of the people hearing them; the space warps and wefts with the
reminder that though you thought the voices were gone, they are still
there, and they might always be. Every time they appear, the space
that remains diminishes a little. I recall what Simon, another voice-
hearer, told me once: "The best way to describe it is, the feeling as if
someone has just stepped over your grave. It's chilling."

Whether presence is a hallucination or a delusion, a feeling or a
knowing—to some extent these are just academic questions, issues
around the naming of things, but little more. When it comes to psychosis, there will always be a question to grapple with, with some
people having a complex mixture of knowledge, expectation, and gut
feeling picking out the uneasy visitor in the room.

What is not in doubt is that this feeling is experienced with a
vividness that cannot be ignored. Alex, Daniel, Keira, and Simon
had all tried to describe it to me, and all had struggled to do so.
Something that is so clearly there but cannot be named; a feeling
that can be recognized but not shared; a story that defies efforts to
be told.

After seeing Alex that last time, I realized that I had to try to understand that feeling. What he was describing may not be new—it may
have been known to some people for a long time—but it might as well
have been the first time anyone had tried to describe it, let alone explain

it. From what I could see, we weren't any closer to understanding this feeling than we were a hundred years ago.

I needed to know more, and for that I knew I would need to look elsewhere. I needed to hear other stories of presence, to hear how others had tried—and perhaps failed—to find the words, to capture an essence. I needed to know how to put a name to a phantom.

"Things Which Should
Never Be Spoken Of"

If you go looking for feelings of presence, the first stories you come across almost always involve snow. Lots and lots of snow. Blank expanses, extreme conditions, the enormity of nature—all seem to combine to conjure silent figures, as if some spaces appear tailor made for feelings of presence.

In these spaces, communities have grown. Presences may not exactly be commonplace there, but they are not unexpected. Mountaineers and climbers form one such community, in which stories of presence are well-known and often shared. These presences usually are known under a different name, though: "The Third Man."

The name comes from T. S. Eliot's 1922 poem, "The Wasteland."

> *Who is the third who walks always beside you?*
> *When I count, there are only you and I together*
> *But when I look ahead up the white road*
> *There is always another one walking beside you*
> *Gliding wrapt in a brown mantle, hooded*
> *I do not know whether a man or a woman*
> *—But who is that on the other side of you?*

In his notes on *The Wasteland*, Eliot recalled reading about "one of the Antarctic expeditions (I forget which, but I think one of Shackleton's)" on which "the party of explorers had the constant delusion that there was *one more member* than could actually be counted."[1]

Eliot was referring to the ill-fated *Endurance* expedition of 1914, on which Ernest Shackleton and his crew attempted to reach the South Pole from the Weddell Sea. They in fact never reached Antarctica, first losing the *Endurance* and then spending many months living on the ice and drifting in the sea's currents. Their journey back to safety culminated in Shackleton and two others trekking thirty-six hours across the island of South Georgia to reach help, something that no one had attempted before and barely since. During the journey, all three men reported feeling the presence of a fourth companion: a figure that walked alongside them, all the way, until they reached safety.

They said very little of it at the time and after, but it stirred a maelstrom of emotion for many years to come. Their phantom traveler created ripples and echoes that, once formed, would not go away. When others heard of it, they shared their own stories of silent companions—across glaciers, down chasms, and at the top of the sky. Immortalized in Eliot's verse, the fourth became the "third": the unknown, hooded figure who arrives at times of need, the one "who always walks beside you."

It might seem a far cry from the mental health clinic, but it was these stories that I came across first when I set out to understand presence. The immediate thing you notice is that these experiences aren't usually terrifying or unsettling—quite the opposite, in fact. Some presences bring encouragement and fortitude; some much-needed momentum on the final leg of a journey. The South African doctor Paul Firth, when descending Aconcagua in Argentina, "felt the powerful sensation of being accompanied by somebody. . . . I kept descending, feeling in some strange way as if I were floating slightly above my body, my invisible companion following behind me, encouraging me to keep on going. Lower down the mountain I felt stronger, and my follower disappeared as mysteriously as he had arrived."[2]

In 1933, climbing Everest without oxygen, Frank Smythe had a similar sensation: "All the time I was climbing alone I had a strong feeling that I was accompanied by a second person. That feeling was so strong that it completely eliminated all loneliness I might otherwise have felt."[3] Smythe even turned at one point to share his Kendal Mint Cake with his companion.

Reinhold Messner has had multiple experiences, as many mountaineers do. There was the feeling of a third climber when looking for his brother on Nanga Parbat in 1970,[4] an expedition that would sadly end in tragedy. And then there were the phantom travelers holding his ropes when he completed the same journey as Smythe on Everest in 1980.

It is likely that such experiences have been happening for centuries, materializing out of blizzards, hillsides, and glaciers, only to dissolve once more. In cases of climbing, the occurrence of hallucinations is often attributed to the effects of altitude. A lack of oxygen in the brain—hypoxia—can quickly induce effects akin to brain injury, alongside panic, disorientation, and confusion. One study of high-altitude climbers found that those climbing over six thousand meters had a disproportionately large number of hallucinatory experiences. For all but one, these happened along with distortions in the sense of their own bodies—like the space around them had dissolved their usual boundaries. For example, one climber described the feeling of another person climbing with them, alongside an "empty feeling" and a "hollowness" about their own body.[5] Fast acting and fatal, hypoxia can encourage climbers to rest when they cannot risk it, or conjure scenes that offer foolhardy bullishness, misplaced comfort, or even feelings of retreat and resignation. The hypoxic brain cannot last long.

If hypoxia can induce such experiences, we might think the story would just end there. Unusual things happen all the time in extreme contexts, especially for people clearly pushed to their limits. But considering only this kind of explanation doesn't do justice to the personal impact that many of these experiences seem to have, particularly for feelings of presence.

Lots of changes to our perception can occur without any emotional impact—they might be bizarre, they might be vivid, but the content of such experiences has little or no meaning or connection for the people experiencing them. Migraines, for example, can produce changes to vision (known as scotoma), but the random things that people see are often not personally significant. Similarly, the most basic kinds of hallucinations just happen—and there might not be much more to say about them.

But when people are in the worst kinds of situations—alone, frostbitten, and exhausted—a sudden change in the perceptual world can be imbued with deep significance. A ghostly figure may lead the way out of a storm or offer companionship at a crucial moment. On the disastrous Everest expedition of 1996, Beck Weathers—assumed not once but twice to be beyond saving, so bad was his frostbite—suddenly saw his family in his mind's eye: "My subconscious summoned them into vivid focus, as if they might at any moment speak to me. I knew at that instant, with absolute clarity, that if I did not stand at once, I would spend an eternity on that spot."[6] Such encounters might reassure and cajole, sound the alarm, or spur one out of a frozen sleep. It is not that they *just* happen; more that they happen just in time.

John Geiger, writing with the psychologist Peter Suedfeld, has argued that, in fact, this *is* the function of felt presence. Reviewing accounts of felt presence in extreme environments, the two concluded that "in almost every case, they [presences] serve as a coping resource in that they aid the individual's efforts to survive."[7]

Whether this is true or not, it is undoubtedly now part of the legend. When I started reading about felt presence, many of the stories I came across seemed to be about saving and surviving, presences that almost seem to take you by the hand and lead you to shelter, the guardian angel by your side. Each telling adds more layers of mystery and meaning, and with each story you can't help but wonder at the capacities of the mind.

But with each of these stories, other things get added too. Wild and confusing situations take on structures, follow certain standard patterns, and have resolutions. Fortitude blends with hyperbole, things end up happening "for a purpose."

It made me wonder what gets missed in those stories. Over time, parts that don't fit the narrative might spiral and break off; feelings of ambivalence and uncertainty, confusion and indeterminacy. Memories of grief and trauma could become buried, but they would still be there—threaded through, like striations in stone. And what if there were some presences that didn't save the day? How would we ever hear about them?

The Third Man looms over these stories, setting the template for them all but casting a long shadow over what *actually* might have happened. I needed to know more about him.

And for that, I needed to go back to Shackleton.

Curious imaginings

The aim of the Imperial Trans-Antarctic Expedition was a deceptively simple one: to traverse the Antarctic continent, crossing from the Weddell Sea to the Ross Sea via the South Pole. The *Endurance* expedition would travel from South America, reaching land near Vahsel Bay. Supplies would be left in advance by the *Aurora* expedition, traveling from New Zealand to McMurdo Sound on the opposite side of the landmass.

It was Ernest Shackleton's third journey to the continent. The first, with Captain Robert Falcon Scott and the *Discovery*, had ended in the failure to reach the South Pole in 1904. Shackleton led the second one: the *Nimrod*, in 1907, reached the farthest point south at that time. Since then the Norwegian adventurer Roald Amundsen had succeeded where the British had failed, reaching the South Pole in 1911. But no one had yet crossed Antarctica or reached the pole from the Weddell Sea.

On August 8, 1914, the *Endurance* set sail for Buenos Aires. There it would collect Shackleton and proceed to Antarctica, its eventually permanent destination. The outbreak of hostilities in Europe, with Britain joining the war on August 4, almost put a stop to proceedings barely a week in. Shackleton had contacted the British government to offer his services to the war effort, requesting only that he and the crew be kept together. The reply that came from the admiralty was just one word: "Proceed."[8]

The *Endurance* left Argentina in October, prepared for a journey that was almost certain to take years rather than months. The coming winter would make the ice impassable: Shackleton hoped to pass through enough of the Weddell Sea to either reach land or, at the very least, to maintain position amid the drifting floes. With winter would come months of darkness and frozen seas, making safe sailing impossible.

Initial progress was steady, with currents and winds constantly forcing the *Endurance* to the southwest. Once in the Weddell Sea, they had sight of land to south and east, but ice floes in all directions stopped their tracks. Tracing leads—cracks in the floes that could be rammed open—required agonizing patience. When surrounded by ice, the boat would squirm and groan, timbers bowing, until it was gratefully released. The rudder would frequently be beset by chunks of ice, which had to be removed as soon as possible to avoid permanent damage.

During the many hours that the *Endurance* was stuck fast, the crew made scientific observations, trained dogs, and played games of football on the ice. The landscape around them was monotonous but also inconstant, with bergs and floes shifting position from morning to night, driving over and under one another like tectonic plates. "The floes grind stupendously, throw up great ridges, and shatter one another mercilessly," wrote Shackleton. "The ice moves majestically, irresistibly. Human effort is not futile, but man fights against the giant forces of Nature in a spirit of humility. One has a sense of dependence on the higher Power."[9] He was also struck by the hallucinatory qualities of their surroundings, describing "wonderful mirage effects," such as icebergs "apparently resting on nothing" and others curiously distorted into "all sorts of weird and fantastical shapes."[10]

The *Endurance* made its final day of forward progress on January 15, 1915. It then drifted in the ice for nine months, tracing the west shore of the Weddell Sea, before finally buckling on October 24, taking on too much water to be safely used by the party. The boat lost, the crew took to the ice, dragging with them their three lifeboats: the *Dudley Docker*, the *Stancomb Wills*, and the *James Caird*.

In April 1916, the crew set sail to reach land. There were islands with supplies dotted around the northwest point of Antarctica, but their progress on the ice had forced the crew further north, with the danger of being pushed straight out into the ocean. Shackleton led the *Caird*, while Frank Worsley, the captain of the *Endurance*, was in charge of the *Dudley Docker*. It was Worsley's first polar expedition, and he was new to Shackleton, but he had quickly impressed with his navigation skills. The man in charge of the third boat, Hubert Hudson, was a navigating officer—but he was struggling badly, on the verge of what his crewmates would refer to as a nervous breakdown. Instead, the tiller of the third boat was taken by the *Endurance*'s second officer, Irishman Tom Crean. Himself a veteran of the Antarctic, Crean had been on Captain Scott's ill-fated *Terra Nova* expedition five years earlier.[11]

The boat journey took five days in conditions that were extremely treacherous, with temperatures far below zero. The surroundings conspired to play tricks of the mind on the stricken party. One looming berg appeared above them as "an icy Cerberus" with "water streaming from its eyes, as though it were weeping at our escape from the clutch of the floes." This wasn't just decorative prose, according to Shackleton:

> This may seem fanciful to the reader, but the impression was real to us
> at the time. People living under civilised conditions . . . may scarcely

realise how quickly the mind, influenced by the eyes, responds to the unusual, and weaves about its curious imaginings.[12]

The voyage brought them eventually to Elephant Island, an un-inhabited and inhospitable rock 152 miles from the tip of Graham Land, the northwesterly point of the Antarctic Peninsula. The island would not be able to support the crew for long. Seals and penguins had kept the crew alive on the ice for many months, but they were absent from the spit of land the crew had settled upon. Wind and snow blasted the beach day and night, and many of the men by this point were suffering from severe frostbite and deep sores on their skin. Two of the boats were upturned to become huts, pitch black inside and secured by animal skins all around to keep out the cold.

Within a fortnight, Shackleton had set out again, this time with only five men: Harry "Chips" McNeish, the expedition's carpenter; seamen Tim McCarthy and John Vincent; plus Frank Worsley and Tom Crean. Their aim was to take the *James Caird* eight hundred nautical miles northeast across the Southern Ocean and reach help at the island of South Georgia—an enormous task for such a small vessel, even with a collection of reinforcements and amendments that McNeish had added to the *Caird*. Crean was originally meant to stay and help Frank Wild, Shackleton's second in command, in maintain-ing morale and supplies on the island. But despite the danger of the crossing, Crean begged Shackleton to take him too.

The crossing took the men seventeen days of hell and toil. To this day it is renowned as a daring feat of sailing and an amazing achievement of navigation by Worsley. They faced waves the size of tower blocks—one so large that Shackleton thought it was a gap in the clouds—and sea spray that would freeze instantly across the deck and sails, each time needing to be chipped away from precarious po-sitions on deck. They would have reached South Georgia two days earlier—on May 8—but hurricane winds blew the boat to and fro when land was tantalizingly in sight.

The crew had four weeks of supplies, Shackleton knowing that taking any more time would mean death for the crew on Elephant Island. But reaching South Georgia did not resolve their troubles. Their uncertain landing had placed them to the south and west of the island—the opposite end to the whaling stations on the northeastern side. The seas were too rough, and Shackleton did not think the party could bear attempting to sail around. They would have to walk.

Accompanying Shackleton were the two remaining fit men: Worsley and Crean. They started at 3 AM on the morning of May 19. The interior of South Georgia has peaks ranging from two thousand to over nine thousand feet in a stop-start pattern of ridges and gullies. All they had to tackle it with was some rope, a pair of compasses, and rations for the journey—but no sleeping bags or tents, and no climbing equipment to speak of. McNeish had installed screws into their boots to give them grip and lent them his adze (a carpenter's axe) for the journey. They also carried a Primus stove and a sled, although the latter was abandoned after three hundred yards, it being too cumbersome for them to drag.

Around 6:30 AM they crossed a saddle of land and saw below them a shimmering lake to the north. The slope down to it looked passable and inviting, but as they neared, they realized it was in fact an arm of the sea—Possession Bay—on the north coast of the island. This required the three men to double back for the first time, losing energy and hours. By 8 AM the sun rose, and the clement weather managed to raise the men too. "It was a prospect of spacious grandeur [and] solitude," wrote Worsley, describing "peak beyond peak of the great Allardyce Range, snow-clad and majestic, glittering like armed monarchs in the morning sun."[13] This was unusual, as the weather on South Georgia was usually terrible.

Through the afternoon, they worked hard to find a passing point for the first main ridge of mountains. The first three gullies they attempted to traverse ended in dispiriting cliffs and sheer drops, forcing them to fall back and move along to a new point each time. It is at this position in his account that Worsley first mentions a mysterious fourth figure:

> While writing this seven years after (almost), each step of that journey comes back clearly, and even now I find myself counting our party—Shackleton, Crean, and I—and who was the other? Of course, there were only three, but it is strange that in mentally reviewing the crossing we should always think of a fourth, and then correct ourselves.[14]

Strange indeed. But rather than dwell on that feeling, Worsley's account moves rapidly on. They had found a fourth gap in the ridge just as the light was beginning to recede. A fog had rolled in, enveloping everything, so their descent was invisible to the three men. From the third gap, it had looked like they could make their way down a steady slope there, so they decided to risk it and slide down while sitting behind one another on coils of the rope: Shackleton, Worsley, then Crean. It was a leap of faith, without knowing what was waiting for them below. Worsley described the first thirty seconds of the speedy drop as the "most scared he had been in his life."[15]

The gamble worked, and they descended around fifteen hundred feet in a matter of minutes, landing in soft, pillowy snow—and ruining their trousers in the process. After firing up the Primus for a brief meal of hoosh (a mixture of snow, biscuit, and pemmican), they set off again. By midnight they had managed to crest a second ridge, and found themselves looking down a long slope to a bay below. They decided to descend to the northeast—but by 2 AM they realized that they had made another error. This wasn't Stromness Bay; rather, it was a glacier to the north and west. Once again, it was time to double back, and exhaustion beckoned.

They marched off, and up, to the southeast, curving to correct their course. Worsley described this as the worst point of the journey: the steady ascent, the deep snow, the knowledge that you were just retracing your steps again and losing precious time. The climb was up a third ridge that blocked their way to Stromness, and by 5 AM—twenty-six hours into their journey—they reached an outcrop of rock where they decided to stop briefly. The suggestion was to sleep for a while, which Crean and Worsley settled down to do. Shackleton stayed awake, and then woke them after five minutes, telling them they had slept for half an hour.

They reached the crest of the third ridge by 6 AM, and not long after they heard their first sound of civilization in eighteen months: the whistle of the whaling station. "Never had any one of us heard sweeter music," wrote Shackleton.[16] They could see the way ahead, with no fear now of overshooting or needing to double back. That didn't mean the danger was over, though: they were still around two thousand feet up at the top of the ridge. Their only way down initially was by cutting steps into a sheer ice cliff. As they descended, Crean and Worsley anchored the rope and Shackleton kicked footholds below him with all his might. Worsley estimated that they managed a thousand feet of descent with this method (although this is likely to have only been two to three hundred feet). Then, after traversing a glacier to the south, they inadvertently crossed a frozen lake, through which Crean fell and had to be pulled out of. Finally, instead of taking another slope that they could have slid down, they missed it and ended up rappelling down through a waterfall instead.

But by 3 PM, their frustration gave way to relief. They were there, finally, walking into town "ragged, filthy, and evil-smelling."[17] Shackleton knew the Norwegian commander of the station, Captain Petter Sørlle, but the captain did not recognize him, such was his condition. They had made it—thirty-six hours, twenty miles in a straight line, with multiple ascents of over two thousand feet—carrying barely anything left between them but their clothes. As Shackleton described it:

That was all of [our] tangible things; but in memories we were rich. We had pierced the veneer of outside things.

We had "suffered, starved and trumped, grovelled down yet
grasped at glory, grown bigger in the bigness of the whole." We had
seen God in his splendour, heard the text that Nature renders.

We had reached the naked soul of men.[18]

That night, a storm rolled in, blasting the island with a south-
easterly gale. Had the men still been out there, they would not have
survived. For Worsley it was proof that "Providence had certainly
looked after us."[19] Shackleton invoked the same sense of fortune and
guidance in his own words:

When I look back at those days I have no doubt that Providence
guides us, not only across those snow fields, but across the storm-
white sea that separated Elephant Island from our landing place on
South Georgia.

I know that during that long and racking march of 36 hours
over the unnamed mountains and glaciers of South Georgia it
seems to me often that we were four, not three.[20]

* * *

WHO, OR WHAT, was the fourth man of Shackleton's party? Based on
my reading of *South*, Shackleton's account of the expedition, I wasn't
sure I was any the wiser.

For the men involved it was clearly a spiritual experience of some
kind. The figure of "Providence," divine, powerful, and mysterious,
was felt to have guided their way through thick and thin. Shackleton
and Worsley's invocation of such an intervention is matched by what
little we know of Crean's experience. According to his biographer Michael Smith, no documentary evidence exists of Crean's own account,
but he did reportedly describe a similar story to his close friends. His
only explanation for the experience was that "the Lord brought us
home."[21]

Given how much had to go right for them to succeed—both on
the final leg of their journey and before—it is no surprise that the

men would fall back on the concept of providence to explain what they had achieved. Had the storm come in earlier, or the rope failed, or their journey into the unknown gone wrong, the consequences would have been fatal for all. Instead, they not only survived the trek, but they also saved all of their crewmates. Every man of the *Endurance* was eventually rescued. After reaching Stromness, it took four attempts to reach Elephant Island—so thick was the pack ice—but the crew eventually landed in Punta Arenas, Chile, on September 3, to cheering crowds and a hero's welcome.[22]

But beyond providence, what we can say? The conditions, undoubtedly, had created a recipe for the unusual and hallucinatory. Despite managing to keep their spirits up, the three men were utterly exhausted and physically debilitated by each step of their polar odyssey. When the *Caird* landed on South Georgia, it took the men many repeated attempts to pull it up onto shore, so weak were they after the sea voyage. To then launch into a mountainous trek was a huge challenge for deconditioned bodies: as Shackleton noted, "We had done little walking since January and our muscles were out of tune."[23] When one adds sleep deprivation and extreme dehydration, both from their time on the boat and on the island, it is a wonder the three men did not experience more hallucinations. Indeed, Shackleton's biographer Roland Huntford attributes their mistakes on the trek—doubling back repeatedly—to their "almost hallucinatory state of mental exhaustion."[24]

Added to the condition of the men was the impact of their surroundings. If the ice had offered mirage-like expanses, and the sea brought the dogs of hell, the island offered an animistic canvas that their minds readily personified. In their accounts, both Shackleton and Worsley refer to the friendly face of the moon guiding their way, while Shackleton also describes fingers of sea fog "reaching after the intruders into untrodden wilds."[25] Shackleton had a poetic streak and was reportedly prone to quoting verse out loud in reflective moments,[26] despite having an almost-telegraphic style of prose when writing. Indeed, the act of expedition itself, and the challenge of engaging with such environments, seemed to represent a kind of poetry for him. He would have needed no encouragement to conjure up the mysterious "fourth."

Seeing such meaning and agency in the world could scientifically be described as examples of pareidolia—in other words, seeing people, objects, or patterns in things when they are not present. It is a tendency that is thought to be very closely linked to hallucinations, another example of the mind reaching out to make sense of its surroundings.[27] It's also something Shackleton himself was clearly aware of, writing: "We had lived long amid the ice, and we half-unconsciously strove to see resemblances to human faces and living forms in the fantastic contours and massively uncouth shapes of berg and floe."[28]

The point about pareidolia is that we see what makes sense to us; a combination of what we are used to, what we need, and what we deem significant. We see faces rather than wheels, hear words rather than whistles, and trace moving figures from mere shadows. If nature abhors a vacuum, the mind will not countenance the incomplete or meaningless. Such conditions make poets of us all.

When our bodies are put under extreme stress, strain, and trauma, other extraordinary things can also happen to the mind. The association of stress with many presence experiences is noted by Suedfeld, Geiger, and others: it is clearly a key trigger of unusual experiences. But Shackleton and his men were not just going through a period of stress—they had endured repeated hardship and uncertainty since they set out from Buenos Aires. In cases of recurrent and prolonged exposure to trauma, a concept that psychologists sometimes call upon is *dissociation*.[29] Dissociation is a wide-ranging phenomenon that is usually characterized by feeling detached from your own body and the world around you. It can include experiences of amnesia, intense absorption, and "derealization," the sense that things in the world aren't real or aren't happening. The corollary to such experiences is "depersonalization," in which the world around you may feel real, but you may not. Whole body parts, or the look of your own face, might not feel like they belong to you.

Thought of as a mental health condition, dissociation has a range of diagnoses associated with it. In some cases, people might receive a diagnosis of dissociative identity disorder, which used to be known as multiple personality disorder. In DID, the disconnectedness of on-going experience is thought to reflect different personas or "parts" of the psyche, each with their own identity and form of expression. It's often what many people mistake for schizophrenia in the popular understanding.

The notion of dissociative experiences as disorders can be highly contested—but most people would agree that dissociation is typically seen as a response to sustained trauma, of various kinds. Faced with un-bearable pain and unimaginable experience, it's like our minds change the channel, allowing our conscious experience to continue unaware. Whether such a thing would represent a useful response isn't always clear—numbing a pain or avoiding a difficult experience in the short term may not always allow it to be processed and manageable in the longer term. But for many people, when dealing with trauma, dissoci-ation may be the only option they have.

When we turn back to that long, thirty-six-hour march, it would be no surprise if dissociation of some kind was playing a role in the experience of Shackleton and his men. Faced with the insurmount-able, managing fear, pain, and fatigue, it would not have taken much to cause their bodies to feel like they were elsewhere, and not their own. A self fragmented, projected onto ice and snow, conjuring com-panions out of a fractured sense of their own personhood. If this is close to what happened, the fourth man would be no mystery. It would be them: Shackleton, Worsley, and Crean.

And yet, the fourth man does not dissolve so easily. For one thing, dissociation often also involves memory problems: one of the features of dissociation included in the fifth edition of *Diagnostic and Statis-tical Manual of Mental Disorders* (DSM-5), the American Psychiatric Association's handbook of diagnosis, is "dissociative amnesia." It has been proposed that the response to a trauma can disrupt the way memories are encoded in the brain. The idea is that, under the stress of a traumatic event, our minds are like a camera trying to take a still image of a moving target: things come back fragmented and only capture part of a whole. Worsley, though, claimed he could remember every step of his journey even years later. Shackleton's account, drawing upon his journal, is equally cogent. The men also described keeping spirits up through jokes and singing. What they recounted sounds like the experience of determined and focused explorers, not ones lost in a fog of unreality.

And perhaps *the* most curious thing about the fourth presence is its number: four. It wasn't just one man pushed to the limit, having this experience—all of them had it, and all claimed to have felt something similar. True, they were all facing the same conditions, but people crack at different times in different ways—many of the rest of the *Endurance* crew already had. It also makes the example, counterintuitively, completely uncharacteristic of what would subsequently become known as "Third Man" experiences. Like Smythe or Messner, these tend to happen to individuals—solo adventurers, creating their own company. Shackleton, Worsley, and Crean had each other, and yet each, apparently, felt the power of the fourth.

In psychiatry, there are examples of unusual things happening to groups rather than individuals, but they aren't the norm. In psychosis, phenomena such as "folie à deux" or "folie à trois" can occur—situations where more than one person has a powerful unusual belief as part of their psychosis, sometimes picked up by another ("folie imposée"). More generally, powerful and charismatic figures can create the right conditions for a number of collective delusions of one kind or another—cult leaders and gurus, for example, or terrorist leaders. But in such situations, what occurs is usually a matter of belief and not of perception. It doesn't surprise us to think that a group could all come to think the same thing, however unusual, given time and circumstance. A clear case of collective hallucination, on the other hand, would seem to be a truly rare thing. Such experiences challenge conventional scientific explanations and often instead invite spiritual or supernatural interpretations.

Perhaps the reason Shackleton's experience has endured for so long, and resonated with so many, is because of what was left unsaid. All we have from Shackleton's and Worsley's accounts of their fourth man could fit onto one page. There is a reticence in Shackleton's attempts to convey what had occurred. When dictating *South*, Shackleton was commended by observers for the precision of his prose—he knew what he wanted to say, and tended to say it clearly and straightforwardly. But when it came to the fourth man, he "swelled up" with emotion and struggled to find the words. There was a sense in which it was something that *couldn't* be articulated, not just because of the difficulties of capturing something ineffable and intangible but also because of the sheer scope of it. At one point, Shackleton even obliquely referred to his experiences as "things which should never be spoken of."[30] And as he tried to recount in *South*:

> One feels "the dearth of human words, the roughness of mortal speech" in trying to describe things intangible, but a record of our journeys would be incomplete without a reference to a subject very near to our hearts.[31]

This sense of an experience beyond ordinary comprehension has added to its mystery, to the feeling that each man was touched by something that went far beyond them. But this makes the Third Man a question rather than an answer. It challenges us to think about how we would feel and what we would do when faced with the extraordinary. Thanks to Shackleton, and thanks to Eliot, that inchoate feeling became a legend; the seed that grew to connect disparate experiences across mountain and sea, wind, ice, and snow.

The archetypal presence—the providential companion, the silent traveler, aiding those adrift in times of need—had been born. But who or what that figure is remains something of a mystery.

3

The Double

It's a sunny spring day when I get the email from George. You often hear from lots of different people when you do research on a topic like hallucinations. Sometimes they ask for second opinions on medication; sometimes they have grand new theories or insights to offer. The most common email, sadly, is from parents—people getting in touch because they are concerned about their son or daughter. Their child might be hearing voices or acting strangely, they might have seen their GP or another clinician and not heard what they wanted to hear. You can't step in and offer consultation or second opinion—that's not your job. The best you can usually do, beyond offering reassurance and sympathy, is point people toward support information or other resources, hoping that something might help.

George's email was different. My Twitter profile lists the kinds of things I work on and what I'm interested in—including felt presence. I had shared a tweet by a team at Vanderbilt in Nashville who were running a new survey, so George decided to get in touch. He had experiences of presence, he said, lots of them. He was keen to learn more about them and help with any research he could.

It took me a few days to respond. This also gave me time to look at George's website, which he had mentioned in his email. It doesn't reflect anything about George to say that my expectations were mixed—an out-of-the-blue email from someone with their own site can end up in some outlandish places. But this wasn't like that at all. George was a collector: he wanted to know more about his experiences, so he had gone looking, scouring the internet for anything that could shed light on the phenomenon. His background is in computing, and his site has directories from which visitors can download libraries of resources: videos, blogs, and any number of research articles. He had read widely too—neuroscience, psychiatry, philosophy. It had been George who had emailed me for answers, but I got the creeping sense that I should have been the one to email him.

We spoke a few days later—evening for me, late afternoon for him. George is from New York City, and he looks a bit like his *Seinfeld* namesake and fellow New Yorker, George Costanza. When we first started talking, he was locked down in his apartment due to the pandemic. But for all that, he had a cheery nature—and was keen to talk.

George had been having experiences of people being present for thirty-five years. They had begun following a grand mal epileptic seizure when he was nineteen years of age. "I was working part time at a retail store and the air conditioning went out. I thought I passed out because of the heat," he explained. He has had epilepsy since he was a child, but hadn't had a grand mal since he was two years old. Various medications had kept his seizures in check throughout his childhood. By his late teens, George had gotten used to a life without the threat of seizures; his medications were being tapered off because it didn't seem like he needed them.

When the grand mal came, it was a big shock to George. He couldn't drive, he couldn't remember his brothers' names, and he struggled to attend college. He'd have to go back on the meds, or find new ones, to fend off future attacks.

And he started recognizing people.

He would be walking down the street and suddenly catch sight of someone coming toward him. An old friend, out of nowhere—how could they be here? He can't have seen them for a long time. A real bolt from the blue. And yet, when he would look again, he'd realize it wasn't them. He must have been mistaken. They looked similar, but it wasn't his friend. It was just a stranger.

This might sound like an everyday experience; something that has likely happened to us all at some point in our lives. We are extremely good, generally, at recognizing people we know, even after years and years of not seeing them. Relatively unfamiliar faces—if we only come across them once or twice—are very hard for us to remember accurately.[1] But familiar faces form very strong traces in the mind.

Still—we all make mistakes, and so did George. The problem was, this was happening to George *a lot*. It might be seeing a face within a crowd, or hearing a voice across a room—each time, George had an intense feeling of recognition, as if he knew the person and they were there with him. "I get onto the subway, and then I'm hearing somebody's voice, somebody that I knew. It could go back like twenty years; I recognize their voice, and then I'm looking around for them. And then I see the person talking—it's not that person," he explained.

It could sometimes take George two to three minutes for him to shrug off the feeling, not the two to three seconds it might take for the rest of us. In those moments, he really felt like his old friends and acquaintances were present. Blasts from the past—ex-girlfriends, roommates, distant relatives—appeared to him as if they had never aged, "frozen in time." The feeling was arresting: "It stops you in your tracks, and takes your attention completely," he told me.

That was what a feeling of presence meant for him—that instant and vivid feeling of recognition; not an unknown "someone" being there but a specific person, present right now. I explained that it wasn't quite like the felt presence experiences that get described elsewhere—those basic feelings of someone being there, but not seen or heard. George had tried to share his experiences on epilepsy forums, but he had struggled to find people with quite the same experience as him. It's a good example of how a term like *presence* can mean lots of things to different people. I wondered if it had stymied George's efforts to link up with others.

George was keen to know as much as possible about what could have changed that day, following his seizure. One of the changes had to do with his body: "At that time I was noticing differences; it's like I felt like my left and my right sides were separated and not connected. I'd be walking one way, and meanwhile a part of my body was going another," he said. At another point in our conversation, he described it almost as if his "mind and body weren't together."

George's experiences might not exactly be prototypical, but they are still very relevant to felt presence. That feeling of immediate recognition that George gets—and had been getting for thirty-five years—went beyond just the seeing or hearing of something. It was as if his "person file" for a particular friend had been activated, but without the right cues or much (if any) supporting evidence: he had recognized them, and that was that. It brought to mind some accounts of presence that I had heard about in bereavement, when people get the distinct feeling that the person who has passed away is suddenly present again, in the room, or in the space around them.[2] They wouldn't necessarily point to a sensory cue—a voice or a body, for example—but they would report a distinct feeling that a specific person had arrived. It's like a presence that comes "identity first," providing instant knowledge that the company of the room has changed.

The other thing that George's experiences suggested was a neuropsychological condition known as the *Fregoli delusion*.[3] It's a condition in which strangers are greeted as if they are an old friend in disguise and unfamiliar faces are treated as mere masks for familiar people underneath. In the Fregoli delusion—and in George's case—it almost seems like a surfeit of certainty has come rushing in instead, giving not just a feeling but a conviction that someone familiar is present.

Where George's experiences differed from the Fregoli delusion was in their hallucinatory quality. I asked him if he would actually *see* the people he thought were there, or whether he just thought it was them: "I see the face, believe me. It's the face, but then after I come to my reality and then observe the person I realize by their behavior, or their voice, or their nuances or personality that it's not them, you know."

I asked George if he had ever had any other kinds of unusual experiences, including something more like a feeling of presence just on its own, with very little sight or sound associated with it. He has—but only once. On the morning of the World Trade Center attack in 2001, he had a vivid experience of his mother visiting him, telling him to get moving, to get away and out of his apartment building that was only blocks from the disaster. George's memory of this experience is difficult for him to recount—he had lost his mother not long before, and the experience was an intensely personal one. It clearly still means a lot to him.

George isn't the only one to have had such an experience during the World Trade Center attacks. John Geiger's comprehensive collection of presence experiences, *The Third Man Factor*, begins with the story of Ron DiFrancesco, the New York broker who believed he owed his life to an angelic presence that had shown the way out of the collapsing second tower.[4] Marooned on the eightieth floor, DiFrancesco had begun to panic amid the intensifying smoke—until someone, somehow, told him to get up. The figure lifted him to his feet and led him down past three floors of flames. He would be the last person to leave the South Tower before it collapsed.

As we have already seen, this kind of encounter with presences—the guardian angel, arriving just in the nick of time, to offer rescue and survival—is a very common one in extreme situations of adversity. But in George's case, his experience that morning wasn't representative of his life with presence. Five to six times a year, for thirty-five years, he had been having these recurrent "recognition" presences instead. Every doctor he spoke to didn't know anything about them, so he resolved to find out for himself, contacting anyone and everyone he could to find out why he would be having such experiences. Again and again and again.

The experiential brain

My conversation with George prompted me to go back to my under-graduate textbooks. One of the first experiments you hear about as a psychology student are those of Wilder Penfield, a neurologist who studied patient responses to stimulation during presurgical assessments. A common procedure would be to open the skull and probe the brain's surface with gentle electrical stimulation, to ascertain whether surgery would likely impinge upon any key processes (such as speech). Penfield's team was surprised to find that focal stimulation of parts of the brain could evoke not just spontaneous sensations, such as hearing a specific sound or seeing something flash before your eyes, but vivid recollections of long-ago events, lost memories that transported the person back to another time entirely.

"I was incredulous," Penfield wrote. "On each subsequent occasion I marveled. . . . I was astonished each time my electrode brought forth such a response. How could it be? This had to do with the mind! I called such responses 'experiential' and waited for more evidence."[5] By "experiential," Penfield meant the immediate and engrossing feeling his patients reported. They weren't just vaguely recollecting something that had happened to them, they were right there, immersed in the memory.[6]

Spontaneous activation is happening all the time in the brain, for all of us. A silent brain is most likely a dead one. Whole fields of research have depended on this kind of activity to establish "resting state" groupings of networks in the brain. We can infer which areas form networks by the way their activity rises and falls synchronously over time; auditory areas tend to hang together, as do visual areas, like they are constantly checking in with one another. But these fluctuations tend to happen slowly, and across large groups of neurons. In contrast, spontaneous and focused activity is less common and often not a good sign. This is what happens in epilepsy. Specific regions fire off, sometimes creating a chain reaction with others, to the point that the brain cannot handle the wave of activity and a seizure takes place.

The seizure can create an "aura" in which the world around someone begins to change, imperceptibly—and unusual things begin to occur.

In some cases, spontaneous epileptic activation can induce experiences that are very much like psychosis. For example, a team in Japan reported on the case of a twenty-five-year-old woman who had been having seizures since the age of two. Despite various treatments, her seizures were frequent and uncontrolled, leading to a recommendation of surgical therapy. To identify the focus of her seizures, electrodes were implanted in her brain, mainly in her temporal lobes (areas of the brain that house our auditory cortex, much of our language skills, but also parts such as the *hippocampus*, which is usually linked to forming memories). While she was in the hospital, she experienced eighteen seizures over two days, after which she started to hear the voices of her parents, even though they were not present. A few days later, she became "restless and frequently expressed anxiety and fear. She could not stay alone in the monitoring room and wandered around on the same floor."[7]

Throughout this period, the most consistent seizure activity was observed in the *left amygdala*, sometimes in concert with other regions. Along with the hippocampus, the amygdala is part of the *limbic system*—an old, primal network that is the seat of how we process emotions (see figure 1). The amygdala itself has historically been particularly associated with fear. It's been argued that involvement of the limbic system is key to such experiences really feeling like they are happening—that they are "experiential" in the way Penfield was referring to. It might be suggested that for a hallucination to have any real force, we have to really feel it too. We can't just see or hear it—it must move us in some way.

Along with hallucinations, epilepsy has a history of inducing ecstatic and spiritual experiences, which again have been attributed to temporal lobe activity. Some researchers have even used epileptic experiences as a model for how religious experiences of presence occur: the neuroscientist Michael Persinger famously developed the "God Helmet," a device that stimulated the temporal lobes in an attempt to induce transcendental and mystical experiences.[8] The science and theory behind these ideas are contentious—but the often positive, spiritual, and overwhelming nature of some epileptic auras is not.

Definitions of "sensed presence" in epilepsy research reflect this: for example, Anne-Marie Landtblom defines it as "the perception that a person or a 'power' is present in the room, often accompanied by a religious sensation of clarity or happiness."[9] Landtblom's definition was

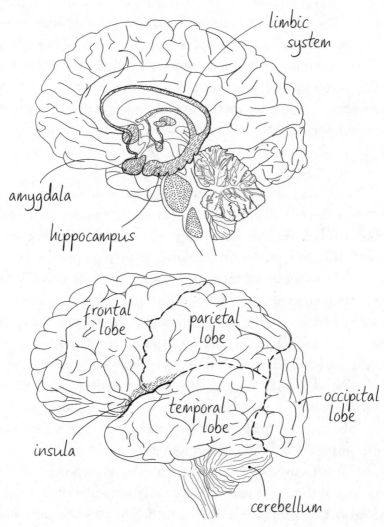

FIGURE 1

based in part on the experiences of a university student from Sweden who had been having seizures since the age of three. During his epileptic aura, the student had the same experience over and over: "I have a feeling that someone stands behind me, someone with a distinct wish to support and comfort me. This person will follow me anywhere I would like to go."[10] Scans and recordings of the young man's brain showed that his seizures originated from a structure called the *anterior insula*, a nested region that sits alongside the hippocampus.[11] The anterior insula is linked to a range of different functions, but this area caught the eye of the researchers because of its association with self-awareness. The insula is thought to be the key component in how we monitor our own feelings, including our own internal bodily sensations (a process known as interoception). This kind of involvement of the insula is also seen in other people with epilepsy experiencing ecstatic phenomena, suggesting that it might relate to the positive emotions that the student experienced during his seizures.[12]

This kind of account—of the lingering sense of someone, being present close by—is quite similar to the felt presences I had heard about in other contexts—it could even be Shackleton's figure of providence. The intense positive emotion was something new, but the basic sense of an anonymous other was nevertheless there. George's experiences, on the other hand, didn't quite fit that model. What he described seemed to be more consistent with another rare phenomenon with a different name: hyperfamiliarity. In hyperfamiliarity, people can become convinced that they recognize everyone—doctors, nurses, other patients—even when told otherwise, and often in the absence of other problems. When this is investigated, the brain activity observed for people with hyperfamilarity can be very similar to epilepsy, particularly in the temporal lobes.[13]

As far as George knows, he doesn't have seizures that start in those regions, so it seems unlikely that exactly the same thing is going on. But what the comparison highlights is how spontaneous changes to the brain can induce quite specific and intense experiences of familiarity, and familiarity alone. All other faculties might be intact, there might not even be any strong emotions associated with it—just an unshakable feeling that you know the person. Recognition is so automatic, usually, that you can't disrupt it, even if you tried. For that moment, you're sure somebody is right there, with you. Like George said—it's a feeling so strong, it stops you in your tracks.

Welcome to mirror world

> The Unknown never speaks; he appears to be occupied in writing on the other side of the wall which divides us. Curiously enough, whenever I move my chair, he moves his also, and, in general, imitates all my movements as though he wished to annoy me. Thus it goes on for three days. On the fourth day I make the following observations: If I prepare to go to sleep, he also prepares to go to sleep in the next room; when I lie down in bed, I hear him lie down on the bed by my wall. I hear him stretch himself out parallel with me; he turns over the pages of a book, then puts out the lamp, breathes loud, turns himself on his side, and goes to sleep. He apparently occupies the rooms on both sides of me, and it is unpleasant to be beset on two sides at once.[14]

Outside of his native Sweden, August Strindberg is primarily known as a playwright. His most celebrated work is *Miss Julie* (1888), the story of a doomed romance across class divides. Alongside his plays, though, he also wrote novels, painted—and dabbled in alchemy. In a period in Paris in the 1890s, while his international reputation was beginning to grow, he was beating a personal retreat. Estranged from his wife and children and in thrall to the pleasures of absinthe, he decided he would attempt to turn sulfur into gold. His companions around the time were the painters Edvard Munch and Paul Gauguin, who were both also growing in notoriety and fame, if not sobriety.

By 1896, Strindberg took to holing himself up in his apartment, creating a home laboratory that would stifle and swell with an acrid chemical fog. Gradually the conditions began to take their toll, and a period of psychosis followed. Strindberg was beset by paranoia, convinced that others were planning to electrocute him if he ventured outside. Every time he saw Munch, he apparently perceived a huge Great Dane guarding his owner (even though Munch only had a cat), and he began to hallucinate the music of Franz Schubert. One day he even thought he had managed to place a hex on Munch when his friend went into a "nervous seizure" after borrowing Strindberg's coat. Munch, apparently, just had a cold that day.[15]

While all this was happening, Strindberg kept an "Occult Diary" to track his experiences of madness. His interest in the limits of physical and mental experience were intertwined with a fascination for the supernatural and spiritual. Throughout his career he had flirted with several major ideas of the day, and his period of psychosis would see him move from engaging with Friedrich Nietzsche to finding wisdom in the writing of the mystic and theologian Emanuel Swedenborg. Contemporaries of Strindberg reportedly even believed that his madness was self-induced or exaggerated to provide material for his next creative project.

The contents of Strindberg's diary became *The Inferno,* a semi-fictionalized account of his wilderness years in Paris. Along with visual and auditory hallucinations, *The Inferno* contains Strindberg's vivid account of his own arresting experience of presence: the "Unknown." This illusory figure was at times a mental companion and even an interlocutor for Strindberg. But it also plagued him with a mirroring dance, imitating his movements for days at a time. In other passages, he describes a fear that the Unknown will attack him in his bed.

Karl Jaspers chose Strindberg for his first "pathography," considering him a prime example for an exploration of creativity and madness in psychosis.[16] In truth, though, Strindberg's experiences could have been caused by any number of things. Along with his heavy use of absinthe, it is highly possible that he exposed himself to dangerous levels of mercury during his alchemical endeavors. Erethism—chronic mercury exposure, or "mad hatter syndrome"—is linked to psychosis, emotional disturbances, and general health problems, all of which were true of Strindberg during that period.

What, though, does a figure like Strindberg add to our understanding of presence? His situation might seem altogether too chaotic: a complex mixture of indulgence, intoxication, and almost-willful insanity. The answer is in the mirror.

The hallucinations of epilepsy that we have heard about so far offer vivid glimpses of presence, but these examples don't clearly offer a model or a theory. It still isn't clear what kind of explanation we get from it, why an apparently embodied phantom "other" would come about. In contrast, the example of Strindberg and his companion illustrates what we might call a "mirror theory" of presences.

One of the foremost researchers of felt presences, Peter Brugger, has drawn upon Strindberg's case on more than one occasion. A Swiss neurologist, Brugger has documented and categorized a wide variety of "autoscopic" phenomena; that is, duplications of one's body that lead to the occurrence of doppelgängers, mirror bodies, and unseen visitors. It is Brugger's contention that felt presences are just one example of such autoscopy, a family of experiences that can be distinguished on the one hand by varying degrees of sensation (the feeling of another body, in another location, perhaps), and on the other hand by depersonalization, or feelings that one's body is not your own. They could be mirror images of face or body (an *autoscopic hallucination*), or a visual experience of another body combined with a lightness or slight detachment from one's own body (*heautoscopy*). Sometimes they might even involve a full visual and bodily detachment from the self or—disturbingly—a feeling that one's own organs are missing (an *inner heautoscopy*).

For Brugger, felt presence is in fact closest to a kind of heautoscopy: that is, the presence is a double, but one that somehow takes something from you. It might not be another body that you see, but you get the feeling that it has somehow come from your body. As Brugger explains, the experience often involves an unusual sense of connection:

Like heautoscopy proper, the [feeling of presence] is usually accompanied by alterations in the experience of one's own body or by some close psychological affinity with the "stranger beneath," who, in some instances, may overly be referred to as an "alter ego."[17]

In contrast to the presences recounted by voice-hearers, Strindberg's figure of the Unknown seemed much more closely tied to him and his body. Brugger's categorization of different types of this experience offers us a way to understand what's happening when people experience a double. If a feeling of presence is in fact a kind of mirroring, then it could reflect from some kind of representation of our own bodies—and by extension, our selves. It's like a map of where we are in the world, an echo of how we experience our body position. And in Strindberg's mind, an echo that has been brought forth to torment him.

Brugger has argued that the majority of such doppelgänger experiences are of the antagonistic kind.[18] In Fyodor Dostoevsky's *The Double*, for example, the protagonist, Golyadkin, initially strikes up a friendship with the unusual, twin-like stranger that he meets in a blizzard. Slowly, though, the other man takes over his life in various ways.[19] The arrival of unexpected doubles is often associated with displacement and replacement. In Duncan Jones's 2009 film *Moon*, Sam Bell is alarmed to be joined on his lunar base by a doppelgänger—who also claims to be *the* Sam Bell. Doubles undermine and subvert our sense of unique and personal identity. A double that takes our image and our movement, and yet still has the potential to act of its own accord, has a freedom and power that we cannot fully grasp. It is like they have all of our agency, and then some more to spare. Doubles, for the most part, are unwelcome guests.

Grouping feelings of presence within this wider family of body disruptions is appealing for two reasons. First, it offers us a plausible explanation of how we could feel like someone is there, even when our senses tell us the opposite. The feeling of someone or something nearby could still be linked or prompted by a sight or sound, but the maintenance of that sensation could be some form of body representation, transposed. We don't have the ordinary language to put such an experience into words, so we are left with the mundane and the minimal. Just a feeling in our bones about "what is there," even without anything else to go on. It is our bodily self noting that something, somewhere, is awry.

The second reason that the "mirror" model might be useful is that it gives us clues about how presence might work in the brain. Different mirror experiences seem to link with changes to different brain areas. For instance, mirror images of faces and bodies would very often be associated with damage to the occipital cortex, i.e., the lobes responsible for the lion's share of our visual cognition. In contrast, the doubling experiences where your own body feels different somehow—what Brugger referred to as *heautoscopy*—are linked to changes in the temporal lobes, the limbic system (like in epilepsy), and a third set of regions: the parietal cortex. Damage to the parietal cortex is very often most associated with changes to spatial cognition. Classic case studies in neuropsychology involving parietal damage lead to conditions such as perceptual neglect, where a particular part of space—for example, things on the left—is completely ignored.[20]

What these patterns of damage and disruption add up to is a recipe for hallucinatory experiences affecting our perception of space and body. Sometimes, this can even involve multiple bodies. In 2006, Brugger reported on the case of a forty-one-year-old man, PH, who presented to his local clinic complaining of fatigue, dizziness, and seizures. He also wasn't quite feeling himself: Upon awakening one night he noticed that he had split into three distinct parts:

(1) the left half of his body, which felt quite normal;
(2) the right half, which felt detached from the left both physically and emotionally; and
(3) he observed "a man" in close proximity to his right side.

This second man didn't look like PH, although he was of a similar age, and he roughly followed his movements. If he looked to the right, so did the double. And he felt connected, as if PH and the man were "sharing the same soul."[21] But the more curious thing was that to the right of the stranger was another figure, in the same position: a fifty-year-old woman with braids in her hair. And a few meters on, there were more figures: two girls, then a boy, all of whom mimicked PH's movements (see figure 2). These weren't his relatives, but he considered them a family. He knew they were somehow connected. And the farther away they got from him, the less connection he felt to them.

After a few days, he couldn't see the family, but the sense of their presence remained. They even passed him messages as he lay in his hospital bed awaiting treatment. Scans of PH's brain indicated a large tumor in his left insula, which had grown to extend into the parietal lobe and areas of the frontal lobe. The messages from the "family" provided comfort—solace that his actual family would be OK following his death. He died sixteen months after surgery.

PH's case is unusual in many respects: the number of presences (a "polyopic heautoscopy"), their different identities, and their positive support for him when facing death. What they illustrate is the wider possibilities of hallucinatory experience following neurological damage, where something spatial also becomes something emotional. A small change grows to something larger, and an internal world becomes external. The unarticulated feelings we have toward others— the ties, roles, and identities that tether us to one another—are made somehow visible and concrete. It is almost as if PH's inner social milieu, a relational imaginary, had been refracted into the outside world, like light through a prism.

This extended mirroring of PH might seem to support an extreme version of Brugger's model—but we could also use it to question the premise, that these are somehow mirrors of PH himself. PH's "family" might have felt connected to him, but they were not copies of him—they just copied his body position. Can we really call them mirrors of a bodily self if they had the different identities he described?

The neurologist Fabienne Picard described a similar story in 2010 that offers a contrasting perspective.[22] This time, a sixty-two-year-old woman with focal epileptic seizures reported that she felt the presence of four of her family members—three grandchildren and her daughter—in the space in front of her, with one granddaughter in particular within touching distance. The experience lasted for several minutes at a time and was generally a pleasant one. These presences were clearly not felt to be her, or to be mirroring her. There were just other people—persons, not selves projected into space.

That kind of example does not negate the many cases of mirroring or their potential relevance to understanding what felt presence might be. But it does encourage us to think past the double, or at least to think more broadly. If felt presence comes from us, why does it feel so distinctly "other"? Could the mirror be a starting point, the first step on an uncanny road? What else might we need to conjure a true case of the Unknown?

FIGURE 2

4

Luke

It was the summer of 2020, and I was standing in a garden in Edinburgh, looking out over the Braids and Blackford Hill. In a strange year, we'd taken the opportunity to come up to Scotland and catch up with friends while we still could, amid lockdowns, support bubbles, and alert levels.

Our hosts, Luke and Hazel, were asking about my research—was I still working on hallucinations, stuff like that. I told them I was. We got talking about Third Man experiences. They are both avid adventurers, and had recently tackled the marshes of Alaska with a kayak and not much else. They seemed to know the old stories well.

"I had those," said Luke, meaning hallucinations. "Like Shackleton. In Antarctica."

* * *

Punta Arenas, Chile. November 2015. Almost a century after the crew of the *Endurance* returned, another journey began from the same town—that of Luke Robertson, on his first expedition to Antarctica. His goal: to ski solo to the South Pole, and become the youngest Briton to do so.

Most of us are satisfied with one life. Some people's lives change direction, or take an unexpected course; some of us look back and wish we had done more with the one we have. Luke, in contrast, is someone who wasn't happy with just one, two, or three. By the age of thirty-five, he was well into his fourth stretch.

I had first met Luke a few years ago—he was getting married to a friend of mine from university. Their wedding was on his family's farm in Aberdeenshire: all rolling fields, massive hedgerows, and—it being northeast Scotland—driving, pouring rain in August. We arrived late on a Friday, and mercifully some friends of ours had put up a tent for us (I was never much of an outdoorsman).

It's not often that you go to a wedding where the groom has recently returned from the South Pole. Even less common is when something like that is one of the less extraordinary things about him.

In summer 2008, like many students, Luke was looking for something to do instead of revising for his finals at Glasgow University. As a fit and healthy twenty-three-year-old, he decided to give blood at a local donor center. On his way out, he picked up a voicemail from his GP. He'd had a few pains in his arm and chest—nothing too severe, but something that was worth checking on, as he soon found out.

The message was startling. Luke would need a pacemaker, with immediate effect. His diagnosis was a complete heart block—a condition where the electrical signals sent between different sections of the heart are disrupted. Without treatment, his heart could beat arrhythmically and even stop: a surprising condition for a man in his early twenties. It was Friday; he was to call the GP back on Monday morning.

A fretful weekend of googling followed. The only person Luke knew with a pacemaker was his granddad, but he was in his nineties. On Monday, a further conversation with the doctor confirmed what would happen next: the fitting, as soon as possible, of a pacemaker into the muscles of his chest.

When faced with the shock of news like that, many of us would have to reassess what we want from our lives. We may brace ourselves for more limited horizons: a life watching what we do and what we eat, pacing ourselves and living with adjusted expectations. Luke had a number of questions for his cardiologist about what he would be able to do, but he was reassured by the positive answer he got. Because Luke was a young man, there was otherwise nothing wrong with his heart—and all things were still possible. He would have to watch how much vigorous activity he launched into—a little less rugby and football, maybe—but he didn't have furred arteries or blocked atrial valves. Provided his pacemaker kept going, he would too.

What his surgeon didn't know—and what nobody knew at that stage, apart from Luke—was that he had a different goal in mind: the South Pole. He had always wondered about going there. He knew all about Antarctica and the stories of Scott and Shackleton. Before, though, he never had a reason to go, and he didn't want to go just for the sake of it. Well, now he had a big reason: life is short, so he may as well get on with it. Some people have bucket lists: bungee jumping, visiting the Taj Mahal—even writing a book. Luke just wanted to go to the end of the earth.

The operation was a success. As he recovered from the pacemaker fitting, Luke repeatedly had the image of the South Pole in his mind. He didn't know how he would get there—he had never done anything like it—but he was determined to go. Over the next six years, he planned, researched, and slowly moved closer to the goal. He got fitter, taking up rowing, and training so hard, his pacemaker had to be removed and placed deeper in his chest. He planned solo training trips to Greenland and Norway. He told his parents and his friends about the plan, even, after a few beers, inviting his best friend to come along (although it was not enough beer to convince him, as it turned out).

He was going, pacemaker and all—nothing would stop him.

* * *

THE PLATES WERE being cleared from our table at the wedding, and tea and coffee were being served. The speeches started, and people had a lot to say. Friends called for toasts, paid tribute to the happy couple, and gave thanks for being all together—especially Luke being there with them, all in one piece.

"It's amazing, really," said the woman seated to my right, "considering all they've been through."

"Yeah," responded a man across from me. "He must be pretty fit—all that with a dodgy heart . . ."

I noticed I had managed to soak red wine into my shirt cuff.

"Well, that and the brain thing," she replied.

I put down my glass.

"Sorry—what brain thing?"

* * *

NOVEMBER 2013. IT started with headaches at work. Maybe too much screen time, or general tiredness. Some blurred vision. Luke hadn't really had headaches before, but he didn't think it was anything to worry about. He went to the GP, then got his eyes checked out at the optician's: all fine. The headaches kept coming, though, then vomiting as well; he couldn't read, he couldn't concentrate, he couldn't work. Surely something must be up.

Many people with pacemakers can't have MRI scans. It's one of the things I have to ask people when I scan them for research studies, along with questions about piercings, implants, and shrapnel ("Have you been doing any welding recently? No?" and so on). Any kind of ferrous metal within the magnetic field of the scanner room will try to move. You hear tales about people getting screened and being cleared for MRI, then remembering at the last minute about the surgical plate they had fitted many years ago or the pacemaker they only had fitted last week.

With the device in his chest, Luke couldn't have a standard scan, even just to check if anything untoward was there. He went back to the GP one more time as his symptoms worsened. The doctor shone a light behind his right eyeball to see if he could identify anything to explain Luke's symptoms.

Luke still remembers the reaction.

The doctor sat back down with a gulp. "Well, you are going to need a CT scan," he said.

"Great," said Luke. "When would that be?" He was relieved that he could finally get checked and whatever was going on could be resolved.

"I'll definitely call you by six tonight about when a scan can be booked in," he replied.

This seemed remarkable to Luke—he had been expecting fairly quick action, but not this quick. But when the doctor called back, it was even more urgent: the scan was booked for 8:30 the next morning.

What the scan showed, beyond any doubt, was a large growth in Luke's brain, directly behind his right eye. At twelve centimeters long, it was pushing on all the brain tissue around it, creating the migraine-like symptoms he had been experiencing. Luke was told he had a tumor and faced between nine months to a year in the hospital, most likely with repeated operations on his brain.

Luke doesn't remember much about getting the news, but he knows that he fainted.

This was massive—different from the news about his pacemaker, a world away from that. Back then everyone at the hospital was surprised by his age, but they reassured him, acted positive, almost. This time the outlook was grave: with an abnormality that large, the prognosis was not good. He faced losing his eyesight, or even the ability to walk. Multiple tests to see whether the tissue was benign or malignant were scheduled to be performed. Luke couldn't believe it—this was something that happened to other people, not him.

Because of Luke's pacemaker, it was a struggle to even know how much of a problem there was and how best to tackle it. Using a technique like CT rather than MRI is much less precise—you can see a large mass, but you don't get the same detail you need for planning surgery. The scan image showed a mass the size of a cricket ball that was pushing against Luke's frontal and temporal lobes and making the right side of his head swell. At one point his doctors even inserted a camera into an artery in his groin and made it travel all the way into his brain to have a look at the site of the tumor. Luke remembers the sound of it clicking away inside his skull as it surveyed the problem.

A long, dark period of uncertainty followed; Luke was faced with a future like never before. His training trips were canceled, his plans in tatters—and the prospect of a completely different life loomed. The South Pole was never farther away.

But then—something else: a lucky break, of a kind. Luke's growth wasn't a tumor: it was an enterogenous cyst. The cyst had swelled with fluid, pushing on its surroundings like a water balloon. It had likely always been there, but something may have prompted it to recently grow—a knock to the head, maybe, or some kind of exertion. When the surgeons opened Luke's skull to remove the tumor, they found a sack of liquid that could be drained and managed. A few weeks of testing later, and they were sure it was benign. He was all clear.

Far from spending nine months in the hospital, Luke would be going home in a matter of weeks. He even stayed an extra night by choice: he had made friends with the other patients on the neuro ward, none of whom were as lucky as him.

"I'm still going to the South Pole," he told his mum and dad.

* * *

I DON'T REMEMBER much more of Luke and Hazel's wedding—I think I got as far as dancing to Chaka Khan at 3 AM.[1] But not long after seeing Luke in his garden that summer, I asked him if he would mind telling me his story of the South Pole. I wanted to know what had happened to him there, to see if his experience could tell me anything more about the Third Man. I couldn't talk to Shackleton, but I could talk to Luke.

In early 2021 we are back in another lockdown, so I speak to Luke over Zoom. He looks every inch the handsome adventurer; whitish hair for his age but a broad, beaming face, and eyes that betray a quick intelligence. He doesn't look weathered or scarred, even though I know he is both these things. There is no thousand-yard stare. He doesn't really *look* like an Antarctic veteran. I wonder what kind of person puts himself in that situation, after everything that has happened. He must have some kind of death wish.

He had arrived in Antarctica in late 2015 amid a flurry of interest and expectation. Media outlets were keen on Luke's story and his expedition, with him taking on such a challenge following not one but two major health scares. Over £35,000 had been pledged to the Marie Curie cancer charity in donations for Luke's attempt on the pole, and he was keen to represent others grappling with serious illness.

"I think there's a lot of stigma about pacemakers" he told me, "You know, I can't give blood. To this day, even though I'm convinced there's no reason why I shouldn't be able to, but they're like, nope, no pacemakers." This was certainly true during Luke's preparations. Getting insurance was a nightmare, and he had to get a special letter from his hospital to give to his trip organizers, Antarctic Logistics & Expeditions (ALE). Would his pacemaker still work in subzero conditions? No one had ever really attempted this kind of thing before. As his cardiologist put it, if the temperature inside his chest got below zero, his pacemaker would stop working—but if that happened, Luke would already be long gone.

On arrival he had to spend ten frustrating days at the ALE base at Union Glacier, waiting for a weather window when he could be flown up the Hercules Inlet, the start of his solo route. (The inlet lies off the Ronne Ice Shelf south of the Weddell Sea, offering a route not unlike the one Shackleton had planned.) Luke spent the time preparing and repairing his kit, ensuring his batteries were well protected. He had two GPS monitors, plus his means of contacting the outside world: two satellite phones for contacting ALE each day, his iPhone for listening to music, and two more basic messaging devices in case of difficulty.

I asked him how he felt in that time just before he set off. "You didn't really have time to think about it too much," he said. "Everything was so busy, getting everything ready." There had been such support for the expedition that he knew he had to go ahead, with the charities backing him and all the media coverage. "You have to go now. You know, you're far too committed . . . the emails I was getting in as well from people who are ill or had had brain surgery, trauma and heart conditions at a young age, all these kinds of things. I was like, there's no way I'm not doing this." He struggled to think of the word that summed up the feeling, but it came to him eventually—"accountable." He felt accountable to everyone watching and waiting at home.

It was only really when he was dropped on the snow at Hercules Inlet that the enormity of his task struck him. The plane disappeared. And then—complete silence. As the vast polar landscape spread out before him, just a few nunataks[2] in the distance, he realized this was all on him and him alone.

"You feel so completely insignificant, and you know that if Antarctica wants to, then it can chew you up and hit you with one-hundred-mile-per-hour winds, and there's nowhere to go," he told me. "It was scary," he said. "Otherworldly."

And then the storm rolled in.

*　*　*

THE FIRST TEN days of Luke's forty-day journey were a whiteout. Each day he aimed for eighteen miles, and each day he woke in his tent, hoping that it hadn't snowed again. But it had.

An El Niño year, late 2015 was particularly snowy in Antarctica. Luke was traveling on long, thin skis perfect for skating over ice and deeply packed snow in the interior, close to the pole. Around the edges of the continent, though, the snow was much newer, softer, and deeper—making it an almost Sisyphean task to pull a hundred-kilogram sledge.

"You can't see in front of your eyes, [and] you're kind of constantly dizzy because you can't see where you are going. You're looking in front of you, and you are imagining all these strange shapes and things because you can't really see your skis," he tells me. He would edge up slopes slowly, then edge just as carefully when going down them, the lack of visibility making every movement cause for anxiety, as if he was about to walk straight into a large, white wall. A keen skier, Luke found himself snow-plowing for no reason, thinking that at any moment he was about to collide with someone or something.

Worse than imagining things, Luke was beginning to fall badly behind schedule. The conditions made progress so slow that he was well behind by day 3, and he began to enter a "calculating panic." Doing less than eighteen miles one day meant nineteen miles the next, or twenty each day for the next few days, but the conditions stayed bad, and he fell further behind. He had built some wiggle room into his schedule—forty-five days of food, and forty-five to fifty days of fuel—but not enough to cover this.

The snow was so bad that he made a Faustian pact with himself. He would eat into his later food supplies—spare bags for days 41–45—while the conditions were bad and make up time later. He wouldn't need it when he got close enough to the base at the South Pole, he reasoned. It was a big risk, but he was so hungry that he felt he had no choice. When he opened the bags, he found that Hazel had left him messages in each one, encouraging him on his final days, given that he was nearly there. It was the spur that Luke needed—he had to speed up and make sure he didn't fall short.

Mercifully, within a few days the storm abated, and conditions improved. Blue skies lit the way, so he could be confident in spotting any looming obstacles. The sastrugi—deep, ridgelike striations in the snow that could easily upend his skis and sledge if not approached with care—were coming up on Luke's route. But he was on his way.

* * *

THE INTERVIEW ROLLED on.

"So, when did things start to get . . . weird?" I ask clumsily. I wasn't meaning to be impatient, but Luke has a way of describing things, a matter-of-factness in his manner. It seemed as if he could take anything in his stride.

"Well, a bit of context first," responds Luke. "I had all these kinds of messaging devices, and they required batteries to power them." He had used these items successfully in Greenland and Norway, and they were supposed to be completely weatherproof. But as he went on to explain, the above-zero conditions on the edge of Antarctica had created condensation in Luke's pack, knocking out three of his four batteries. He needed his satellite phone working to radio in his position each day—otherwise, ALE would assume the worst. But he had to cut back on what he could, including dropping regular contact with home. He also couldn't listen to anything on his iPhone during the long march across the ice.

On day 12, his phone died, and silence descended. The weather was still good, but Luke's internal climate was changing imperceptibly.

The first time it happened was a few days later. Luke's eyes were down on his skis, as they were all the time. He looked up briefly to his left—and saw green fields. They were the fields from home, from the farm in Maryculter. Looking down again, he felt like he knew the lands all around him; he was surrounded by familiarity. Looking to his left, he felt like he could see the house and the garden he grew up in. It freaked him out.

"I hadn't read much about hallucinations or anything before I got to Antarctica. I had been aware of how being by yourself can cause things, but hadn't really thought about it too much," he tells me. It was toward the end of the day, and he could rationalize it away—he was tired, and strange things can happen. It was scary, but it was also oddly comforting. He knew he was seeing things, but at least the things he was seeing were known to him. "[It was] somewhere I recognize—it wasn't this crazy place where there's no one around for hundreds of miles," he explains.

This feeling was a new one for Luke. The sensations he was having up to that point—like when he was anticipating collisions in the snow—he'd had before, back home in Scotland. They may have been a bit more intense in Antarctica, but qualitatively they were the same thing. Any kind of adverse conditions can do that to you, even in a familiar place.

Seeing the farm, though, was like crossing a line, both inside his mind and outside his body. It was like a splash of color in a monochrome scene; a door had been opened and was now left ajar.

A brief interlude of relative normality came on day 20: Christmas Day. Luke phoned into *BBC Breakfast* to publicize his trip, but everything had to be synchronized to the minute; he had no battery to spare. Happily, he had been making good progress and been feeling strong—the sledge was getting lighter, the snow denser and more packed, and his muscles were adapting to the conditions.

I ask Luke about strategies. Without anything to listen to, how did he occupy himself? Did he talk to himself? Imagine songs, even films? I know I would have been lost in a web of inner dialogue by that point.

He shrugs and says he didn't do any of that. Songs were going round in his head though, stuck on a loop. The climber Joe Simpson famously got Boney M.'s "Brown Girl in the Ring" stuck in his head when he broke his leg and became trapped on an expedition in the Andes.[3] Luke didn't have any Boney M., but he did have the theme song to *The Flintstones* (I'm not sure which would be better). He remembers that one because it came with visualizations too: one morning, when he was looking up from his skis, he saw one of the Flintstones up ahead of him on the horizon.

Looking down wasn't necessarily any better. The constant swirl of snow and wind over the ground, snaking into the distance and under Luke's legs, created ever-changing patterns for his eyes. He saw animals of different kinds moving around below him: lions, dogs, and birds. They became so familiar to Luke that they were part of the daily routine: illusions on the snow and hallucinations on the horizon. These didn't feel familiar to him—not like the fields from home—but they became the norm.

The knowledge that these kinds of experiences can occur in polar conditions seemed to help Luke keep calm. They might still give you a jolt, but being ready for them, knowing they are part of the territory—all that helps someone to ready themselves for tricks of the mind.

But some experiences are much harder to ignore. We don't always get to choose how we respond, no matter how much we rationalize it or tell ourselves to feel differently. And for Luke, that came with a voice.

On most days, the only sound breaking the silence was the squeak of Luke's skis. But on windy days, the whistle of the air across the ice created a shifting and unsettling soundscape. And around day 25, Luke began to hear something. A voice calling his name, just now and again, from behind. A male voice, maybe, someone trying to catch his attention. Almost like his own voice. He remembers the first time it happened: "I dropped my poles and looked behind. *Who was that? What just happened there? Am I going mad?* Then I was like: *OK, there's no one here, there's no one around. Just focus, focus, focus, focus. This is just the wind.*"

But it kept happening, multiple times throughout the day. Luke would talk himself down, but every time it happened, he had to turn around. He couldn't shake the feeling that someone was there, just behind him, over his left shoulder. Catching up with him, close enough to touch. He couldn't not look.

"I had to keep turning round, because I told myself, if there's ever anyone behind me and I get a tap on my shoulder, I would collapse— like, the pacemaker's not going to save me."

A presence being able to stop his pacemaker had not been in the letter from the hospital. I wondered at how that felt—to be out there on your own, constantly feeling like someone was there. It sounded like something out of a horror movie; the ever-approaching figure, never gone but never quite reaching you. A heart stopping with fright when the touch finally came.

At first, Luke was more irritated than anything else. It was unnerving, but most of all he was frustrated that he couldn't stop himself from looking behind him. "I felt like it was so real . . . it's so bizarre thinking about it now. I had to keep looking round and reminding myself, *There's no one there, there's no one there, there's no one there . . .*" Luke says this with his hands to his face, as if turning away from a dream.

Many voice-hearers with psychosis describe this sort of experience. The inability to turn away from a voice—the way it grabs your attention, whether you want it to or not. We all get this, to some degree; researchers study the "cocktail party" effect where we suddenly pick our name out from the sounds of a crowded room, full of conversation.[4] It feels like there is something fundamental about how we respond when called to; we can tell ourselves to ignore it and not react at all, but you can never quite switch off that reflex, that urge to look. Someone is there, even though you know each time that there can't be.

"Eventually, it just became the norm, and I just accepted it," he goes on. He explains how he told himself that it didn't matter what these things were or why they were occurring—it was just a question of whether they would go away, and if they wouldn't, how then would he live with them. "As long as I'm thinking these thoughts, then I'm alive and I'm skiing. So everything's not as bad as it sounds or as scary as it feels," he said.

This all sounded remarkably levelheaded to me. I feel like I would have been going out of my mind. It could be a post hoc rationalization, I suppose—it's never pleasant to think back to a time when we aren't in control, when our mental experience becomes unpredictable and alien, and we may no longer be the author of our own thoughts. This could be "calm Luke" now telling me everything was fine, but I wanted to know what it was like for "freaked-out Luke" on his carpet of ice animals.

But Luke's philosophy of acceptance—if we can call it that— seemed very genuine to me. Toward the start of our conversation he talked about how he viewed a place like Antarctica. "There's a phrase that I think gets overused, a little bit, which is 'conquering' something: conquering Everest, conquering the South Pole, whatever it is. I've never tried to use that phrase before because I just don't believe in it. I think if you try to conquer something that is unconquerable, then you get yourself into all sorts of trouble. You work with those environments, you work with nature, you adapt to it. It's in control."

On the trip, Luke's conditions continued to worsen; more white-outs, plus he had arrived at the sastrugi. A false move now and he could break a ski, a leg, or worse. His sleep was worsening too, going down from six hours a night in the first week to little over three hours a night in the final ten days. Any kind of sleep deprivation is bad for your physical and mental health, but it's particularly bad for increasing your propensity to hallucinate. Most of us will begin to see or hear things that aren't there if we stay up for more than two days straight—our brains are just not cut out for constant waking.[5]

Luke's food stocks were getting dangerously low; he was losing weight and losing energy, a lethal combination. The final climb to the South Pole reaches three thousand meters above sea level, and it gets much, much colder. At two hundred miles out, Luke was getting worried, and the voice behind him was getting more frequent. Luke started to show signs of frostbite, something he kept from his contacts at the ALE base. When he spoke to them, they were worried. Everyone knew it was a hard year, the conditions were terrible, and Luke, after all, was essentially a novice. At the end of the call, they put a familiar voice on the line—Steve Jones, an Oxford-based coordinator who had helped Luke set up the trip. He reassured Luke that he was doing well, and noted that he was at the most dangerous point: "summit fever." He wanted Luke to stay safe and wished him well.

The call was a real boost, the first contact Luke had had for days with someone other than the people taking his daily coordinates. Before setting off once more, he sat down on his sledge for a moment. He looked across at a hill in the distance. It was a hill from the farm, from home. It looked just like it. Except, obviously, it wasn't. It was like the feeling of his conversation had seeped out into the snow, springing up shoots of hope, bringing back that sense of familiarity again.

With just over three days to go—three days before all of Luke's supplies would run out—he realized he needed to ski seventy miles, effectively nonstop, if he was going to make it. He planned to sleep for three hours, then ski around thirty miles, grab another ninety minutes of sleep, then attack the remaining forty miles—over forty-eight straight hours. He could barely sleep in any case, his mind whirring with anticipation. The Antarctic sun at that time of year is constant, so night and day become meaningless.

When he rose after that first stretch of sleep, he packed up and checked behind himself, making sure he hadn't left anything, and set off. Five kilometers later, he put his hand in his pocket for his GPS monitor. It wasn't there. He checked his other pocket, then another one. Then his pack. Not there either. He couldn't believe it. He had a backup one, but it had less battery, and he couldn't risk something happening to that one—if he lost both, his journey would likely take much, much longer. Exhausted and despairing, he lay down. Time to calculate the cost once more.

To go back to his camp would be a four-hour round trip—losing rather than gaining ground.

He didn't have time to go back, but he couldn't risk going on. And more than anything else, he just wanted to stop. Just . . . stop.

And then he heard it.

Another voice—different this time. Female, maybe, in a different tone. Ahead of him, not behind. Thinking back now, he can't remember what it said, but he remembers the meaning. It was something like, "Come on," "You got this," or "Get going." The voice was comforting, just like the hills from home. This wasn't the wind, or the snow—it was a voice with an authority that came from somewhere else entirely.

He told himself he had to go back, that he couldn't take the risk of losing his equipment. He rose, raced back, and found the GPS a few hundred meters from where he had camped. Now he had the GPS, he started feeling lighter and quicker as he sped along. And something else happened: the "Luke" voice—his first voice—started up again. But there was no wind to speak of this time. The voice was just there, with him, for the final stretch.

I try to ask Luke about the second, female voice, but he struggles to describe much more. He remembers it being distinctly different from the first voice behind him, and it didn't give him that sense of presence, on his shoulder, not in the same way. It was hard to say if it existed in any space at all, and it only came at very specific times: once, when he had to turn back for the GPS monitor, and once more, for the ultimate push.

"This was about thirty-five hours into the day [his final, sleepless forty-eight-hour ski], and I remember wanting to give them an update. And I was like, I'm not going to sit down on the back of my sledge and fall asleep." He made the call to the base, reassured them that he was OK and only about twelve hours away, and hung up. "I was just so tired, I couldn't even stand, my legs were fading. . . . And I sat down. I shut my eyes—don't even remember shutting my eyes, but I obviously blinked, and they stayed shut for longer and longer. And then I was woken, by a voice. . . . The same voice as the day before. And it said "Oi!"

Luke had fallen asleep, for only a matter of seconds. Anything more and the consequences could have been fatal. Even that close to the camp at the South Pole, it would have taken hours for anyone to find him. "At that point it was probably minus thirty-five, minus forty. It's not where you want to be when you want to fall asleep," he explains, with characteristic understatement. That simple call, from the second voice, gave Luke the strength to get up and finish the journey. "It was like, I can't sit down again. You're so close, you've one percent of the journey left, do not mess this up, do not fail everyone that's been backing you."

Luke made it up the final slope and skied into the base amid another storm. He was so used to hallucinating by this point that he assumed the pylons of the base—the suspended Amundsen station—were also tricks of the mind, appearing to him as if they were the legs of a spaceship. A member of ALE had to call out to him to bring him in, as he couldn't work out where he was.

He was the only person to finish the journey on their own that season.

Forty days. As if it was ever in doubt.

*   *   *

AFTERWARD I ASK Luke again about the two voices that spoke to him. It strikes me that these weren't quite the same as the kinds of presences described by Shackleton and others. They seemed to have presence, but not in the same way. They came and went, doing different things at different times, in different conditions. And there appeared to be two of them—but who they were, Luke couldn't say.

"Did you ever think someone was actually there with you?" I ask.

"Yeah, I thought for sure towards the end. I felt it was quite strange because it was always behind me. I felt as if I was leading them. It was kind of my duty as they were relying on me. . . . I wasn't following someone, I was making sure that other people were safe . . . like I needed to get them to safety."

This surprises me for two reasons. First, the presences described in most Third Man accounts don't follow, they lead—or, at least, they accompany their hosts. We are used to guardian angels intervening, showing the way in times of need. They don't turn up to add to the burden, surely? Second, Luke says he was leading this voice, saving it, almost. And yet—this was the voice that was about to tap him on the shoulder if he didn't turn around. A presence that could have stopped his heart, apparently. It made no sense.

He goes on. "The only points where I felt like I was being led were those two instances we talked about." He means with the second voice, which had sent him back for the GPS and that woke him from sleep. He described it as if it were "his turn" to be led. This sort of thing was much more like the accounts of people like Beck Weathers or even Shackleton and his sense of providence—something beyond Luke, stepping in just in time. I ask him how aware he was of these other accounts, but other than reading *South*, he knew very little about them. He hadn't even thought about hallucinations, really— not before, and not much after. In fact, I was one of the first people he had spoken to about them.

Luke seemed to have been thinking of others a lot on the ice— what they would think, what they would expect. That he was there *for* them and they, somehow, were therefore there *with* him. I ask Luke if that was right.

"I actually had never thought about it, but I guess. Whether or not that voice could be related to feeling like they were there with me, I don't know." He pauses. "But at the same time—I was the only one that could lead them because they weren't there, and that accountability was there as well. . . . It definitely helped, that voice. After the initial frustration of looking behind me, it was just, this is how it's going to be."

There's that word again. Accountable. Even here, thousands of miles away from almost anyone, a man with a pacemaker and a surgical scar across his scalp carried the weight of many over the ice. One ahead, one behind, and him.

Who is the fourth?

I couldn't stand in Luke's shoes and experience what he had—any number of conversations would not allow me to do that. But I could look him in the face and catch a glimpse of what couldn't be said— what baffled and dumbfounded Luke, and what was shrugged off as immaterial.

His experience was clearly different from Shackleton's in many ways. Luke's visitors were not silent companions—far from it—and in fact he experienced a range of hallucinatory phenomena: illusions, visions, voices, and presence. He was traveling on his own, not with others or with a larger expedition. He wasn't making a journey after over eighteen months of hardship and survival; his journey was days and weeks, not months and years. Perhaps most significantly, for

Luke this didn't seem to be the transformative, lasting experience that the South Georgia party had alluded to. Or maybe I'm just a clumsy interviewer.

Nevertheless, the presences Luke experienced raised a number of questions. They surprised me in their distinction—both in form and function. The figure behind, both chasing and following Luke, had a sense of needing to be led. Luke was responsible for that figure, and it had a feeling of presence, albeit with a voice. In contrast, the voice ahead that only spoke twice—that voice led Luke. The second voice didn't seem to have a sense of continued presence in Luke's description, but it acted in many ways like the archetypal Third Man; saving him from disaster, from a frozen sleep. Together, these two figures pushed and pulled Luke to his ultimate goal—but they did so in very different ways.

If not all presences take the lead, how might we look back at the accounts of Shackleton, Worsley, and Crean? Is there another way of considering their experiences and the synchrony of what happened to them? Could there be another piece of the puzzle, provided by the experiences of a young man nearly a century on?

The main thing Shackleton is now celebrated for is his leadership—he's the man who lost no men, who saved the whole crew of the *Endurance*. One of the main things his biographers agree upon is that Shackleton was supremely committed to the men under his command. This was the case on each of his expeditions, but particularly on the *Endurance*. As described by Roland Huntford: "Shackleton did not want others to suffer for his ambition. He felt an intense and very personal responsibility for anyone who served under him."[6]

Added to this picture are the circumstances in which *South* was written. When he met Sørlle in Stromness, Shackleton and the others were amazed to find that the war was ongoing and its scale was so large. It took them many weeks to adjust, although Shackleton had to learn quickly, as his requests to the British government to provide help in rescuing the crew from Elephant Island fell on deaf ears. Shackleton's reception by the British public was mixed at best, with many people questioning the worth of expensive and resource-sapping adventuring at a time of dire need. Many of the crew served in the war almost immediately after their return—Shackleton and Wild ended up in Murmansk, on the North Russian front. Despite Shackleton's offer at the start of the war, there was still a degree of guilt and embarrassment that the *Endurance* expedition had taken place amid the greatest war ever seen.

Everything we know about "the fourth" was told, heard, and written down in this context. It must have been hard for Shackleton and his men to explain and justify the hardships they had faced, let alone what they have achieved. How could they possibly do so when thousands were dying on the front every day? This isn't to say that the experience was a post hoc creation, that something didn't happen to Shackleton, Worsley, and Crean on their journey across the island. They claim to have shared their experiences not long after, and they had no clue what was happening in the wider world while they were trudging over ridge after ridge on their long march. But the interpretation of their experiences, as they looked back, would inevitably have been colored and shaped by a whole gamut of emotion, encompassing guilt, shame, wonder, and grief. It's hard to separate those kinds of feelings from what can be said about the experience itself.

Leaving aside the war, each of the men had reasons to already be experiencing these feelings when they set out that morning on May 19. It had taken months and years to reach that point, and they still weren't sure of safety—and not just their own safety, but the lives of the rest of the crew. Accounts of the South Georgia trek don't tend to dwell on those men left behind, but it is surely significant that Shackleton, Worsley, and Crean were the last men of the *Endurance*; the only hope left. How must that have shaped their thinking, their prayers, their desperation? How could they not have the other men on their minds?

Shackleton died from heart failure in January 1922 during a final visit to Antarctica, and he was buried in Grytviken cemetery on South Georgia. Later that year, his friend the journalist Harold Begbie

published a collection of conversations with Shackleton, "a little essay in Shackletonian psychology."[7] One quote from Begbie's book
has been used repeatedly in discussions of the Third Man: the title of
chapter 2 in this book, Shackleton's reference to "things which should
never be spoken of." But there is another, longer quote that is barely
discussed, although just as important:

> Do you see, Begbie, it was like this: the thought of those fellows
> on Elephant Island kept us going all the time. It might have been
> different if we'd had only ourselves to think about. You can get so
> tired in the snow, particularly if you're hungry, that sleep seems just
> the best thing life has to give. And to sleep out there is to die, to die
> without any pain at all, like Keats's ideal of death.
>
> But if you're a leader, a fellow that other fellows look to, you've
> got to keep going. That was the thought that sailed us through
> the hurricane and tugged us up and down those mountains. Of
> course, I couldn't say all this in the book. I couldn't give the mental
> side of the story. But that is the side, looking back, that interests me
> the most.[8]

Luke's presences weren't just saving him; they needed him. He had
a responsibility to them. His experiences remind us that relating to
others is not a one-way street; duties, hopes, and desires go in both
directions. It stands to reason that if our minds somehow create others, then our feelings toward them will reflect that complexity.

Ultimately, we cannot know who the fourth man was for Shackleton, Worsley, or Crean.

But some presences lead. And some are led.

5

The Presence Robot

Talking to Luke had opened up something new. Whatever it was that had accompanied him, it wasn't clearly just about coping, or providence. It was something messier than that, something to do with the bonds that tied him, the weight he felt upon him. The experiences he had were tethered not just to his body but to his heart. That idea of presence having a "feeling of connection" for the perceiver seemed more relevant than ever.

And yet, like the tales from neurology clinics, these strange stories don't always offer a clear path forward. Each individual case fits some sort of model, but it also generates new questions. There is such a variety of different experiences that it can seem that any theory can be supported through careful observation. This is particularly the case when we are trying to make sense of things retrospectively. We can probably find an explanation for anything, and we don't always get the chance to test our explanations. To do that, we would have to somehow create a presence.

Some scientists think we already can. In 2006, a team of neurologists led by Shahar Arzy and Olaf Blanke reported on an unusual case of felt presence. A twenty-two-year-old woman was having a pre-surgical evaluation for epilepsy treatment, and she had given consent to have her brain stimulated with electrical current, just like Wilder Penfield's patients many years before. Among the sites stimulated was the left *temporoparietal junction* (TPJ), an area of the brain behind and above the ear where the back of the temporal lobe meets the lower side of the parietal lobe. When the experimenters probed this area, a striking thing happened: a strong feeling of a shadow presence befell the woman, occurring directly behind where she was sitting. When they tried it again, she described "a 'person' as young and of indeterminate sex, a 'shadow' who did not speak or move, and whose position beneath her back was identical to her own."[1] They then tried stimulation while she was standing, then in a different sitting position: each time the presence mimicked her, and at one point— unpleasantly—she felt it embrace her. Like the presences of PH, or August Strindberg, this shadow figure was not her, but its movements were inextricably tied to her own. What had produced this phantom?

The answer to this question seems likely to lie in the integration of signals from several different parts of the brain. The TPJ doesn't handle sensory or motor signals itself; in fact, the TPJ is one of the points of the brain that is the farthest away from our primary sensory or motor regions.[2] In other words, it is in a position to provide an abstracted overview of what's going on. Despite its name, it is actually close to the joining of three lobes: temporal, parietal, and occipital. There it can process information on sound and language via temporal regions, information about body, touch, and space via parietal areas, and visual information via occipital cortex. It also receives input from the limbic system and the thalamus, a key nexus that lies deep in the forebrain and acts as a relay for sensory and motor signals. The TPJ is a crossroads-like area where all these signals can meet and be combined, enabling us to do many complex things. In an MRI experiment, we might expect to see the TPJ involved when people are tracking gaze, tracing hidden intentions, or viewing things from other perspectives. And building selves.

Based on a range of evidence, it has been suggested that the TPJ might provide a simulation of where we are in space. Think of it like a map of our body position, our movement, and our direction at any one moment. Right now I am seated at my desk, slightly hunched over my laptop in a way that I shouldn't be. The TPJ is adding up all the information I have about my body and placing that in a perceived space: Ben is upright(ish), sitting, with two feet on the floor and his hands on the table in front of him.

This isn't likely to be a single representation of us but the product of a range of information about our senses and bodies, distributed across the brain in a network (Brugger likes to call this the "neuromatrix"). The TPJ seems to be important in linking all this information together, and interrupting its function disrupts the whole scheme. Thus, when Arzy and Blanke stimulated the left TPJ, interfering with the usual neural activity in that region, integration became disintegration. The patient's simulation of their own body map—sitting down, passively waiting—became a mirror instead, a shadow presence transported.

Stranger still, something similar might be happening for out-of-body experiences, when people suddenly feel they are floating above their body or are able to observe it from the outside. You might have come across this kind of thing before when people talk about near-death experiences: on the operating table, or in the midst of a serious accident, the person might feel like they have drifted away from their body momentarily. Blanke and colleagues had previously observed seizure activity in the TPJ of a person with epilepsy and frequent out-of-body experiences, and of people imagining being in that kind of situation.[3] Crucially though, this was observed in the right TPJ, not the left, as if the two areas were doing something similar but subtly different. Both areas seem to be able to handle signals about where our bodies are in space. If we interfere with the right TPJ, it's like we zoom out from our bodies, suddenly able to see them from the outside looking in. If we do the same for the left, our bodies zoom out from us—producing another figure, a presence.

You don't even need to directly stimulate the brain to induce these kinds of effects. Sensory integration depends on timing—all these signals, coming in all the time, must be combined seamlessly, harmonized and consistent with one another. When they cohere, they are thought to create a unified sense of ourselves. But when they are delayed or disrupted, the self seems to go astray.

Imagine if you were to clap your hands now in front of your face and you heard the sound a split second before your hands met. What would you think? Did you make that sound . . . or did someone else? How uncanny or unusual would it feel if one sense got there before the other? I know what belongs to me, I know where my body starts and stops, in part because all the senses and all my muscles are playing the same tune. Things happen in lockstep, effects on the wider world are predictable. But when the timing goes wrong, so does the confidence in what belongs to us. Famous effects like the "rubber hand illusion" rely on this principle: if I stroke a rubber hand with a brush at precisely the same time as your actual hand is being stroked, I could probably convince you that the rubber hand was yours, provided it was in a realistic position.[4] The synchrony of the cues from what you see and what you feel can override everything else you know about where your hand actually is, so this new rubber hand becomes part of you. I have used this illusion many times in public science events to demonstrate the shakiness of our sense of body ownership. It usually ends with the experimenter threatening to strike the rubber hand with a hammer, at which point the volunteer recoils because they think it's their hand being attacked.* It doesn't work for everyone, but it does seem to for many of us: momentarily, a new object becomes part of one's own body, enveloped into a body schema, to solve an unusual coincidence of timing. It's a surprising example of how open some of the boundaries of the self can be.

The invisible touch

In 2014, Blanke and colleagues offered a more detailed model for how this process works for presence—this time, with the help of

---

* This, incidentally, is probably the only time you are allowed to attack members of the public with a hammer.

a robot.[5] First, they used a technique known as lesion mapping to explore where, in the brain, feelings of presence were coming from for a group of neurological patients, the large majority of whom had epilepsy. For some of the patients, presences just occurred from time to time (most likely due to localized epileptic activity). For others, the feeling could be induced via focal stimulation, as in the 2006 experiment with the shadow figure. By combining the data for all the sites at which this occurred, Blanke's team came up with three regions that seemed key to producing a feeling of presence: (1) the insula, (2) TPJ, and (3) another area, higher up in parietal cortex, known as the *superior parietal lobule* (see figure 3). When they then compared this collection of areas to data from patients with other kinds of hallucinations, only the last area—the superior parietal lobule—was unique to feelings of presence.

What, then, does this tell us? From epilepsy case reports we have come across the insula before—it's an area we rely on for information on internal states and self-reflection. The importance of the TPJ seems to involve both space and integrating the senses, potentially into a kind of body map. But what of this third area, in the parietal cortex?

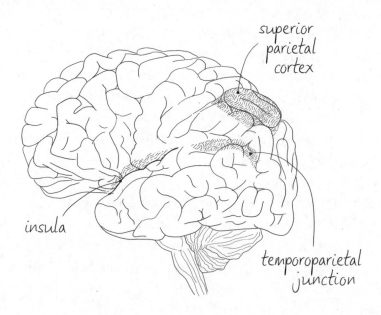

FIGURE 3

This region is known for often working in tandem with parts of the frontal lobes to support action and attention. Blanke and colleagues argued that this area is significant because it suggests that presences might be linked to *sensorimotor* processing—specifically, planning and executing coordinated motor actions. This, they say, is the bit that is missing from other experiences, like autoscopy, but key to feelings of presence—the plans and expectations of our own motor system and the sensations we expect when we move around.

To test this idea, they deployed a novel contraption—a presence robot. Imagine you are facing a wall with a button in front of you. When you push it, you expect a bit of resistance back. What you don't expect is to be touched yourself, from directly behind you. This is what the presence robot does (see figure 4). When you push the button, a "master" robot activates a slave system behind you, transferring the touch back to you. Sometimes this happens in sync, but sometimes it doesn't (an asynchronous touch). Sometimes you feel pushback on your finger, but sometimes you don't (a "no force" condition).

Various "full-body" illusions are well-known to be induced with such synchronous movements: touching something and being touched in sync can make you feel transported forward, or you may feel as if you are touching your own back—a bit like an extension of the rubber hand illusion to one's whole body map.[6] Blanke and colleagues reasoned that, if feelings of presence were dependent on our motor system, then maybe disrupting usual patterns of synchrony could induce the experience of a presence.

This is exactly what they found. Touches in sync gave the sense of touching one's own back and feeling transported forward. Self-projection, in other words, but without presence. But *delaying* the touch of the slave robot seemed to do the opposite, pulling the projection backward instead. Initially, without even asking about felt presence, nearly half of the participants (five out of twelve) spontaneously described a distinct sense of a figure standing behind them. Another person was felt to be there, delivering the touches instead. When they tried the experiment again and asked people to specifically

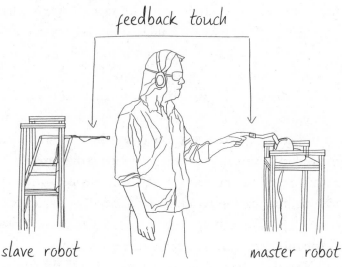

feedback touch

slave robot   master robot

FIGURE 4

rate whether a presence was induced, three-quarters of participants endorsed the feeling.[7] This was particularly apparent when no force (i.e., pushback) was felt on the fingers—so participants were pushing into a feeling of thin air, and yet they were feeling touches on their own back after a delay. This kind of "sensorimotor conflict" creates a baffling scenario for our bodies—we are acting, but we aren't getting the right feedback, nor at the right time. Confound the expectations of the motor system and you change the body map; change the body map and you conjure the other. The authors argued that it is the first ever successful experimental induction of felt presence.

We have moved, then, from spontaneous activation and epilepsy, to mirror figures and body maps, and finally to sensorimotor expectations. If Blanke's team is right, felt presence appears to be a combo of all three—a spontaneous change in our expectations of where our bodies *and* our movements should be. Could this explain the presences we have come across in other contexts such as psychosis and schizophrenia?[8]

The first thing to notice is that the robot presence relies on touch and motor movement—but it isn't clear that the presences of psychosis are as closely linked to touch as that. Thinking back to chapter 1, we recall that some people report touches, but what people describe often seems to be more about someone being *in* their space—it's a creepy feeling, but is it a touchy feeling? Maybe if your sense of your body was really disrupted, it wouldn't even need a touch, you would just feel the existence of the other—but it would be hard to show that. A second point to consider concerns the role of emotion. The procedure used by Blanke's team gives us *a* kind of presence. But is it the presence we are looking for? The robot presences of the lab seem far from the chilling figures recalled by Alex or the mysterious family described by PH—if anything, they just seem neutral. Experiences with these phenomena seem somehow colorless; they lack a certain magnetism. Where is the affinity, or the menace, in these presences?

I don't know how convinced I am about this model being able to explain presences in psychosis. They don't always operate by touch, or even mirroring—instead they have identity, intention, and meaning. But the Blanke experiments do something else hugely important by showing the way toward a model of how such a thing can occur. They demonstrate the fundamental malleability of body, space, and self. This is a kind of self that we are constructing all the time, but it's a temporary structure, susceptible to sudden, unpredictable winds and currents. It seems highly plausible that conditions like schizophrenia and epilepsy could disrupt this construction process, this subtle orchestration of mind and body. We need to know more to understand presence—but it shows how such bizarre and confounding things are even possible.

The Art of Presence

Following the publication of what Blanke and his team had found, a piece in the *New Scientist* in November 2014 triumphantly announced, "Ever felt a ghostly presence? Now we know why." The ability to successfully induce such experiences and to localize them to specific areas of the brain appeared to be a great leap ahead. Far from paranormal, the ingenious methods of experimental psychology were allowing us to chart one of the more uncanny corners of human experience.

One of the people who read the *New Scientist* article was the interactive media specialist Naomi Lea. She was studying for a new kind of master's degree at Bartlett School of Architecture in London— "Design for Performance & Interaction"—and she became fascinated by the prospect of trying to create such experiences. The reports of the presence robot might sound like science fiction, but for Naomi they recalled another world of conjuring: that of spirits and the spaces in which they dwell. Over the course of five installations, she set about simulating the uncanny feeling of being joined by another. The pieces were exhibited each time as a walk-in installation, a series of spaces and artifacts designed to bring forth shadowy companions.

I was about two years too late to try out the exhibition myself, but I managed to talk to Naomi about her work. I was keen to know what brought her to the topic of felt presence in the first place. Her first aim was to create an environment that interacts with you in a simple way. This resulted in a drawing machine that would start writing in sand when it detected someone entering the room. Movement by visitors would prompt movement by the machine—a relatively simple task providing you have some proximity sensors at hand— and a lightbox under the sand would make it appear as if words were bursting out from below.

"A lot of people still think that that was my most successful project, maybe because it was the most intuitive," she explained. "I think the thing that really intrigued me as I was looking at it was actually this emotion or feeling of awe." For visitors to the first installation, the sudden appearance of magical writing, out of nowhere, captured people's imaginations, but sometimes in ambivalent ways. Naomi became interested in what it really means to feel awe of this kind: "There were a lot of people trying to define the emotion of awe in relationship to the 'sublime,' but when people encounter something that's sublime, there's also a sense of fear. So, it's not just a solely pleasant experience—it's actually that there's a bit of the unknown that is kind of unsettling."

The reaction to her first installation prompted Naomi to delve deeper into the theory and science behind inducing presences. She was struck by the idea of constructing the self via sensory integration, and by the way it appeared to come so easily apart, like pulling at a loose thread on a sweater. As she continued working, her thinking changed. "I initially thought it's just something you can construct, almost like a ghost or a spirit-like configuration. But it actually had a lot to do with yourself," she said.

By this, Naomi meant that people's reactions differed from installation to installation and person to person. After her first attempt, Naomi experimented with shadow and movement to varying degrees of success before having more consistent results with her final installation. In this iteration, you sit at an underlit tabletop across from an empty space. As you reach across the table, shadows of your arms and hands appear—but from the other side of the table. At first the shadows are in sync with your movements, but they become asynchronous over time. These asynchronous movements are still your arms, but they are random prerecorded snippets, played at the wrong time, to give the impression that they belong to another person. If you touch the shadow, you feel it—haptic feedback (i.e., buzzing and vibration) is built into the surface just for those moments.

Naomi's installation had many similarities with the presence robot setup: the use of synchrony and the mirroring of movement, with unpredictable disruptions, gave a feeling that another person was in the room. In contrast, when she looks back at her first installation, she thinks that a lot of the surrounding cues added to the effect. The rest of the room was dark, and the writing machine made a quiet, scratchy noise against the surface of the sand. Naomi thought that, for some people, personal expectations were shaping their response to the unknown scribe. "It's hosted in this black box, and it's lit from underneath, and there might be I think just a simple case of cultural connotation, where people may be relating [it] to some of the other cultural references from their background, from films, for example," she explained.

The piece that really worked for Naomi herself was a collection of wooden sticks hanging from the ceiling that would drift delicately through the air when visitors entered the room. They had no connection to specific movements or touch. It didn't quite create a feeling of presence for everyone who encountered it, but it did for Naomi. It reminded her of a Shinto temple she had visited in Japan, when she had lived there for a period. At the center of this temple stood a gateway, and through it an altar-like area. Behind that, there was an opening with a shimmering white curtain. Every now and again the wind would catch the curtain, causing it to drift toward the observer—as if an unknown figure was there waiting, even welcoming. To reach the curtain, one must pass through many gates along the way, and at the final gate the curtain is framed at a distance from the observer. The setting, the preparation, and the expectation combined to create something otherworldly. Even when she thinks of it now, Naomi feels as if her encounter with the temple brought forth a spirit of some kind.

Naomi's encounters with presence act as a timely reminder about the nature of this phenomenon. In trying to understand mysterious and unusual experiences, one can have a tendency to look ever further into individual cases, seeking cognitive processes, brain regions, cortical networks that can explain hallucinatory happenings. The evidence would seem to suggest that the sense of our own bodies is important to understanding presence, but our bodies aren't inert objects, placed in a vacuum. They are defined—at least partly—by the spaces around them.

Thus, when visitors came to see Naomi's exhibits, some worked for them, and some didn't. For those that didn't, maybe the lighting wasn't quite right, maybe the room was too warm, maybe the sound wasn't quite what they expected. But for those that did, different sensations, in different environments, combined to hit a sweet spot; a mixture of expectation and perception that subtly undermined the sense of space.

Our brains might create a bodily self—but that body has to exist in space. Some spaces will make our bodies grow or shrink, contract or relax. Where we draw the line, where we distinguish ourselves from others, these things will shift with the space we are in. The presences we encounter might be familiar companions, or unsettling doppelgängers, or just neutral entities, but the conditions around us have to be right for them to appear at all.

6

"I'll Set the Table for Three People When It's Just Me and My Wife"

In 2002, an essay by psychiatrists Dennis Chan and Martin Rossor appeared in the *Lancet* medical journal. Its title "—but who is that on the other side of you?" was a reference to Eliot's Third Man, and it called for attention to two conditions affected by felt presence: Parkinson's disease and dementia with Lewy bodies (DLB).

The two diseases are closely linked, both involving "Parkinsonian" changes to motor functioning, such as tremors. They also involve changes to mood, thinking, and behavior—but whereas the course of Parkinson's can be slow, developing sometimes over twenty years or more, DLB moves fast, with its major symptoms appearing within two years. This is because of Lewy bodies—bundles of a protein called alpha-synuclein—that appear in brain cells. These Lewy bodies cluster in disparate parts of the midbrain and cortex, disrupting ordinary signaling and changing the way people think and feel.

Visual hallucinations are known to occur in both conditions. This is particularly the case for DLB, but their relationship with Parkinson's may be surprising. In contrast to some of the hallucinations reported in psychotic disorders, they are often experienced as silent and unthreatening, and they don't appear to have the same emotional impact as voices and visions do for people with schizophrenia. Based on this observation, Chan and Rossor suggested that the kinds of hallucinations reported in DLB may bear comparison to the silent presences described in Shackleton's case, plus similar accounts from elsewhere: presences visiting shipwrecked sailors and mountaineers, among others. Silent like sentinels, feelings of presence drifted through these disparate examples—could they shed some light on the nature of dementia?

Chan and Rossor were used to asking about visual hallucinations when talking to people with DLB. To their surprise, they found that several of their patients also endorsed feelings of presence when asked about them in the clinic, particularly the presence of someone "behind or beside them." One patient described:

A sensation that someone was sitting on his left side when he was driving or at his desk but, when he turned round to inspect the person, nobody was to be seen. This ghost-like presence was always silent and emotionally neutral, in that the patient was neither alarmed nor reassured. On no occasion did he experience a visual hallucination.[1]

The last sentence here is important: presence occurring without visual hallucinations. It is significant because something as nebulous as a "feeling of presence" could simply be a sign of something else, another way of describing the feeling anyone would get after seeing something they can't explain. Frequent visual hallucinations of a face or a full person, for example, could just prompt a sense of presence as a form of expectation. It would be logical to think that someone was there with you. It wouldn't even take that much—how many of us have caught sight of something briefly, or heard a faint voice, and immediately searched for the source? It is a natural reaction to a glimpse of something uncanny or uncertain. We have already heard of examples like this: Luke's main encounters in Antarctica, for example, began with voices, and the feeling of their presence came later. If that was the case—if that was all that was happening—it could be that there is nothing particularly unusual about the experience. In that situation, when we talk about "presence" we would just be using a different kind of language to refer to some of the vagaries of everyday perception.

But a presence on its own—a *pure* presence, in a sense—marks it as something in and of itself: not a redescription, not a misunderstanding of words, but an encounter. It is something that can stand alone, and that warrants its own explanation—even if, confusingly, it doesn't seem to have much by way of any clear content. When people describe presences in this way, it is as if we can experience personhood abstracted from overt signs of a voice, a face, or a body. It's as if simply "being there" is something separable and basic to be understood.

Until recently, there was very little research available on presences in conditions like Parkinson's. A small handful of studies had documented such experiences, and fewer still had sought to systematically explore them. In 2000, a study by Gilles Fénelon and colleagues in France had surveyed 216 patients with Parkinson's. Thirty-five had experienced presences, "commonly as vivid as a hallucinated scene and . . . described as a 'perception.'"[2] The language the patients used for the experience was often visual, but of an impossible kind: one patient said, "I see someone arriving—I turn back but nobody is there," while another stated that "the image is behind me."[3]

Such examples almost sound like vivid cases of mental imagery— the mind's eye creating a person and placing it in the world. But some examples weren't perceptual or imagistic; instead, they were of the "purely felt" kind. Fénelon and colleagues described a case study where a seventy-one-year-old woman, living on her own in Paris, felt as if her sister was in bed with her every morning and night. Even though she knew this wasn't the case, she had to lift the covers and check each time. The feeling wouldn't go away, despite every part of her rational mind telling her that it couldn't be. This happened every day—and it had been happening for six months.

In 2007, an international working group from the National

Institute of Neurological Disorders and Stroke (NINDS) and the National Institute of Mental Health (NIMH) grouped felt presences with a list of other experiences known as "Parkinson's disease psychosis."[4] Presences were often referred to as minor hallucinations, a category that also included various kinds of visual illusions and a phenomenon known as "passage" experiences. The latter are glimpses of movement out of the corner of your eye, as if something is moving in your peripheral vision. These experiences were thought of as minor because they contrasted with the more clinically significant, full-blown visual hallucinations that can occur in Parkinsonian disorders.

The 2007 working group argued otherwise, noting that such experiences could be a sign of a worsening underlying pathology. Even if the hallucinations weren't having the same impact on people, or didn't seem to hold much content, they were still potentially important and far from minor. These experiences were all connected. The feeling of a presence might not in itself be distressing, but it might be the first step along the way to a more hallucinatory world.

Larger studies on presence and Parkinson's soon followed. A newer study by Gilles Fénelon—this one from 2011—reported on a sample of fifty-two patients with felt presences.[5] The presences were described as mostly fleeting, lasting only a matter of seconds. They were often placed specifically behind or to the side of the person experiencing them and were mostly anonymous. Sometimes they worried the subject, but they were not especially distressing. The patients were also compared to a group of seventy-eight people with Parkinson's but no experiences of presence. The researchers found that the patients with felt presences were more likely to also have visual hallucinations and illusions, supporting the idea that they were on a "continuum" for unusual experiences.

These kinds of studies show that presences can occur in Parkinson's and DLB, but they don't tell us much about the scale of the phenomenon. After all, even if they aren't minor, presences could still be incidental—"epiphenomena" that happen to be occurring alongside other, more significant and more prevalent symptoms of disorder.

Like the experiences themselves, their trace through the literature was elusive.

And then, out of nowhere, a huge study in 2015 reported from a survey sample of over five hundred patients with Parkinson's and related conditions. Its claim, stated in the title, was striking: "Fifty Percent Prevalence of Extracampine Hallucinations in Parkinson's Disease Patients."[6]

Fifty percent. Could the proportion really be that high?

The Presences of Parkinson's

Parkinson's disease affects millions of people worldwide, with a prevalence of 1–2 percent in those over seventy.[7] It often begins with changes in movement: hand tremors, gait problems, clumsiness in basic motion. Following this are cognitive and emotional changes, and eventually, in many cases, dementia results. The full cause of Parkinson's isn't known, but we do know a fair bit about how the disease works, and it all has to do with dopamine. You may have heard of dopamine in relation to reward—the "pleasure" neurotransmitter—but dopamine does a range of different, complex things across the brain. (A lecturer of mine once likened the question of asking what dopamine does in the brain to asking what the letter "e" does in the English language.) In Parkinson's patients, the neurons responsible for making dopamine begin to slowly decay, disrupting its usual availability around the brain. This is turn means that neurons across the brain begin to fire differently and not always at the right time. The main impact is actually on movement, making motor processes more difficult, poorly timed, and imprecise. This is reflected in its first clinical descriptions, where it was referred to as a "shaking palsy."

Treatment for Parkinson's typically aims to counteract the falloff in dopamine. Levodopa—a dopamine precursor—can be prescribed to sufferers to generate more dopamine and lessen the main symptoms. The treatment works, insofar as it reduces the disease's impact on motor functions,[8] but it can also have side effects. Hallucinations have long been suggested as possibly being one of them. Reports of hallucinations in Parkinson's patients were rare before levodopa began to be used in the 1960s. Then, in 1970, Gastone Celesia and Arlene Barr reported on a sample of Parkinson's patients who appeared to have various psychotic reactions to the medication, including hallucinations.[9]

The Northern Irish poet Frank Ormsby was diagnosed with Parkinson's in 2011 at the age of sixty-four. Rather than retreat, he followed his instincts and wrote about his experiences, saying that he felt "little inclination towards the morose, the lachrymose, the sentimental or the elegiac."[10]

Presences drift through his poems, like in one titled "Side Effects 1."

> *Wherever I sit, at the corner of my eye,*
> *they fade-in, fade-out, melt into elsewhere*
> *before I can see their faces. Who is that girl*
> *I sense at my shoulder? Who is that dancing lazily*
> *on my table until I look up?*
> *Are they playing a game? Do they mean me any harm?*[11]

In "Hallucinations 3," he captures presences again in verse.

> *They have the fearsome*
> *patience of invalids.*
> *Whatever it is they are waiting for,*
> *they will wait for ever.*[12]

People with Parkinson's often come to their own conclusions about the side effects of their medication, choosing what to avoid or minimize, and how much they can put up with. Subsequent research has identified little causal evidence to demonstrate a clear link with levodopa, but there are still findings that might be considered suggestive of a connection. For example, when Fénelon and his team compared the Parkinson's patients in their 2011 study, those who reported presences were also on significantly higher doses of levodopa. It's possible that levodopa—and other medications—could somehow boost the likelihood of unusual experiences, in effect amplifying hallucinations rather than causing them, specifically for individuals already susceptible to them.[13]

Even without levodopa, though, it seems that hallucinations often emerge as Parkinson's takes its course. Lots of patients with the condition will start to see people or animals, particularly in the later stages of the disorder. Why, then, might this happen?

To answer this question, it's important to consider who receives a diagnosis of Parkinson's or DLB. Although these are not conditions that exclusively affect older people, the large majority of patients will be in their seventies or older. And aging itself would seem to increase the likelihood of unusual perceptual experiences. As we age, our hearing and vision worsen, and this often corresponds with a rise in aberrant and unusual perception. For example, reductions in hearing capacity increase the chance of auditory hallucinations: a study in Holland[14] found that over 15 percent of people using a clinic for hearing impairment had experienced auditory hallucinations over the previous month, whereas most estimates for the prevalence of such experiences usually fall between 5 and 15 percent.[15] Over half of the respondents with hallucinations reported hearing voices, but a third of them heard music, and a quarter heard other sounds like doorbells and telephones.

Charles Bonnet syndrome (CBS) provides a kind of visual counterpart to this phenomenon. In those with CBS, disruptions to sight—either partially or fully—can prompt a range of hallucinatory visual effects: repeating patterns or swirls (known as "simple" hallucinations) or images of people, places, or things ("complex" hallucinations). Charles Bonnet was a naturalist who wrote about his grandfather's hallucinatory experiences following cataract surgery. These included "astonishing images of men, women, carriages, and buildings. The figures appeared in movement: approaching, receding, becoming larger or smaller, disappearing then reappearing. Buildings would rise in front of his eyes, showing their exterior construction."[16] CBS is also a common consequence of macular degeneration. Up to half of those suffering from macular degeneration report experiencing visual hallucinations, and other forms of peripheral degeneration can create similar effects.[17] The experiences might be annoying or confusing, but they are not necessarily distressing—once people know what they are.

The most accepted theory of why such hallucinations occur in these situations is a kind of sensory deprivation. In the absence of the usual sensory signals coming into the brain, either partially or fully, brain centers continue to fire to make sense of the world. Usually this is balanced out by new signals coming in, but without them the brain has free rein to create new forms. In those with Parkinson's and DLB, it is possible that something similar and rather basic is happening. Hallucinations could just be the brain's response to changes in its usual sensory signaling—a knock-on effect of dopamine disruption, perhaps, or the spread of Lewy bodies. This wouldn't occur in the main sensory areas of the brain, those handling visual and auditory signals, but further up the chain, affecting regions and networks responsible for perceiving people or objects. The brain would be compensating from within, putting form and meaning to things it doesn't need to. In this way, it could be that Parkinson's is accelerating a process that might otherwise happen with age.

Taking those factors together, high rates of hallucination in Parkinson's patients wouldn't seem out of the question. But a rate of 50 percent for something like felt presence would seem implausibly high for this kind of condition—that is, one that isn't primarily known for psychiatric symptoms. Our team at Durham University had seen a similarly high rate of presences during our analysis of people using psychosis services, but they had a whole range of unusual experiences happening to them.[18]

The 2015 survey that reported the 50 percent prevalence statistic for extracampine hallucinations in Parkinson's was led by Dr. Ruth

Wood, a researcher at the University of Sussex in the UK.[19] Over five thousand people were invited to take part in an online survey via PatientsLikeMe, a service for people with complex health conditions. Of them, 569 responded to take part: all of them had a self-reported diagnosis of Parkinson's, but they were excluded if they reported anything else that indicated either dementia or problems with their vision. After excluding various people on these and other grounds, 414 people were included in the eventual study.

Did half the sample report extracampine hallucinations? Well, in a way—yes. But it wasn't as straightforward as that. In fact, only 24.6 percent reported "feeling or imagining a presence that was not truly there," while 45.9 percent reported a "feeling of movement," as if something was passing them. The latter sound like "passage" experiences rather than presence: glimpses of motion in other words, not a basic feeling of a hidden person. When the authors counted these experiences, combining all people who either reported one or the other, they reached a figure of 208—50.4 percent.

There isn't anything wrong with referring to presence and passage experiences together as extracampine hallucinations: many researchers and clinicians would do so. But grouping the phenomena in this way makes it hard to gauge what the presences were like for the people experiencing them. Categorized as such, the extracampine hallucinations were mostly experienced as people (70.7 percent of cases), but sometimes as animals (20.2 percent), and they were more likely to be unfamiliar than familiar, at a ratio of two to one. The survey did gather more specific information about the emotional response to presence: like the cases Chan and Rossor had drawn upon, and the presences reported by Fénelon's team, the presences reported on PatientsLikeMe were mostly experienced as emotionally neutral in nature—silent figures, and seemingly harmless.

Even grouped with other experiences of hallucination, this data tells us something. It seems likely that not an inconsequential number of people with Parkinson's are having this kind of experience—it might not be 50 percent, but it could be as many as a quarter of all cases. And even with just a quarter, that's almost like there's an army of invisible people out there, waiting to be discovered.

It doesn't tell us enough, though. It doesn't tell us what it's like to feel this experience on the inside—or, considering the nature of the hallucination, on the outside. It doesn't tell us how something so strange could also be so mundane. I wanted to know more—to really get a sense of what the experience was like for individuals involved. When I thought back to the people I had spoken to, it baffled me to think of these experiences as neutral. Perhaps if they happened every day, and only briefly, you could get used to them. They would be part of the psychic furniture, in a way.

But would you want a silent figure on your shoulder?

An ill portent

To find out more, I got in touch with a former colleague: Dr. Jennifer Foley of the National Hospital for Neurology and Neurosurgery on Queen's Square in London. Jennifer is a clinical neuropsychologist—in other words, someone who specializes in the changes to the mind's faculties following damage or degeneration of the brain. If you have a head injury, or a stroke, or a disorder like Alzheimer's disease, a neuropsychologist will assess how your cognition has changed and what can be done about it. In some cases, the tests used in neuropsychology can identify highly specific processes that are impaired. Isolated impairments can be contrasted with others to provide "double dissociations"—evidence that two psychological mechanisms lie separately in the brain.

In many cases, the picture is a lot more complicated than that. Changes to the brain can, but don't often, solely affect specific processes. Many things can change at once. And they keep changing—cognitive aging is a movable feast, particularly when conditions like dementia are involved. When it comes to understanding something like the neuropsychology of Parkinson's, the challenges are sizable.

Jennifer is one of the lead clinicians at the Parkinsonian syndromes clinic at the hospital. In 2020, Jennifer and two colleagues—Erin Reckner and Lisa Cipolotti—published their own phenomenological survey of presence in the *International Journal of Geriatric Psychiatry*.[20]

I call Jennifer on a cold wintry day at the start of 2021 to chat about her paper. We're talking on Zoom because of the third COVID lockdown in the UK. Jennifer answers the call from her flat in North London, where she is working from home for the day. I'm wedged into a corner of my attic, with an oil heater by my side. Her video connects, and she waves hello past a pair of 1950s-style tortoiseshell glasses.

I start by asking about the kinds of experiences she and her team come across in their day-to-day practice. Would presence be part of that? "So, patients would never, ever proffer it," she explains. "I would have to ask—do you ever have the sense of someone standing over your shoulder, but they're not actually there?"

I immediately get the urge to check behind me.

"And either they just look completely blank or you get complete endorsement." She explains that she would ask them to say something more about it, but the conversation would stop. "They might say something like, 'Well, it's just *there*.' They sort of struggle. I think it is hard to have the vocabulary to describe a sense that doesn't really have much more about it."

This can happen a lot when asking people to describe unusual experiences. We don't usually have to consider what our thoughts, feelings, or senses are acutely like on an everyday level—they just are the way they are. What do your thoughts feel like? How do you know your friend is really *there*, or anyone for that matter? These are things that philosophers might consider, but they are a tough prospect for the rest of us. They are the kinds of questions that don't really make much sense the harder you think about them.

Undeterred, Jennifer and her team wanted to get more of a grasp of what this experience was like for their patients in the clinic. They devised an interview that would be flexible enough to let them explore a whole range of aspects of the experience—how it made people feel, when and where it happened, whether the presence was familiar or not. These topics had been covered in other studies before, but not always as thoroughly. The in-depth nature of this kind of work makes it necessarily much smaller in scale, so rather than five hundred patients, Jennifer and her colleagues interviewed seventeen people about their experiences.

Their interviews turned up some familiar themes. As in the Patients-LikeMe survey, most presences were felt as human in some way (88 percent), but up to a third were animals. Again, most were experienced as unfamiliar and mostly benign. There were some differences, though: Wood and colleagues had reported that extracampine hallucinations were most likely to occur off to the side, but Jennifer's study found that they almost always occurred behind the person. It's hard to say why, but it seems likely that respondents in Wood's survey were really talking about passage experiences, not actual presences.

One of the motivations for Jennifer's study had been to explore the reactions that people had when the presences occurred—could they really be as neutral as prior research has suggested?

"I suppose what really struck me was that these people often *are* distressed," Jennifer says, "but they weren't distressed for the reasons that I had thought." Instead, it was how people interpreted what was going on that had the greatest impact on the experience, and what came after: "You can see how people's previous experiences really start to impinge upon their understanding of their sensory experience," she said.

Those in the study who were most perturbed by felt presence were already in a state of emotional distress. Jennifer drew a comparison with "Othello syndrome"—another type of neuropsychiatric condition you can sometimes see in people with Parkinson's. In Othello syndrome, people develop intense feelings of jealousy and imagine that their partner is committing various infidelities—just as Othello had suspected of his wife, Desdemona. The group of patients Jennifer saw had been given dopamine agonists—drugs that mimic the way dopamine works in the brain as a way to counteract the effects of Parkinson's. It's a typical treatment for the disorder, but one that can have some unusual side effects, including hypersexuality. In a number of cases, the patients would end up requesting an increasing amount sex from their partners, only to then be rejected. From this, a delusional jealousy would spiral, with the patients typically growing more and more suspicious of their loved ones. Crucially, though, this tended to happen only if their partner had *actually* been unfaithful in the past. "There's no smoke without fire" would be the reasoning; even if the infidelity had happened many years ago, their reactions were fueled by a spark that had lain long dormant.

In such a situation, the psychiatric symptom—a delusion—spirals out from a historical concern, prompted by a medical treatment. Experience and illness dovetailing in distress. It might seem obvious, intuitive, even, that when faced with a major change to our lives, of course we would fall back on past experience. Why wouldn't we?

But this isn't always the starting assumption for conditions like Parkinson's. Along with dementia and Alzheimer's, Parkinson's is considered an "organic" disorder, indicating that we know the specific neural pathology that underlies what is going wrong. Conditions like schizophrenia or bipolar disorder—mental health conditions in general—aren't considered organic in the same way; we can't point to clear biological markers of someone having them even if we spend much time and effort trying to do so. Instead, these are considered "functional" disorders in the absence of established evidence for a clear biological change.

This distinction means that the role of experience can be overlooked sometimes when it comes to organic disorders. The thinking goes that change is happening to the brain whether we like it or not; it's irreversible, and it's consistent across individuals. Experience doesn't get a look in—even when it might turn someone into an Othello.

What of presences, then—how were prior expectations playing a role, in Jennifer's view? Were people offering their own interpretations of the uncanny—spirits or ghosts, for example? Or maybe lost loved ones? "I think we had twenty-five patients, and only one person thought, 'I've always had this extrasensory perception . . . so this hasn't been a change for me,'" she explains. When Jennifer asked that patient about presence for the first time, he informed her in a conspiratorial manner that he saw dead people. He was disappointed to learn from her that it could, possibly, be a result of a condition.

"Most of them sort of just attributed it to the Parkinson's," she goes on, "but the ones who were distressed by it seemed to be linking it to a harbinger of doom, like it's a sign of Parkinson's marching on." I ask if that's an expectation thing, or if someone had told them to look out for these experiences as a sign of things going wrong. But that generally wasn't the case—instead, it was usually their own interpretation. "Some people described it as being a sort of malevolent force where they felt like someone was going to come in and knife them in the night, which was associated with a lot of heightened anxiety," she explains, "but those people were anxious to start with. It was like the *presence* of the presence was the sense of a threat—a sort of increased threat system firing off." She pauses. "But that was rare. It was mostly just a sense of sadness."

Sadness. Sadness about the fact that your mind is changing; sadness as your experience of the world around you becomes more unpredictable, slowly slipping from your grasp. The presence is here, and it is telling you something you can't bear to fully entertain. Some quotes from Jennifer's study capture the gradual slide from reality on the day-to-day level.

I will ask for water and no one takes notice . . . then I know it is not real.

I feel worried that I don't have enough food for them.

I'll set the table for three people when it's just me and my wife.[21]

There seems something almost absentminded about these situations; lapses and forgetful moments, preparing for dinner guests who may never have existed. It's like the patient simultaneously knows someone isn't there but has it in their mind anyway that they are; as if the attendance of the presence is something that isn't just hard to explain or articulate but hasn't even *been* articulated yet. A lingering thought, left to its own devices in the back of their mind.

These kinds of examples also demonstrate the tricky role of insight in assessing and managing the experience. Do the people know that the presence isn't really there in that situation, or don't they? "It's in the middle," explains Jennifer. "There's no one there, and they are all right. And then later, they'll still be sort of questioning: Who, who is it?"

As the Parkinson's progresses, many people will lose their insight about their health, falling back into the autumn of dementia. This can take many years—unless it occurs in someone with DLB.

"When you ask people with DLB about [whether they are having] extracampine experiences, they often say no," says Jennifer. "And then you do cognitive tests with some of them, and you realize—it's not possible that these people don't have hallucinations, because their visuospatial system is *completely* broken." What Jennifer is talking about here is not some sort of extreme kind of denial, but a genuine lack of awareness of what is happening. In psychiatric terms, this is what is meant by "insight"—the ability to recognize you are ill or are experiencing a specific symptom of a disorder. People with DLB might not have the insight to realize that the things they are experiencing are hallucinations—so the answer comes back "no."

It is a situation that will be familiar to many who work with psychosis patients. In this context, the question of insight is highly contentious, as being accused of lacking it can come across as undermining, invalidating, and dismissive. But there is something about hearing voices or seeing visions, if they are close enough to everyday perception, that makes them incredibly hard to distinguish from a wider, shared reality. If you ask someone how long they have been hearing voices, they often can't tell you. If you thought the voices through the wall were your neighbors for six months, only to find that they had moved out much earlier, how would you know when things had started to depart from the reality that others experience?

I ask Jennifer for an example of how a DLB patient might differ from someone with classic Parkinson's, when they present to the clinic. "Well, there was one patient, and it was a bit like an M. R. James story," she says. "He was living in this big house out in the country, all on his own, and he was convinced that there were people outside going around his house. He had been referred because he had a little hand tremor—but nothing else, no Parkinsonism." She explains that they weren't sure what to make of his condition at the clinic: it sounded more like a psychiatric condition of some kind, although the neurologist suspected DLB.

"And then we got an email from the local police. They had been called out to his house due to complaints of an intruder. They got there and asked him what the problem was—and he pointed to an empty armchair."

In Jennifer's study there were seven patients with DLB, and all had difficulty with distinguishing reality from fiction, particularly when it came to presence. Some people had the constant feeling of needing to check that no one was there. Some were convinced the presences were deceased relatives, while others described presences that could also touch them at will. And all the patients experience presences—whether they had DLB or Parkinson's—did worse on a set of cognitive tests than they would otherwise be expected to. General scores for verbal and nonverbal IQ were lower, as were tests of visuospatial skills, speed of processing, and measures of "executive function."[22] Together, these things suggested that the occurrence of presence could point to someone's cognitive health—most likely for the worse.

I felt like I was beginning to get a sense of what presences really meant for people with Parkinson's. The experience itself might not be much more than an annoyance, but if you were already worried about your health, an irritation could become a portent. The absentminded setting of a table is yet another sign that things are ever so slowly coming apart, that you and your relation to the world are changing. The presence itself doesn't need to be any particular person or prompt any specific emotions. But it can be an unwanted reminder, a looming future of a lost self.

Right now, asking about presence is not part of routine enquiry in the treatment of Parkinson's or DLB. It seems, though, that presence could be an important sign of something—just as the 2007 working group had argued, and just as some patients themselves are concluding. Jennifer Foley and her colleagues will definitely be focusing more of their research on it, with the aim of understanding the specific psychological components that can create such experiences.

"There's so much more work to be done," she says, "and it's such an important predictor of how the person is going to fare in their disease, because the dementia is the most expensive part to Parkinson's for the NHS. And the neuropsychiatric element"—the hallucinations and delusions, she means—"is the most expensive part of the dementia."

The Flowery Man

After speaking to Jennifer, I kept thinking about that space between knowing and not knowing; the feeling that something is there, but knowing it isn't. The sense of there being an ever-widening gap: between realities, and between where your faculties are and where you would like them to be. For a lot of people, that change, that awareness, just becomes too much to bear.

The actor and comedian Robin Williams died in 2014. His death was a suicide, and immediately after, the inevitable media reports surfaced fueling rumor and speculation: money troubles, addiction, the clown who was really in agony on the inside. The family did not comment much on the circumstances of his death until months later. What wasn't widely reported at the time was that Williams had been diagnosed with Parkinson's disease in the months prior to this death, and this only after a number of months of physical and emotional upheaval. This wasn't the cliché and stereotype of a performer "losing a battle" with drink or demons. It was someone losing their mind, bit by bit, day by day, and being fully aware of their descent.

Autopsy reports revealed that Williams's brain was permeated with Lewy bodies to a degree that specialists had rarely seen. We know this from the editorial his widow, Susan Schneider, wrote for the journal *Neurology* in 2016.[23] It is a moving and heartbreaking piece, detailing the different stages of concern, physical ailments, and cognitive slips that preceded Williams's diagnosis of Parkinson's. Problems with learning lines for a film led to prolonged periods of paranoia and anxiety; sleep problems and stress kindled further feelings of fear and insecurity. And when Williams was finally diagnosed, he wasn't satisfied. He knew how far and how fast things were changing inside. He wanted to know if he was developing Alzheimer's disease, or even schizophrenia.

In such situations, it is not uncommon for highly capable people to hide what is really happening—even from those who are closest to them. As Schneider notes, her husband was a Juilliard-trained actor who tried as hard as he could to shield others from what was happening. It seems significant, then, what he chose to hold back: "Throughout the course of Robin's battle, he had experienced nearly all of the 40-plus symptoms of Lewy Body Disease, except for one,"[24] wrote Schneider. "He never said he had hallucinations. A year after he left, in speaking with one of the doctors who reviewed his records, it became evident that most likely he did have hallucinations, but was keeping that to himself."[25]

In Williams's situation, unusual experiences hadn't been the first sign of something untoward, unlike the cases of DLB described to me by Jennifer Foley. But that is clearly no consolation. If anything, it seems *worse* to have a steadier descent, knowing that you are being pulled into a whirlpool, into the maw of unreality.

Friends and relatives get pulled this way and that too, traveling alongside the sufferer in a desperate attempt to understand what is happening and determine what can be done. In a piece for the *New Yorker* in 2021, literary professor John Matthias describes how he ended up in a psychiatric institution himself after trying for many months to care for his wife, Diana. She had been suffering from a number of vivid hallucinations as a result of DLB, including visits from a range of alarming houseguests: "three women [who] were hanging in her closet and refused to leave," "rude people who masturbated into a dresser drawer and had sex on the living-room sofa," and a mysterious "Flowery Man" who "roamed the house." When things became too hard to manage, Diana was moved into a facility for people with advanced dementia, while Matthias was also urged to get help. Initially admitted for exhaustion, he ended up being kept on a ward longer than planned and having to plead to check on the welfare of his wife. He only finally secured his release with the help of an advocate, after which he returned to an empty home:

> In [the] ambulance, driving back the same way Diana came, I consider asking the attendants riding alongside me if they have heard of the Flowery Man, the topiary trees, the little people—any of Diana's hallucinated cast of characters. For years I have tried as hard as I could to see these things, to share Diana's view of the passing world. In her absence, returning to the home where I must now begin to live by myself, I long all the more to understand the reality that she inhabits.[26]

Thinking of these situations—these people, their families and loved ones—I was not surprised by some of the reactions by people in Jennifer's study. If I knew that this is one of the possible outcomes, one of the paths ahead, I would feel the same. A presence on my shoulder wouldn't be neutral. It would be dread personified.

What can be done about an experience like this? Treatments for psychotic experiences for either Parkinson's or DLB patients are few and far between. A key problem relates back to dopamine once more. Ordinarily, psychotic experiences would be treated with an antipsychotic. But these medications act to inhibit the flow of dopamine—the opposite of what you want to happen if you want to treat the motor problems that occur in Parkinson's. Treat one and you exacerbate the other. And that's before you consider the wide range of side effects associated with antipsychotic medication or the problems that arise with long-term use.

Things might be changing, though. Recently, a new drug has been trialed and approved in the United States for treatment of hallucinations and delusions in Parkinson's: pimavanserin, or to give it its brand name, Nuplazid. Pimavanserin works differently from other antipsychotics by targeting the neurotransmitter serotonin rather than dopamine. The first randomized controlled trial to show benefits of the treatment was reported in 2010: it showed a significant reduction in "global" scores for hallucinations and delusions compared to a placebo control.[27] A larger trial followed in 2014 showing similar improvements—albeit with slightly different measures.[28] So far, the side effects profile of pimavanserin seems acceptable as well, although subsequent trials haven't shown as much success as those initial studies, and some commentators have questioned how strong the evidence really is for pimavanserin.[29] As such, despite calls from patient organizations such as Parkinson's UK,[30] pimavanserin is still to be approved for use in the United Kingdom.

Filling gaps and expecting presences

Beyond drug treatments, we also need to know more about how the brain creates hallucinatory experiences in patients with Parkinson's or DLB. If we know the brain networks and cognitive processes involved, then assessments can be followed up by targeted treatments.

Most of what we know here is based on visual hallucinations. Studies of brain changes that correlate with hallucinations in Parkinson's and DLB patients often pick out the areas in the brain that primarily handle visual information.[31] Sometimes *less* activity is seen in these regions than there should be.

If this seems strange, consider again how brains react when faced with CBS, in which the ordinary sensory signals aren't being received properly through visual channels. In these instances, the brain seems to overcompensate, filling in the gaps with its own patterns. In patients with Parkinson's and DLB, it's possible something similar happens following changes to parts of the brain that deal with more complex visual information (such as seeing particular people). In the absence of the usual information it *should* be receiving, the brain is filling in the gaps in a different way.

We can see how this works via experiments that require our brains to fill in gaps. A team at University College London (UCL) recently tested the visual skills of people with hallucinations and a diagnosis of either Parkinson's disease or DLB.[32] The experiment involved looking at a series of black-and-white images and picking out those that featured animals or people. These were images that would be very hard to recognize unless the subject had seen them before—they would just look like random patterns. A famous example of this is a two-tone image of a Dalmatian in the snow[33] (see figure 5). When we first see it, it just looks like a collection of shadows, but once we know where to look—once we know how to connect the dots and fill in the gaps—our brains become very good at finding the signal within the noise.

This kind of phenomenon is well-known in psychology as an example of "top-down" influences on perception. If we just rely on the information coming in to us ("bottom-up"), it is often difficult, if not impossible, to work out what we are looking at. But once we have more information—prior knowledge of what to look for, where to look, and so on—we can complete the picture ourselves, like a jigsaw puzzle that relies on you turning up with a few of your own pieces.

The UCL experimenters showed these kinds of images to patients and healthy control participants, asking them each time whether they

FIGURE 5

saw anything. Neither group did particularly well. They were then quickly shown the original color images—which makes it much easier to spot what is there—and then tested again with the black-and-white images. Both groups did better once they knew more about what they were looking at. But crucially, the DLB group got *a lot* better.

How do we make sense of this? Why would one group do so much better? Imagine an old-fashioned scale—the kind you might use for baking, with weights on one side and a dish on the other. We manage incoming information a bit like this type of scale, weighing new information against old, what we are seeing anew versus what we expect to see. It's best to try to keep a balance, adjusting what we expect based on changes to what we see in each situation. Sometimes we see a little more, or a little less. If we don't get enough information coming in, the scale will tip—and we have to fill in the blanks ourselves to make sense of what we are seeing. Like when we wake up in the dark and try to make out a shadow across the room, we have to try out different solutions. Is it a person? A coat? A wardrobe?*

For people with DLB and hallucinations, the idea goes, the scales are already a bit tipped. Why? Because the usual sensory signals aren't coming in properly or being weighed in the right way. Instead, prior knowledge and expectations about what to see—the other side of the scales—is already being given a bit more weight, already filling in the gaps. Sometimes this might be helpful; expecting the Dalmatian helps you to see Pongo. But if this were happening even when we don't need it to, we would often see things that just weren't there. In other words, hallucinations.

When it comes to the task in the UCL study, when both groups know where and what to look for, the scales are being tipped for both groups. But for the patient group, the scales tip even *further,* and they perform even better. For a task that *requires* top-down information, they don't need much encouragement to see the world that way. It's like pushing a swing that is already in motion; the momentum is already there.

The theory is part of a wider set of ideas known sometimes as "predictive coding" or "predictive processing."[34] It's an exciting and controversial framework that argues that the brain's whole business is in predicting reality based on our expectations, the top-down factors that shape our perceptions. It's the brain taking an informed guess at what's out there, even if that involves cutting corners sometimes. This kind of idea has some startling conclusions, including the idea that none of us might need to be experiencing the world around us as it really is. It's less like we are taking a photo of the world, and more like we make do with a sketch. Provided that sketch is good enough and fits with what others are experiencing too, we can make do. It means—as the neuroscientist Anil Seth puts it—that our experience of the world is a kind of "controlled hallucination" that we happen to call reality when we agree.[35]

---

* It's actually your bathrobe.

This finding almost exactly mirrors something also seen in psychosis patients.[36] In the UCL team's study, adding new prior expectations—new knowledge about what could be found in the black-and-white scenes—led to people with psychosis really boosting their performance. Taken together, these kinds of findings push us to think more about prior expectations being tightly aligned with hallucinations. It also fits with that broader question of how people's prior experiences shape their responses to unusual perception and ill health—all these things will be feeding into the kinds of hallucinations people experience if the brain is in the business of filling in the gaps, not just some of the time but potentially all the time.

Results like these are suggestive of a specific story of how presences come about—but not much more than that at this stage. It gives us a rough idea of the brain regions likely to be involved in presences, and it gives us a potential mechanism for them to occur.

We also have to be cautious about drawing conclusions too generally. Even with more evidence about Parkinson's and DLB, this data could just be telling us about how hallucinations work for those conditions. Lewy bodies comprise a specific kind of pathology that is unlikely to be part of the story of presence in psychotic disorders, or other contexts. I can see how presences have an impact in these conditions—and the need to understand them much better, to support those affected—but they raise as many questions as they answer, questions that are likely specific to the brain changes we see in a condition like Parkinson's.

But, in considering the examples of Parkinson's and DLB, we now have at least two slightly different theories to consider. In chapter 5 we learned about the bodily self and how disruptions to expectations about our bodies can induce momentary experiences of an embodied presence. We can call this the *body* theory of felt presence, and it reflects how we think the motor system works. It might not fit all accounts of presence, but it provides a plausible explanation of how presences might be possible in very particular situations and conditions.

From the evidence in this chapter, we also have an alternative theory of presence based on the broader idea of "predictive processing." When we see, hear, or feel things around us that aren't there, our brain attempts to fill in the gaps based on some kind of ingrained expectation. That might not be something we're consciously expecting—it's more like a learned response. It's the way our perception is used to working, or the best way our brains can make sense of the world, based on our prior experiences. We can call this the *expectation* theory of presence.

These models might not be mutually exclusive. For example, we can think of the bodily self as requiring integration of lots of different expectations—multiple cues about our bodies and senses, how we feel on the inside and out. In that case, a body theory could be one part of a broader expectation theory.

An expectation-based theory of presence wouldn't have to be based on our motor system or confined to bodies. It's potentially something with a wider reach, something that drives the whole of our experience of the world and everything we feel around us. But the broader we go, the vaguer the story might get. There is always a trade-off involved.

Both of these theories could be playing a role in the presences of psychosis or Parkinson's. They could potentially explain different examples of presence, or they could work in concert in some way—one laying the groundwork, the other offering a finishing touch. To understand their role, though, we need to think beyond the clinic. It's time to look back out into the world.

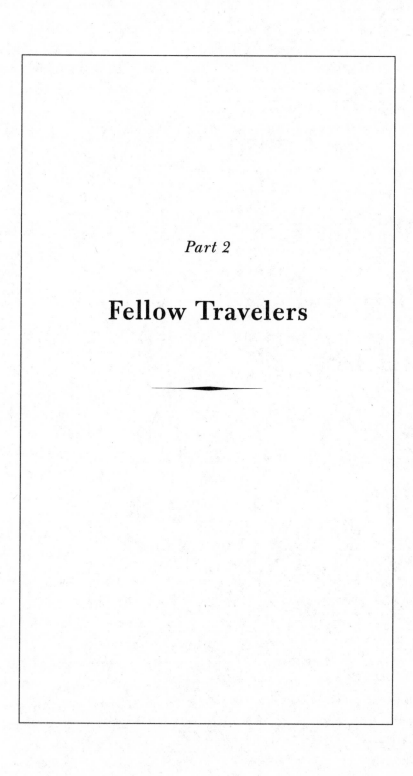

Part 2

Fellow Travelers

7

The Walnut of Reality

It's mid-December 2005, and the heat is rising off the dock in Scarborough. Not that one, the other one—Scarborough, Tobago. A strange man has appeared: his face round and red, his beard wild, brown, and shaggy, and his eyes bloodshot. There were no passenger boats due that day. Where had he come from?

The man wasn't making any sense, and he looked like he had been run over. The sea that day was the color of burning copper. As the stranger stared out across it, he claimed he had rowed here. But from where, exactly?

The police were alerted, and they took the would-be sailor into custody. He seemed confused, drunk even, and he couldn't provide any papers to say why or how he was in Tobago. He kept saying he had rowed the ocean. Not the Caribbean Sea, but the whole Atlantic, all the way from Europe. A likely story—this man looked like he had fallen asleep in a paddleboat and been swept out to sea.

The police weren't sure what to do with him, so they locked him in a closet on the dock while they made further enquiries. Eventually, a man in the port came forward, claiming he knew the prisoner. They had met in Cadiz, he said, and the man was telling the truth: he had indeed rowed to Tobago all the way from Spain.

His name was Leven Brown.

Back in the closet, Leven took in his surroundings. He had been at sea for four months, and he had faced sun, rain, lightning, and hurricanes to row solo across the Atlantic. He was supposed to have landed in Trinidad, but conditions had blown him off course at the last moment. Compared to his cramped and rolling boat, the closet was a five-star hotel. He could sit down, lie down even, and not worry about his progress, or the weather, or any unwelcome visitors. He had made it. He wasn't sure how, but he had.

The door opened, and a police officer came in, apologizing profusely. Out in the hall, another couldn't stop shaking his hand. They still couldn't quite believe that he had rowed all the way there, but they didn't think he was drunk anymore.

* * *

I'VE ALWAYS BEEN in awe of people who can push themselves to the limits of endurance. I've wondered what makes them different from the average person. I don't really mean physically, but mentally different, how they have a certain kind of outlook that redefines the challenges in front of them. I don't doubt that these people have huge reserves of discipline and willpower, but that's not quite what interests me either. Even deciding in the first place to take on things like polar expeditions or ocean rowing seems like such a foreign act to me; these are the acts of someone perceiving things very differently from the rest of us. What kind of person sees the world in that way?

Shortly after I had spoken to Luke Robertson, he recommended I contact Leven Brown. Leven is a five-time Guinness World Record holder for ocean rowing. Born in Scotland, he took up rowing in his midthirties, and his trip from Cadiz to Tobago in 2005 was his first-ever major expedition. He had been bored at his office job and wanted a new challenge. He knew of military people attempting things like solo ocean crossing, but, in his own words, he wanted to see if someone "ordinary" like him could do the same. So, he stepped off the corporate ladder and into, well, the sea.

I wanted to talk to Leven to understand more about the link between endurance and presence. Once you start looking, you come
across so many accounts of experiences that sound like presence for
extended pursuits done solo: ultrarunners, free divers, long-distance
swimmers, and sailors, for example. But what drives that connection? Is it just isolation, leading us to conjure companions? Is it about
people being pushed to the extremes of their limits, mentally and
physically? Or is it something more individual than that, something
unique to the people who have these experiences?

Some of the encounters that get reported are quite similar to
the classic "Third Man" experiences we heard about in chapter 2:
shadow figures and saviors, turning up in the nick of time, saving
people with a word, a touch, or just by being there. But unlike those
encountered by mountaineers or Antarctic adventurers, these kinds
of experiences aren't always about survival. They have a similarity in
that they come about in adverse situations, but they occur more in
continuity with everyday life. Some might happen closer to home,
physically and psychologically. And compared to those of a Messner
or a Shackleton, the stories recounted by endurance athletes are altogether more diverse, taking place across sometimes wildly varying
conditions.

Hallucinations of various kinds are common when people are
pushed to their sporting limits. A recent study tracked 48 runners
tackling the Mont Blanc trail, a 106-mile single-stage race across
peaks in France, Switzerland, and Italy.[1] Over half of the runners saw
unusual things—typically black-and-white people. But the key difference seemed to be race strategy: 25 runners adopted a no-sleep
strategy for the run, and 84 percent of them experienced hallucinations (compared to only a quarter of those who got at least some
sleep). One study even documented it in a 91-hour charity game of
five-a-side football. By the second night, two of the players started
having visual hallucinations, while all players ended up seeing things
by the end of the game.[2] Like mountaineering, where the effects of
hypoxia can lead to hallucinations, endurance activities offer prime

biological conditions for perception going awry, including heat exhaustion, dehydration, and sleep deprivation.

Less studied are specific examples of presences encountered during endurance activities—although they would seem to be reasonably common in anecdotal reports. Our team in Durham ran a survey—led by psychologists Jamie Moffatt and Kaja Mitrenga—on these kinds of encounters that we published in 2022.[3] Eighty-four people responded to an online survey, and the most popular physical pursuits that came up were diving and caving. Some of the experiences reported were quite benign, but others were unsettling, to say the least. One cave diver reported the feeling of a "Doom Fairy" watching them die—the experience occurred on two occasions when they had made potentially fatal mistakes. Others spoke of experiences out in the open air:

> Sometimes I would find myself whirling around, looking for the presence I felt. It sometimes would happen when I was running in the dark on a trail, and I'd find myself peering around, or thinking I'd see someone in the distance ahead of me. I don't know how to describe it other than just the feeling or aura of a presence, such that I'd again whirl around looking for the presence that I could feel.[4]

The challenge with these kinds of activities is in picking out the common threads. The variation in what people are doing clearly means that they don't all face the same challenges or the same scenarios; they all have their own peaks and troughs, their own specific hurdles to clear. That makes it much trickier to pin down what happened when and why. Talking to a man with as much experience as Leven—someone who had really been there and done that—felt like a golden opportunity to make some progress and start piecing together a few things.

When I speak to Leven, he is faring much better than he had been that day in Tobago. His voyage in 2005 led to him losing seventy pounds—nearly a third of his body weight—and even his eyelids had been burned by the sun, leading to his alarming look when he arrived on the dock that morning. In 2021, having spent various lockdowns sequestered in his house in Scotland fourteen miles from the nearest neighbor, Leven is no longer sunburned or emaciated, and he is back at a normal weight. Appropriately, Leven has a beard reminiscent of Captain Haddock, but a face somewhere between Oliver Reed and Jack Black. He looks every inch the sea captain you might expect.

We get talking about unusual experiences—the things that happen at sea that everyone knows about but only talks about occasionally. You might share a story late at night over a whisky, but still not even tell close friends or relatives. We decided to focus on his first voyage because so much happened, although he's had these kinds of experiences multiple times, on many trips across the world.

Like Luke Robertson's, Leven's experiences started mid-expedition and consisted of individual sounds and visions of things: animals, objects, occurrences on the horizon.

"It started with dogs barking," he explains. "And then flashes underneath the boat, which I thought was a squid. But they were enormous, absolutely enormous!" he adds, with a roar.

"On the solo voyages it was much more prevalent than it ever was in the team events. I was never quite sure why. On your first ocean row, you would be subconsciously more nervous, I guess?" Leven likens it to a ski jumper getting ready for his first jump, with all the anticipation building up to that point. I ask him how he prepared for that—had he ever done anything like it before, any training voyages? "There's not much you can do to build up the distance. It's a little like you can't really practice a skydive by gradually jumping off at five feet, then ten feet. At some point you just have to believe that the parachute will open."

The journey to the starting line in Cadiz hadn't been long in terms of time—around eighteen months—but preparation had involved a number of ups and downs for Leven. He could control his physical preparation, but getting all the equipment and backing he would need was a stop-start affair. At one point he had maxed out all his bank accounts to get the boat he needed; then he missed his connecting train home and had to spend a cold November night on a park bench in Newcastle. This might sound like a real setback to most people, but as Leven explains to me, it was all part of the preparation process. "It was lovely having that sort of rifle-shot direction. It gave you the power and energy to overcome small inconveniences. Rather than being rudderless in the corporate world, just drifting along with the flow, you had this focus—what seemed like sacrifices to other people didn't seem like sacrifices to you."

On his voyage, Leven had struck out west from Cadiz and traced the coast along to Portugal, after which he needed to cross the shipping lanes coming out of Faro. His boat had a tiny cabin with mostly army rations that he had managed to acquire from a friend. He had just two books with him: Hemingway's *The Old Man and the Sea*, and the Bible. The Bible had been given to him by a drifting John Wayne type in Cadiz who said that Leven looked like he needed it more. I don't know if I would have found that reassuring or not.

His initial progress was very slow. The local press called him "El Loco," and the *Daily Mail* back home referred to him as that crazy guy, rowing nowhere. He remembers following the coast one Saturday and seeing people playing on the beach. He thought that he could just drop anchor, swim ashore, and get an order of fish and chips for himself.

Something stopped him, though. Not tiredness or discipline, but a sense of something almost unreal about what he could see. "It was like these people were on the other side of a screen, or on a TV; something you could see but couldn't touch." He refers to it as a sense of "warped reality," and he remembers it as the first instance of something odd happening on the journey.

Things really started to ramp up after the shipping lanes. The plan was to get to Faro, sleep for a while, then cross in a seventy-two-hour sprint. He would have to play *Frogger* by hopping each lane in short bursts to ensure he wouldn't get run down by one of the gigantic ships passing through. But the sleep never came: the winds changed, so Leven had to move fast, and he did the next three days on almost no sleep. Once out in the ocean, he was so tired he couldn't remember how to open a bag of chips (he sat on them instead).

Not long after that ordeal, the dog barks came. The squid came too, with other visions as well: Spanish galleons, UFOs, lights in the sky. As Leven explains though, they didn't feel real to him. As they flashed before his eyes, "it was like there was a walnut in my head that says—well, you know that UFO isn't really there." He describes being so tired that it felt like his eyes were moving independently, defocusing without him realizing.

So far, so hallucinatory. The way Leven talks of these experiences, almost in passing, betrays their lack of significance for him. They might sound outlandish, but we can think of them more like mirages or other illusions—the natural product of frazzled senses and a tired brain.

Once again, though, things changed with the arrival of a voice. It was a mid-voyage period of calm amid a season that would see four hurricanes hit the Atlantic (and Leven). "Interestingly during the most stressful times, none of it happened—it was actually more during the calm times, not going through tough physical periods," Leven explains. "When you're distracted by danger, you don't have time to contemplate life, the universe, and everything."

The day the voice came, it was flat calm. The previous day Leven had reached the Canary Islands—approaching close enough to see people driving around in cars—but the last breath of Hurricane Vincent spat him out of the way, setting his progress back four days. He had to batten down the hatches and wait it out until the calm came again. And while Leven was alone on the voyage, he had consciously taken someone with him: his grandfather, who had fought at the Battle of Nijmegen in World War II. Leven had his grandfather's dog tags, marked with the sign of St. Christopher, the patron saint of travelers. If a voice had spoken to him, he would have liked it to be his grandfather.

But it wasn't. It was a voice like he had never heard before, although at the same time it felt familiar. It wasn't male or female, and it didn't say very much, but what it said was reassuring: he would be OK, everything would be alright, he would see tomorrow. It was as if someone were close by, whispering into his ear. In Leven's words, it was "orbiting" him, coming before or after moments of duress, rather than right in the heat of the moment.

Whatever that voice was, it had a sense of reality that made it stand out from the other experiences. The things Leven had seen before—the UFOs and the galleons—had had an "etching" quality to them, as if they were rendered on the landscape; they were there but they weren't, and Leven understood this.[5] This voice, though, was something else; it felt irreducibly, undoubtedly real. It was there, with him, right at that moment.

The only other experience that matched that level of reality for Leven was a kind of waking dream. One morning he awoke to find that another boat had pulled alongside his. He got out from his cabin to see a character like Ben Gunn from *Treasure Island,* weather-beaten and seasoned, leaning over the rail to check that he was OK. Leven reassured him he was, and off the other boat went, with Leven satisfied that someone was concerned for his welfare.

Except the encounter didn't happen. It can't have happened. Leven's boat was the only thing for hundreds of miles around and no small boat could have tracked him to the middle of the ocean. It was a dream, but a dream so vivid, so real, that it took days for Leven to realize that it didn't happen.

A similar type of encounter—spoiler alert—happens in Alfonso Cuarón's film *Gravity.* In the film, Sandra Bullock's stranded astronaut is suddenly joined in her capsule by a returning astronaut she thought had been lost. Her companion, played by George Clooney, offers her comfort and reassurance, providing her with the push to get her to safety. But it's all in her mind—it has to be. The only way anyone could get into her capsule would be to open the door and depressurize the cabin, removing all oxygen in an instant. Even in a fictional story, the event is impossible.

The crucial point about Leven's waking dream is that, for him, it was in the same category as the voice. Both felt so real, and the message was consistent: others were with him, and he would be OK. The only difference between voice and dream was in something unusual about their relationship to Leven, in time and space. "With all these things, like the person shouting from the boat, it's like you're in this little capsule with things coming towards you. With the voice, it's like they've never left, they're not physically coming to you." In other words, a voice with a constant presence; a voice that was there, for him.

Once again, the hallucinatory and unusual come in waves and degrees. There is no single switch to unreality, no flip to an "upside-down" world, but subtle changes in the screen through which the world is viewed. Unreal etchings gradually appear alongside hidden companions, dreams seep into waking life, and feelings of reality, familiarity, and purpose wax and wane.

Spurred on by the voice and the dream, Leven completed his voyage after 123 days at sea, covering 4,278 miles. Apart from losing his sunscreen, he was unharmed, despite rowing during the busiest hurricane season on record for that time.

After the storm

In some ways, Leven's experience is a classic example of the Third Man phenomenon: an entity or figure that comes to you in a time of need and adversity. Leven's voice and the encounter with the other boat didn't come in the form of shadow figures or lingering feelings of someone "just" being there, but it isn't hard to see the parallels between his story and Shackleton's. or Luke Robertson's. Like the many encounters of isolated mountaineers, the "Other," whatever that may be, comes on the brink of the journey ending in tragedy, of them not quite making it, not quite getting there. In function—as in the *use* of these experiences, their utility to the person undergoing them—Leven's experiences on his first voyage are classic and prototypical. The reassuring figure. The calming voice. The steady hand on the tiller.

We can also count the now familiar factors that brought Leven to this point. The first is exhaustion—Leven missed the time he had scheduled to sleep before sprinting across the shipping lanes off Faro. When he finally got past them, he slept for fourteen hours instead of the one hour he intended. The next factor is dehydration—Leven had plenty of water, but the combination of exertion given to rowing every day and the ever-beating sun overhead would have taken its toll, especially without sunscreen or his sunglasses, which he had managed to lose along the way. And third, isolation—four months at sea, just Leven, his boat, and thousands of miles of gray, undulating ocean. Being alone for all that time can lead some to deliberately create companions—new friends like Wilson the volleyball in *Castaway*; for others, solitude can sometimes bring forth unbidden visitors.

And then there is the adversity—but this one is a bit of a puzzle, for Leven and for me. Clearly, he faced different challenges all through the voyage: preparing mentally for the prospect of setting off, alone, across such a vast space; navigating the onslaught of hurricane winds; even avoiding being mowed down by other ships. The lightning storms were the worst, with some strikes hitting the water less than one hundred meters from the boat. (At one point he tried to fashion a makeshift Faraday cage—a mechanism designed to divert the lightning around an object rather than through it—by wrapping wire round his mast and along the edges of the boat, away from him and the cabin. He was never sure if it would work—one strike and the whole boat could be aflame.)

The puzzle here is similar to Sherlock Holmes's question in "The Adventure of Silver Blaze." The case concerns a missing race horse and the murder of its trainer, and its resolution rests on an inference Holmes makes based on a "curious incident" involving the watchdog at the stables. The curiosity came from the fact that the dog did not make any noise during the night, meaning that whoever stole the horse must have been familiar.

In Leven's case, we have to work out the answer to the mystery of what happened to the voice in the storm. All Leven's encounters were before or after moments of peril, when the ocean had settled again. He describes his experiences orbiting times of stress and adversity, not specifically accompanying him during them. They seemed to have kept him going, but not in a way that spurred him on at the moment of greatest danger: these were more like postgame reflections, ways of working through what happened and preparing for the next challenge. The voice that came to Leven and the Ben Gunn character who visited him were less like guardian angels and more like coaches, keeping him on task, shouting encouragement from the sidelines, and getting him ready for more.

From a psychological perspective, the function or purpose of Leven's experiences seems familiar. But the circumstances under which his experiences occurred, coupled with his own reflections, point to the important role of attention. When he was focused, under pressure, these things didn't happen—no one joined him. When he was recovering, when he reflected on what had happened, it was *then* that the Other came for Leven.

Changes in attention can lead to unusual things being experienced. For example, psychologists sometimes describe the states of focused attention as "flow," when someone is fully immersed in— and often enjoying—a skilled activity.[6] When in flow, people describe losing a sense of themselves as part of this singular focus; they are at one with the activity they are engrossed in. Many athletes describe having some of their best experiences when in a flow state, and in some cases this involves transformative and mystical elements.[7]

The timing and nature of Leven's experiences don't quite seem to fit that picture. If Leven was experiencing some kind of flow state, we would again probably expect his companions to join him in the midst of the action, when he was fully focused on the job he needed to do. That didn't happen. It seems plausible, though, that such intense periods of sustained attention, when under threat, could have had a knock-on effect in those periods of calm. A focused state under peril could relax the moorings for what comes next, allowing the boundaries of the mind to drift in the current. And when the mind is allowed to wander, a voice may emerge.

We also have to think hard about the kind of person Leven Brown is. He started our conversation by explaining to me that he wanted to see if an ordinary person, like himself, could do something extraordinary. But how ordinary was he, even at the start of his very first voyage?

The area of Scotland Leven grew up in, the Borders, is miles and miles of rolling farmland, mostly well away from any sea. The Borders produces cows and rugby players, but in Leven it produced something else. As a teen, he got the idea for crossing an ocean from a chance encounter with John Ridgway, the British sailor who had rowed the Atlantic in 1966. Leven met Ridgway when staying at a survival-based boot camp in the northwest of Scotland. His father sent him there when he was fifteen to challenge him, but he loved it; the hardship, the isolation, the chance to do something different. He and some other boys were given the task of fending for themselves for a few days on "Survival Island," a barren rock that contained no food whatsoever. Many would struggle in that situation, but Leven's solution was to swim to the next island, collect a load of mussels, and then swim back. He was already like that at fifteen: ready to do whatever it takes when faced with the sternest of tasks.

Before he attempted his first ocean row, Leven's father again set him on a challenge: go up to the Hebrides—the scattered and isolated islands off the northwest coast of Scotland—and spend a few days on his own, just him and a tent, to see if he could hack it. For some people, that would be hell. For others it might sound idyllic—but they might begin to feel different upon facing the monotony of the situation. Again, though, Leven loved it: the space, the focus, the self-sufficiency.

I ask Leven if, when he got into that boat in Cadiz, he wasn't stepping out into the unknown but into something more like home. Was the boat his place, where he was supposed to be, away from everything and everyone else?

He stops and thinks for a moment. "That's a hell of a question," he responds. "I mean, there were many emotions swirling around—part of me was terrified, thinking, *What have I got myself into?*"

He goes back to the moments before he set off: putting his boots and gloves on, leaving the hotel, walking the last few steps down to the boat. "There's that great expectation, and yet, you are trembling in this combination of terror and excitement, trying your best to keep as calm an exterior as you can for your family. I cast away in the boat, and that's when I thought, *This is great.*" As other boats peeled away, and Leven got out into the open ocean, he felt not fear, but relief. He could drop the mask and finally focus on the task in front of him.

It takes someone quite unusual to harness all that energy, to face all the challenges that lie ahead, and feel relief. How one chooses to respond to such feelings can vary hugely from one person to the next, with great consequence. For some, the surge of adrenaline, pulsing through their body as they approach a precipice in their life, pushes them back, overwhelming them with a wave of feeling that makes them freeze, or flee. For others, like Leven, they ride that wave, embrace that energy—it's a sign that they are on their way. But that wave could so easily break in the other direction; someone ready and waiting to ride it can instead end up turned over in the surf, just another wipeout.

The psychologist Lisa Feldman Barrett has argued that all our emotions work like this.[8] We might think of emotions as basic universals that are the same for everyone, but in fact they are constructed—they are the result when our bodily feelings and our knowledge and expectations about the world meet. We might think that we know and understand our emotions, that they couldn't be any other way, but in fact they are a series of signals, impulses, and urges waiting to be interpreted like tea leaves. Barrett's theory takes the logic of predictive processing—wherein our expectations rule experience—and applies it not to the outside, sensory world but to the inner world of heartbeats, gut feelings, and goosebumps. This world of sensation features prominently in many of the stories of presence we have already heard.

Talking to Leven, the feeling I get from him is an overwhelming sense of mission. Through emotion, adversity, roaring storms, and flat calm, Leven's arrow did not allow him to stray from his path: he had a goal, and that goal helped him to accommodate all that an ocean could throw at him. And while he clearly approached the task with a certain set of expectations, their influence on the changing world around him seems indirect. He didn't actually hear his grandfather's voice, for example, even if he would have dearly wished to. Instead, his expectations provided him with a framework to hold his experiences, to make him even stronger: he heard a voice, and it gave him support, it stayed with him, it was his strength. That was the point of the voice—it was not a matter of who it was.

I felt like our conversation had begun to clarify some things for me, but I was left with some nagging questions. Is it stress or adversity that prompts these experiences, or do they tend to occur for a certain kind of person? Do you have to be someone extraordinary already—willing to swim to the next island—to enter this realm, to pass through the screen separating the everyday from something else?

And if you do need to be a certain kind of person—how can the experience ever be separated from the individual?

8

The Marathon Monk of Billingham

A footbridge looms over my head, and it seems to sway in the air for a moment. It is a second or two before I realize it's me who is wavering; I shake my head and tell myself to focus. I look down at the sticky tarmac in front of me, as the road ahead appears to swell and heave with numbered figures. A sign is rigged on a pedestrian bridge: 6 MILES in fluorescent letters. My whole body feels full and uncomfortably warm, like an old beanbag left out in the sun.

Welcome to the Great North Run 2018.

I'm not much of a runner. I started in 2014 for something to do. In the beginning, getting going with any running was an exercise in self-deception. I had to listen to the radio, podcasts, music—anything that would take my mind off what I was doing. To my surprise, that strategy worked. If I focused on someone or something else, I would get into a rhythm, and before long I would run five or ten kilometers without thinking much of it. What I had considered a "long" distance collapsed in my mind as I grew familiar with different routes, inclines, and times. I wasn't fast, but that wasn't the point—I was just pleased that I could complete a run without stopping. I mostly did the same course, but even when I didn't, I always needed to know in advance what the route was because I had to remove all thinking, all decisions, all prospect that I had a say in what was going on. It all had to be out of my hands—this was the route, and the only way it ends is by reaching the finish.

By 2018, I was ready for more of a challenge, and on an impulse I signed up for the Great North Run, perhaps the UK's most famous race after the London Marathon. My training had been going well, and I'd been given a tip: underestimate your expected finish time by a little, then you don't get stuck at the start in a big scrum of runners who might be slower than you. I aimed for something ambitious and turned up early to find the section of the starting area who had picked the same target as me. As it filled up, I looked around at the other runners. They all looked serious, focusing into the distance, wearing shirts with names of local running clubs and hi-tech gear of all kinds. They also didn't quite look like me—they were leaner, probably faster. I started to wonder if I was in the right place.

My brother—a more experienced runner—had advised me that I might get a bit emotional at the start, and that I should look out for it. I wasn't sure quite what he meant. I assumed he was talking about nerves. I was tingling with anticipation and desperate not to get injured. I really wanted to get going, and to do well.

Before I knew it, we were off—over the starting line in no time. The day was surprisingly hot, the sun not just beating down but braising me in its glare, holding everyone in individual spotlights. As we streamed over the Tyne Bridge, it felt fantastic.

But with all the elation of starting, I realized I had made a mistake. I had gone off too fast, running the first mile almost a minute too quickly (and almost as quickly as I could run any mile). I kept trying to pick runners ahead of me to act as pacers, but they were always slightly too fast. I knew I needed to rein in my efforts, plan ahead. The race is a half marathon—13.1 miles—and everyone knows miles three through six are tough ones: an unending incline of straight road that you just have to plod through with your head down. When we hit that section, I knew I really needed to get into a lower gear, and I steeled myself for the grind.

The miles ticked past: three, four, five. My times were beginning to slow, but I knew I was nearly through it. Soon we would hit flatter ground and I could kick on, knowing the worst was out the way. After the incline there was a ramp down toward the road leading up to the mile 6 marker. As I ran down it, I was waiting for relief and my legs were burning; the heat was really beginning to sap all my energy, and I couldn't help but obsessively check my pace on my watch.

And then I realized the problem.

I didn't have any kick, no reserve of energy. I had over half the race left, but I was spent. The pace and the excitement at the start had drained me far more than I expected. Crowds at the side were shouting to all the runners, offering encouragement, drinks, everything— but I didn't want anything to do with them. Instead, I had a sinkhole inside of me, a creeping, yawning sense of dread. The sun smashed down on the road like a hammer on an anvil—I felt like I could crumple under it at any minute. As I entered the seventh mile, all I could think was, *What if I need to stop? What happens then?* I hadn't had that thought in nearly four years.

I spent the rest of the race in a hot, miasmic fog. At ten miles the screen of my watch froze up—I had managed to get moisture in it from one of the water stations along the way—and at eleven miles I had to stop for a minute as I nearly collapsed. Later on, when I checked what my watch had logged up to that point, I saw that my heart rate had averaged 175 bpm, peaking at 190 at that six-mile mark. Having my heart going at that pace, for that long, was within a normal range—but probably only if I was being chased by a tiger.

I managed to finish the race eventually, and in the end I only missed my time by about ten minutes. That ten minutes might not seem like much, but to me I might as well still have been running. I thought I was prepared for the challenge, but I wasn't prepared for how it would make me feel, or the strange mental place that my body would put me in.

Despite all the crowds, and all the support from friends and family, I felt completely and utterly on my own.

* * *

AFTER MY CONVERSATION with Leven, I kept thinking about the nature of loneliness and isolation, and what they might tell us about presence. We often talk about feeling lonely and being isolated as if they are the same thing, but they don't have to be. There can be times when we are surrounded by people but feel completely alone. And then at other times we can be completely isolated from everyone—in the middle of an ocean, perhaps—and yet not feel alone at all. It didn't sound like Leven felt alone when he described his voyage to me. He had sought out a kind of isolation, but he looked for and got connection with others, even if that happened in unexpected ways. And that seemed as much to do with him as it did with the situation.

Rather than asking when or where these experiences occurred, I felt like I needed to know much more about *who* these people were—who puts themselves in those kinds of situations? There is a process of matching going on, between individuals and environments, and I needed to know more about it.

Leven's experiences reminded me of the practices of members of religious sects and movements that seek out various forms of privation and self-sacrifice. Anchorites wall themselves away from the world. Hermits—taking an almost opposite path—leave themselves exposed to the elements of it. But the effect is often the same: deprivation leading to revelation, isolation conjuring communion. The tradition of searching for spiritual and mystical experience by enduring conditions of extreme physical deprivation is a long one. And while some remain essentially static in this process, others use movement to bring about the necessary states of meaning and enlightenment: the Japanese monks of Mount Hiei, for instance, complete eighteen- to twenty-five-mile runs every day for one hundred days as part of their training. Some then graduating to a thousand-day challenge, and forty-six monks have completed the full course of runs and prayer since 1885.[1]

Few research studies have explored the experiences of monks

during their marathon runs, but a recent study from Italy can give us a flavor of the kinds of things that might occur. The Tor des Géants, a trial run in the Aosta Valley in Italy, tests runners over 205 miles and must be completed in under 150 hours. A 2020 study of twenty-one runners on the Tor documented them experiencing extensive pareidolia (seeing their surroundings "as fantastic beasts, such as dragons, goblins, or gremlins") and reporting a number of hallucinatory phenomena. For one runner, these included visions and conversations with his family, who entertained and advised him along the way. Another runner was joined by a helpful presence who "preceded him and escorted him up to the finish line. However, as the records show . . . the previous runner completed his race several hours before the arrival of this proband."[2]

I had learned about the marathon monks after talking to Paul Burgum, a PhD student in my department at Durham. Paul's an ultrarunner, regularly tackling 20-, 40-, or 60-mile training runs, and sometimes running as far as 160 miles for endurance races. Paul has taken an unusual path toward studying for his degree. A mature student, he was a promising semiprofessional sportsman until a period of crisis led him to reassess his life. Problems with alcohol and depression left him in a rut—but one that he pulled himself out of by pushing himself to the limit in various ways.

Paul has had a number of unusual experiences in his life. He's even used them, in different ways, to achieve the tasks he sets himself—not just as strategies of last resort but almost as tools he has in his locker, useful things he knows he can apply to get himself through pain and adversity.

The most pertinent experiences have come during Paul's long-distance walks. In 2013, he challenged himself to walk the length of Italy, with no money and not much more in the knowledge of the Italian language. His aim was to force himself to ask for help, to make himself be dependent on others. "It was kind of a misplaced attempt to go on a journey and rediscover myself," explains Paul. "It was to make me practice asking for help. Before that I was in a place that was very macho, you couldn't feel any pain—stupid bullshit. I worked out it was just a massive failure."

Things hadn't been going well for a while. He had been in the construction trade when the financial crash hit in 2008. His marriage broke down too, and he ended up living for a period in the old flat his grandparents owned in Billingham, on Teesside in the northeast of England. The walking was a response to that, and the Italy trip was in fact his fourth long-distance challenge that he had taken on since the crash. The aim of this new expedition was to force Paul to face a new kind of challenge. He deliberately took very little kit and didn't speak the language. He would be vulnerable, at the mercy of strangers, and he would need to learn to accept that.

Paul's trip began in the city of Reggio Calabria—if Italy is a boot, this starting point is at the toe of the shoe, just across from Sicily. Suitably enough for the odyssey Paul was about to undertake, day 1 of his walk would see him reach the town of Scilla—where its name-sake many-headed monster Scylla menaced Odysseus and his crew as they passed through the Strait of Messina. The worst thing Paul came across in those early stages of his walk—on more than one occasion—was finding that he couldn't join a particular route or road. Each day when Paul walked, he would regularly need to be hitchhiking by the end of it. He was often dehydrated and heavy-legged, but he couldn't just stop anywhere; he needed to find somewhere to sleep.

To keep himself going, he got creative. "It was almost like I needed to summon up another motivational source," he tells me. What Paul did was draw upon what he calls his "angry juice": he would remember negative experiences from his life, but in dwelling on them he would transition them into positive things—people and events from his past that brought love and reassurance. Out of this, Paul would find an impulse to keep going, a power born from the energy of frustration. But he found something else too.

It was a Saturday afternoon, two weeks into Paul's walk, when he reached a bar in Futani, a small town in the hills south of Salerno. A group of old men were watching football: Hull versus Chelsea in the

English Premier League. Paul had been nervous going in, needing to once again charge his phone, ask for directions, and try to make the one drink he could afford last as long as possible. Luckily, the men there took to him. One of them (appropriately named "American Tony") had lived in the United States for thirty years and acted as the group translator, and the conversation quickly started flowing. Paul finally had an afternoon of rest and comfort.

As evening approached, he knew he needed to get going again—he still had many miles to do that day—and he couldn't let the light fade. Before long, he was on the road again.

As he walked, a desire grew in Paul to turn the day into a success. Before Futani, he had had one of his hardest days, with routes and plans constantly being derailed. After that afternoon in the bar, being in the company of others (and maybe more than one beer) had renewed his spirit. He felt energized as he aimed for Vallo della Lucania, twenty kilometers to the northwest.

At this point, I'll hand the story over to Paul, who recounted his journey in his memoir, *Jumping the Cliff to Simply Be*:

It was pitch black as I absolutely smashed through the hills that surrounded me, even though I had walked at least a marathon already. . . . I was breathing so heavily and sweat was literally pouring down my face. My breathing was getting heavier and heavier as I drove onwards. I began to feel almost like I was drowning, I simply couldn't catch my breath, as water began to pour from my eyes. I wouldn't say I was crying as it felt like I was no longer controlling what my body was doing. The coldest of shivers was running down my spine, but I felt no fear. I was eating up the ground underneath my feet and feeling like I wasn't even in control of my own movements.[3]

When he checked, Paul had covered six miles in an hour, double his usual pace, and he couldn't explain what had happened to him. He says it felt like a spirit of some kind had joined him that evening, pushing him along like the perfect tailwind. Like Dr. Paul Firth on Aconcagua, being propelled down the mountain by an invisible companion (see chapter 2), a presence made of speed and strength had come forth. For Paul, exhausted and shivering on a dark hillside in Italy, this was something with an intensity and otherness that he had barely experienced before.

I had to ask him—did he have any sense of who or what that was? He says he did.

When Paul had ended up at his grandparents' flat in 2009, it was his job to clear the place and get it ready to be rented out. Throughout his childhood, Paul's grandad Fred had been a constant source of support. He even has inscriptions to his grandad tattooed on his body, markers of the debt he owes him.

The flat, Paul explains, was an important place for him. "It was my safe space when I was a child—a place of tremendous peace." Paul, along with his brothers, worked hard to renovate the place, but inside he was struggling. The others didn't know, but he had been having suicidal thoughts. Focusing on the flat was a welcome distraction.

Paul got to work, shifting furniture, sorting ornaments, stripping wallpaper. Then, one day, something began to happen. First, Paul began to smell something: a distinct smell of pipe smoke. "It was so strong that I'm almost getting it now, [causing a] tingling down my back." Then, along with the smell, a sudden coldness—the kind of temperature change people often report when there is a sudden change in a room's atmosphere or energy. And then finally, a feeling of reassurance, of familiarity almost. This wasn't a haunting—not quite—but a joining, a visitation of some kind. It felt like an embrace.

Paul had needed something right then in his life—so much else was going wrong. This was something to hold on to, something significant. It was an experience, for him, that came straight from his grandad Fred.

That night in Italy, it was Fred that Paul had been thinking of. Before that ghost-like impulse took him, before he went storming up the hills of Salerno, he had been thinking about how proud his grandad would have been had he still been alive, how he would have understood what Paul was trying to do. Paul had deliberately brought Fred to mind, and then had managed to walk faster and harder than on any previous occasion.

Even at the time, he was unsure of how he should feel about what had happened. He couldn't really explain it. Now that he is studying psychology, he finds it even more unusual to think about and share. It's not really the sort of thing many psychologists would easily talk about, or at least not those who have been trained to think about psychology as an experimental discipline, an empirical science. It doesn't fit with what we can think we can test, measure, or give evidence for. And yet, there are always things that are hard to explain, that don't slide easily into the boxes of what we think possible and observable. What gets left is an uneasy sense of ambivalence; the crashing together of how you feel and what you think you experienced on the one hand, versus what you know, or what you are supposed to know, on the other hand. We might like to think we know how things work, but the mind—and the world—often has other plans.

Paul did talk to one person that night. After the experience, he called his friend John, back home in Teesside. John had been helping Paul as a kind of coordinator, helping him plan the route and pick the right pit stops, willing him along the way. John was a big reason Paul was doing this walk, as along with the challenge to himself, Paul was walking in memory of others who had passed recently. That included a member of John's family—a relative who had been tragically killed in a car accident.

When Paul had been at his lowest, John was one of the friends who helped to get him going again. He also gave him a sense of community, introducing him to others; Paul in fact had a whole team of supporters like John back home, all willing him on. When Paul rang John that night, it wasn't the first time—in fact, almost every time Paul failed to get onto a road, or found out that the road he wanted was a motorway, or made a mistake—it was John he rang. When he called John from Salerno that night, his friend affirmed what Paul had suspected: that he had had a spiritual experience.

John himself is a spiritualist; someone who believes that the spirit of people endures and can be communicated with. This might seem quite unusual or old-fashioned, but there are many people who would describe themselves as spiritualists. From a movement that began in the mid-nineteenth century in upstate New York and grew in popularity in the early twentieth century, spiritualism now only exists in pockets around the United Kingdom and the United States. It's hard to say why and how spiritualism boomed in that period—some have argued that it reflects the retreating influence of more mainstream churches, or an interest in establishing scientific evidence for unexplained phenomena.[4] But I don't think it's hard to understand its enduring appeal, particularly in the face of loss. A need to believe in something that offers comfort and solace, something that offers a way for loved ones to endure, is an understandably human response.

Paul was, and is, one step removed from that. I am not sure he would call himself a spiritualist; but he is someone who has had spiritual experiences. And the influence of this kind of thinking, this sort of idea, cannot be ignored when it comes to understanding Paul's experience of presence.

In his own account, Paul's description of the moments just before his Salerno experience don't just contain thoughts of his grandfather. They start with thoughts of his childhood, difficult experiences with members of his family, things that are still painful now. This is the "angry juice" he described. But once he moved on to thinking about formative, important relationships, things he values and feels lucky to have, he felt a sense of gratefulness. "My thoughts were more and more going to the people who no longer walked this world," he writes.[5]

When put like this, it's almost too easy to connect the dots. Physical exertion. Isolation. Imagination. Expectation. Paul has planted the seed for his mind and body to grow in new ways, just like a polar explorer or an ascetic monk might in their own particular situations.

And he has a huge reserve of emotional energy, a burning desire to achieve something for others. The way Paul describes his experiences, it's hard not to think of our minds filling in the gaps with what we expect, want, and need. It's like the journey or the situation took Paul outside of himself, and an "other" was created to fill in the gaps. He needed someone at that point, and Fred stepped into the breach.

But like many things, it isn't as simple as that.

Paul also had another strong and vivid experience on his Italy walk, but this time it wasn't of his grandfather. At another point of his walk—a point at which the same thoughts and memories were being invoked—he once again felt that a spirit had joined him, but it didn't feel like someone he knew; rather, he felt that it was actually one of John's relatives. Again, he had been speaking to John a lot, and again, we can draw the lines between preparation, expectation, and experience straight and true. But for Paul, this experience didn't have the same effect. It was uncomfortable. Why was that? I ask him.

"This was a new person, a different person I had never met before," he explains. "It was quite surreal. I didn't have any sort of relationship to them directly." Something about that experience didn't feel quite right—it didn't feel like it was *for* Paul. He attributes it to the conversations he was having with John and with others: "His words were incredibly resonant, and I think the constant conversations were building a picture in my head which wouldn't otherwise be there," he says, wondering out loud as he speaks. "At the same time, it was almost a community support, you know, a group of people coming together, to connect with spirits and things. *It's not just one person saying something.*"

Paul's experiences illustrate an important point. If you go seeking inspiration, actively looking for companions, and put yourself into states that blur the boundaries of self and other, you might not always get to choose what happens next. A presence could be invited in, but who or what they are isn't always up to you—the process might even *require* you to give up that kind of control. And it might be shaped by others around you.

Nowadays, Paul doesn't use these kinds of strategies and techniques, and it sounds like he is in a different kind of place entirely. He has a new partner, and a son, and they offer all the fuel he needs for his expeditions. He'd recently completed a 160-mile ultramarathon—probably most people's idea of hell—and he described it as "a 157-mile warmup, followed by a 3-mile run with my family."

He still gets unusual experiences too, but not the same kind of presences. When he is ultrarunning, he mainly gets visual experiences, particularly when he runs at night: things bound toward him, animals and other shapes. It's a very common experience for those stretching the definition of "a long run."

He has a recurring experience on those runs, which he does with a friend of his named Dave. "When we get into the later stage, we always try and catch them." Phantom runners, he means, people just up ahead. It's a well-known technique for runners—pick someone out up ahead and try to reel them in, except usually the runners actually exist.[6] "I always say, 'Let's just catch them,' and Dave doesn't even bother to say it anymore—that they aren't there!"

I ask Paul if he has ever had a distinct feeling of presence when he is running, anything that spurred his momentum in the same way that happened to him during his Italy walk. Surely the conditions would be perfect for something like that.

"No—you know what?" he says. "I wonder about those experiences. Particularly in a foreign country, not knowing the language, [that] versus a very social experience. Ultrarunning for me is a highly social activity, it's such an amazing community."

So even in some of the most extreme conditions, key things about our outlook or mentality seem to play an important role in shaping what kinds of experiences we might have. How our bodies and our minds respond to hardship and adversity might be very different depending on our need for others in that moment, depending on the answer to a simple question: Do you feel alone? It's like presences come about from a meeting of the physical and social worlds, when there's just enough flexibility, just enough traction, to allow thoughts, ideas, and beings to pass back and forth. Sometimes this happens in an intentional way, and other times it is out of our control.

In any case, from what Paul is saying, he doesn't need those kinds of experiences anymore. Angry juice for him was like "nitric oxide"; it led to him failing races, it burned him out too quick. He takes strength and meaning from the experiences that he has had, but he doesn't rely on imagined others to get him through that wall anymore. Now he tries to get himself into a constant, meditative state while running mile after mile after mile—just like the marathon monks of Mount Hiei.

And that's who he is now—the enlightened Paul Burgum. Always running, never alone. And stronger than ever before.

* * *

THE STORIES I had heard from Luke, Leven, and Paul left my mind swimming in its attempt to understand the complexity of presence. We know that certain situations, measured by certain statistics, seem to create the conditions for hallucination—but we also know that specific kinds of people seek out those scenarios. They do that for different reasons. It might be for the challenge, or to feel a sense of belonging, or even growth—but person and place align to set the scene for a feeling of presence.

People enter that scene with different expectations, and those expectations undoubtedly have a big part to play in the kind of experiences people have. But strikingly, even when someone anticipates a particular feeling (like Leven) or willfully conjures it (like Paul), they don't always end up with an encounter that makes sense for them.

When we turn back to our two hypotheses about presence—one about the body, and one about expectation—both can easily still be playing a role in these stories. But for the expectation hypothesis, it feels like we need something subtly different. It's not just about expectations but about people: social entities, agents in our environment, things we can relate to. And it might not even be about specific people; we probably don't get to select who arrives. I think that capacity—that ability to conjure someone, you just don't know who—is probably true of all us, whether we are an extraordinary person or not.

And if it is something true of us all, something potentially universal, its source seems likely to lie closer to home—I needed to think about what that might be. Our time with the fellow travelers was over.

Well, nearly over.

Ally

It's April 2021, and the pubs have reopened again in the UK. Not only that, but I am back to running, and I have just run ten miles: my longest distance since that day in 2018, for the Great North Run.

I am sitting with a friend, Ally. Ally is a serious runner. Born and raised in the northeast, he has done the Great North Run over twenty-five times. Despite being in his sixties, Ally still regularly runs huge distances. He is the only person I know whose vacation schedule is organized around marathons. Pre-pandemic, he might have been found jetting off to Boston to do the marathon there—ensuring he turns up in time to do the half marathon the day before as well—then heading off to do the Burj Khalifa marathon (twenty-six miles up and down stairs . . .).

Over a pint, Ally and I get around to talking of running strategies: What keeps you going, what works for you, do you focus in or zone out, do you run with others? Inevitably, we end up talking about hallucinations. I explain some of the questions I've been thinking about, some of the accounts of runners being joined by phantoms.

Ally looks over his pint with a raised eyebrow and a knowing nod. "I know what you mean," he says. "There's a place on the Great North Run. I could never get my head round it. People would get all sorts of funny things happening to them, seeing stuff, you know?" I nod.

"And it's happened to me a few times." He pauses again. "I would see my grandmother. Not my mother, mind—sometimes I would kind of talk to her in my head, or hear her, she was always in my ear giving me this and that. But seeing my grandmother, that was different. She wouldn't talk, I would just see her there. I always got on with her."

He takes a sip. My legs are cooling down from the run, and they are beginning to shiver.

"And I couldn't work it out for years. But the last time I ran, I realized as I reached that bit. Where you turn there, where you hit that bit, you know where you turn off that road?" I nod again. "The tarmac is always really, really hot and sticky. And I noticed you can see the heat coming off it as you run, you know like the air goes wavy? And I wondered whether that could be it, people seeing stuff."

He shrugs, seemingly baffled by it. If anyone was going to notice this sort of thing, it would be Ally; he's done the race enough times. And where was the place that he was talking about, this hallucinatory hotspot?

The six-mile mark. The anvil. Where I was alone, Ally was not.

Come bring your imaginary others, see your lost ones, loved ones, and longed-for ones, pushing on heavy arms and jelly legs, right through the eye of the storm. Or, you know, nearly have a heart attack.

You choose.

9

Seeing Darkness

It is among the most unsettling things that can happen to a person. An experience to make you reconsider what is possible, one that takes you back to childhood fears, forcing you to recall a kind of imagination that you had tried to forget. Whole worlds and entities, once packed out of sight, far under the bed, are pulled back out once more. It is a reason to be afraid of the dark again.

You wake slowly one morning. You open your eyes and see a weak shaft of light coming through the curtains. You feel like you were in the midst of a deep dream—something significant, but you can't quite remember what. You stir and think about lifting your hand to rub the sleep from your eyes.

But you can't.

In fact, you can't move any part of your body. It feels like you are held down, restrained, locked somehow. A slight pressure builds on your chest. You struggle to breathe. You try to stay calm, but your body has other plans.

And then you feel it. It's there—and it's watching you.

Sleep has stalked through the tales of presence that we have heard so far, a shadowy figure that keeps appearing and reminding us that our waking life is, and can only ever be, half of the story. The integrity of our daytime world depends on its nocturnal twin. Sleep grounds us, renews us, and places much-needed boundaries around our experience.

And, when it comes to the uncanny, sleep is the great unifier. As anyone who has stayed up too long can testify, our brains just aren't designed to function on too little sleep.

After talking to Leven and Paul, I realized that I had been neglecting sleep, even though it is potentially one of the most powerful sources of presence. We have already seen just how easily sleep deprivation can conjure phantom phenomena, but most research on hallucinations and sleep doesn't involve keeping people up for days on end. Instead, it has focused on experiences that occur during normal sleep patterns. Typically, these involve the boundaries of sleep. *Hypnagogic* phenomena refer to experiences that occur when one is going to sleep, while *hypnopompic* experiences happen during emergence from sleep (the two are sometimes referred to collectively as *hypnagogia*). You might have had one of these experiences yourself—a shout from nowhere, or a call of your name. A jerk, just as you are drifting off, with the sudden sense of something you need to pay attention to. Or the very brief dash of randomness in your thoughts as you close your eyes for a split second longer than usual.

Sometimes these experiences are persistent and alarming. "Exploding head syndrome" (EHS) is the outlandish name for the sudden experience of loud noise that some people get when falling asleep and waking up.[1] It's completely harmless, but it can be distressing and unsettling when people experience it frequently and don't know the cause. Not unreasonably, you as an adult might think something odd was happening with your hearing, or even your mental health. As a child, it can feel like a herald of something: a warning of the oncoming night, with a world of the unknown ahead. This happened to a colleague of mine, who battled through the experience for years in his childhood, being afraid of going to bed each night for fear of the

strange and sudden sounds that could occur. He was nearly forty—
relieved, amazed, and somewhat frustrated—when I told him about
exploding head syndrome for the first time.

Like some of the more basic auditory and visual hallucinations,
those related to sleep are often fleeting and quite simple in form.[2]
Single words might be heard, for example, rather than any kind of
full dialogue. In people who have hallucinations around the boundaries of sleep, they can also be consistent—a similar sound or vision
might recur at the same time each night or be promoted by the
same kinds of conditions (such as overindulging or burning the
candle at both ends). What's experienced might also reflect what's
on someone's mind as they go to sleep. On several occasions, I've
had an experience familiar to many new parents: phantom cries
from the baby, just as I drift off. Some people might even see or
feel their baby in bed with them, even when the child is fast asleep
elsewhere.

We don't know the exact cause of hypnagogic experiences, although
there are a range of plausible hypotheses. Compared to the variety
of hallucinations that can occur in clinical disorders, the consistency
and relative simplicity of some hypnagogia make them easier to
try to explain. The most popular theory of EHS, for example, is
a reduction in activity in the *reticular formation*, a set of neurons
in the brain stem.[3] This structure is thought to be important for
regulating consciousness and arousal, including how different areas
of the cerebral cortex relating to movement change their activity as
a person moves from wakefulness to sleep and back again. If this
doesn't happen in sync, it's possible that sudden bursts of activity in
sensory parts of the brain could be misinterpreted as real sounds—
including explosions.

This kind of model could also explain a range of hypnagogic phenomena, but we don't know for sure.[4] Our sensory systems staying
on and experiencing random activity while other parts of our brain
shut down sounds plausible, but showing it experimentally is another
matter. What we do know is that these states involve a series of gradual

transitions happening in the brain, with different stages of conscious experience each emerging and receding in their own time. And many strange things can creep into that transitional space.

The best demonstration of what happens in that space is also one of the most unnerving examples: sleep paralysis. Sleep paralysis is a naturally occurring phenomenon affecting around 7 percent of the general population at some point in their lives.[5] It involves waking from sleep and not being able to move your body, like you have been temporarily immobilized.

The existence of sleep paralysis itself isn't considered any great mystery. When we sleep, our brains enter into different stages of processing, which are characterized by a change in our brain wave patterns. The brain's oscillations—neural assemblies firing and resting—shift to a much slower and more synchronized pace across different brain regions.[6] In the first half of the night, we pass through various stages of "slow-wave" sleep—when our sleep is deepest and our bodies go through the core business of restoration and repair. In the second half of the night, we progressively cycle through shorter stages of slow-wave sleep coupled with periods of rapid eye movement (REM) sleep, during which parts of the cortex show rapid and spontaneous patterns of activity.

REM sleep was once considered synonymous with dreaming, and many of the dreams we can remember will occur during REM periods in the early hours of the morning. But we now know that we can dream during non-REM periods of sleep too, even in the middle of the night.[7] The dreams we have don't tend to be complex or bizarre, and they might be hard to remember.[8] (Experiments on non-REM sleep usually require waking participants suddenly and asking for immediate recall of what is happening in their dream.) During REM sleep, in contrast, is when we have our more complex, story-like dreams: multistage plots involving goals, conflicts, and other people. And when we are in REM sleep, our muscles are in a state of paralysis that stops most of us from acting out our dreams.

In sleep paralysis, our conscious awareness emerges from sleep.

But due to an accident of timing, the knockout of our main motor functions is still in place when we wake. When that happens, we feel awake, and we feel like we should be in charge of our bodies—but we aren't. Sleep still holds us down, pinning us in position (usually lying on our backs), and locking us into a combination of dreamland and reality.

That might sound alarming in itself, but the strange thing here isn't the paralysis. It's what happens next, when we are stuck in place. Consider the following experience, from Herman Melville's *Moby-Dick*:

> At last I must have fallen into a troubled nightmare of a doze; and slowly waking from it—half steeped in dreams—I opened my eyes, and the before sunlit room was now wrapped in outer darkness. Instantly I felt a shock running through all my frame; nothing was to be seen, and nothing was to be heard; but a supernatural hand seemed placed in mine. My arm hung over the counterpane, and the nameless, unimaginable, silent form or phantom, to which the hand belonged, seemed closely seated by my bed-side. . . . I knew not how this consciousness at last glided away from me; but waking in the morning, I shudderingly remembered it all, and for days and weeks and months afterwards I lost myself in confounding attempts to explain the mystery. Nay, to this very hour, I often puzzle myself with it.[9]

As the shudder of the narrator attests, the presences that come with sleep paralysis aren't like most of the presences we have met so far. These visitors are much more likely to be experienced in a negative fashion. They are perhaps most comparable to the voices we began with: the silent voices encountered by Alex and Keira, for example. They are not here to save you, or keep you company, and you certainly won't be setting a place for them at the dinner table. The combination of paralysis and the appearance of a shadow figure can be excruciatingly intense and frightening.

Here's another example, from the felt presence surveys we ran at Durham University:

The very first time; in bed, feeling that I am awake but unable to move and completely aware that there is a malevolent presence moving towards me and I can't move or look at it or even scream. I managed to get my fingers to move then I could move and it went. But it completely freaked me out and left me terrified that night. I did not know what had happened so called my dad and asked him about ghosts. He explained that it was probably stress causing night paralysis, that I thought I was awake but really asleep. This made it easier to be less terrified however they came nightly for months.[10]

This kind of reaction is not uncommon; I know friends who have responded in the same way. Against all sense or reason, they feel they must ask someone about ghosts or spirits; things they haven't thought about or entertained for years or even decades. The vividness of the experience, and its extreme sense of reality, makes people challenge their core assumptions about what is real and what is imaginary. The repetition of the experience is common too; it can happen again, and again, and again, no matter what.

The presences encountered during sleep paralysis are often reported to take up a specific physical location in the room, and they sometimes move progressively closer to their host. Their identity isn't necessarily known, but, more than perhaps any other kind of presence, their intent is perceived almost immediately.[11]

They are pure malevolence, watching you, stalking you as you lie prone.

They do not mean well.

Find the light switch

As a child, I was always afraid of the dark. I had an overactive imagination, and for years I went to sleep with the light on. Luckily, I never experienced anything like sleep paralysis or the presences that accompany it.* But a friend of a friend—Helen—has had repeated experiences of both sleep paralysis and presence over a three-year period. I spoke to her to get a sense of what it's like to have recurrent visits of this kind.

Helen is in her thirties and works with deaf children as a communication support worker. She lives with her husband and seven-year-old son. Despite undergoing the usual few years of sleep deprivation and stress that accompanies raising a young child, her sleep paralysis experiences hadn't started until more recently.

I start by asking her what the experience is usually like; could she describe it for me? "What happens is that I wake up, and I know that 'they' are there. It's really hard to describe how I know, but with every little bit of my being—like in the same way I know my husband is in the house now—I know that someone's in the room," she says. "For me it becomes imperative that I turn the lights on, because I have to see—I have to expose this person who's in the room. But I am unable to move."

While this is happening, Helen is acutely aware of her unwelcome guest. "The fear is incredibly overwhelming because the person who's in the room is not benevolent—it's one hundred percent malevolent. This thing, I know, is there to hurt me."

Beforehand, I had explained to Helen that this idea of *knowing* that a presence is there versus *feeling* a potential presence was something I had been grappling with. Is this definitely a "knowing" thing for her? "It's just so apparent to me that there's someone there. It's the knowing that comes before the fear. So it's not as if I wake up fearful—I wake up and think, *That thing is there*, and that's when the fear begins. So the feeling is secondary to knowing that the entity is in the room."

In many ways, Helen's experiences offer a typical account of the presences that can come during sleep paralysis: shadowy figures of ill

---

* The closest I ever came to sleep paralysis involved overindulging at a family wedding, a four-poster bed, and a field of particularly loud nocturnal cows.

intent, consistent in when and how they come, but faceless and un-knowable. In other ways, though, Helen's attacks of sleep paralysis are even more unusual. For example, the spell usually breaks as soon as the sufferer can finally move. But Helen's experiences don't end there.

"Eventually I am able to move, but the problem is that, then, I don't know where I am. And I don't mean like when you wake up in a friend's house you are momentarily like, *Where am I?* I don't even have any concept of my house, my room, or who I am."

This is something I hadn't considered before. Where does our sense of "us" go when something like sleep paralysis occurs? It's a question that isn't often asked—perhaps because one's attention is always focused on the intruder in the room.

Helen reflects: "I have no idea in the whole world. I don't know what the room is like, so I spend a long time reaching out, and quite often I can't feel anything, and then I might get my hand on a bedside table. You would think that you could work out how to get out of bed, but I just can't."

It's like Helen's mind has entered a vacuum, floating weightlessly in space, free of its moorings. Helen doesn't know how long this process goes on for: it may be seconds, or even minutes. Eventually she manages to find the light switch, and as soon as she presses it, the feeling of the presence dissipates. But up until that moment, she can think of nothing else—she must get the light on. This has happened when she has been sleeping alongside her son, but she even loses the sense of who *he* is in that moment.

What Helen is describing sounds like she was still asleep in some way, and that perhaps this was an episode of sleepwalking following the paralysis. She has been a sleepwalker since she was a child, al-though she has never experienced anything like the anxiety or fear of the presence visiting during a period of sleepwalking—it always comes with the paralysis.

I ask Helen if she has any thoughts about why it occurred. Were there any kinds of triggers that seemed to bring the attacks on?

"Once I realized it wasn't normal, I was able to look back. Every episode that I have had has been during a time of bad mental health or particularly stressful situations." Helen's most recent experience has been only the week before our conversation. The first in a while, this one came the night before she was due to take her son on a camping trip on her own. Anxious about how it would go and if they would manage, she instead woke up to the presence—while still dreaming that she needed to get out of the car.

Stress is often considered a trigger of sleepwalking episodes, although there is stronger evidence for a hereditary predisposition.[12] If you have a first-degree relative who sleepwalks, you are ten times more likely to do the same.[13] Chillingly, Helen's mother would often scream in her sleep.

Despite how alarming Helen's experience of presence might sound, for her it has become manageable—explainable, even. "I've always really seen it as my brain doing super weird things," she tells me. I'm not sure I would be as calm about it as she is.

The final thing we talk about is who that person or thing could be. This is the bit that really intrigues me about sleep paralysis—why is the intruder so often experienced as this malevolent other? Where does that come from? For Helen, it doesn't have a gender, nor is it familiar. At times she refers to it as a monster, and probably not human. One thing I knew coming into the conversation is that Helen is a born-again Christian, and I wondered whether her beliefs were relevant at all for her in how she manages her experience or makes sense of it.

I finish by asking her about the origin of the thing visiting her—does it feel like it fits within the world of her beliefs? She thinks a while about this—but her answer is clear. "No, I do think it's a different category. I think if you believe in the concept of spiritual beings outside of our realm—which Christians do—I don't think that a demon would come to visit me very sporadically at night. I'm not sure that's how they operate." I am impressed at how Helen so casually weighs up the modus operandi of a demon, as if it were the most natural thing in the world to do.

She went on. "I feel I can sort of sense spiritual things. For me this doesn't fall into that category—I don't wake up and think, *Gosh, I need to really pray about that!* you know?" I nod, but I know I would be terrified if it happened to me.

"It feels very much part of my psyche rather than part of my soul," she says.

* * *

ABOUT A WEEK later, I receive an email from Helen.

> Hi Ben, I thought I would share with you a first from last night, I had my sleep paralysis/sleepwalking again. But as soon as I was able to move I put my hand out and grasped onto a cactus that [my son] had moved next to his bed. Never have I woken up so quickly!! There are still two spines in my thumb I can't get out as I grasped it so tightly they've gone in deep 💀. Not sure it's a long-term solution, but it did cut the experience short!
>
> Helen

If you are similarly affected by sleep paralysis, please do not try this method at home.

A deadly visitor

If you're someone, like Helen, who has an explanation ready, then I can see how sleep paralysis might be something you could ride out. It could even become normal, in a strange way—particularly if you knew it was a momentary thing, something brought on by poor sleep or bad diet. But for others, the experience retains its power, and that power can even grow.

The occurrence of these nighttime visitations has been recognized for centuries across many different cultures, with a large folklore based around them. Stories of the "nightmare" have been attributed to hypnagogic phenomena, as have visits by incubi and succubi, which sometimes sit or press on the chest of the sleeper. Different cultures have identified and interpreted the experiences in different ways, and the sinister intent of such nighttime visitors is a common thread across all of them.

Among the Yoruba of southwest Nigeria, unpleasant hypnagogic experiences have been attributed to *ogun oru*, a malevolent female spirit that seeks to poison the sleeper during dreams.[14] In Brazil, the *Pisadeira*, "a crone with long fingernails who lurks on roofs at night in order to trample on the chest of those who sleep," comes to visit.[15] The *Pisadeira* has been suggested to come from the Portuguese idea of the *Fradinho da Mao Furada*, or the "little friar with the pierced hand." The friar, legend has it, enters through the keyhole of the bedroom door, bringing with him the worst nightmares. By placing his hand on the sleeper's chest, he stops their ability to scream, locking them in place.

Among these examples, one group has stood out to sleep researchers for special scrutiny, for deeply disturbing reasons. In the 1980s and early 1990s, a spate of sudden deaths occurred during sleep among Hmong Laotian communities in the United States. Those affected were found lying on their backs with their faces contorted into grimaces, but there was no clear explanation for what had happened.

It was like they had been scared to death.

In Hmong culture, there is talk of a malevolent spirit that visits when sleep paralysis and night terrors occur. *Dab tsog*, or the "night spirit," attacks by crushing the victim's chest and causing difficulties breathing, an action known as *tsog tsuam*. Sometimes the spirit is directly perceived during an attack, as in the following example:

> I was in my bed at night. There were people at the other end of the house and I could hear them talking. . . . But I knew that someone else was there. Suddenly there comes a huge body, it looked like— like a big stuffed animal they sell here. It was over me—on my body—and I had to fight my way out of that. I couldn't move—I couldn't talk at all. . . . I was trying to fight myself against that and it was very, very, very scary. That particular spirit was big, black, hairy. Big teeth. Big eyes. I was very, very scared.[16]

The striking thing about *dab tsog* was that many Hmong apparently believe that the experience can literally be fatal. This prompted the interest of American anthropologist Shelley Adler, who interviewed a number of affected individuals for her 2011 book *Sleep Paralysis: Night-mares, Nocebos, and the Mind-Body Connection.*

ADLER: Can *tsog tsuam* actually kill people, or does it just frighten you and make you feel that you might die?

INTERVIEWEE: It always scares you and you feel that you will die. Usually people don't die the first time. After it happens once or twice, you go to a shaman and they help you. If it happens a few times and a shaman doesn't help you to find out why, then the spirit may be very angry and *tsog tsuam* can kill you.[17]

This was one of the more curious ideas that came up in Adler's interviews: it wasn't the shock of the first encounter that was understood to be dangerous, but repeated attacks bode ill. Other curiosities also stood out. Along with a need for a shaman to resolve the issue, the rates of sudden death observed were strongly biased toward males rather than females. And while *tsog tsuam* attacks occurred in Laos as well as in America, it was specifically Hmong immigrants—many of them refugees following the Vietnam War—who were susceptible to the fatal attacks. This spirit of death was selective in who it came for.

Through her research, Adler was able to identify some key factors that provide clues to this pattern. First, the Hmong community has been traumatized and displaced. Those living in the United States in the 1980s had fled not just war but also ethnic cleansing, as their alliance with the Americans and South Vietnamese had led to them being targeted by North Vietnamese forces. It is possible, indeed likely, that the stress of their experiences made Hmong individuals especially susceptible to sleep disruption and more serious health problems. In that context, something like heart failure could be a plausible consequence of chronic stress. Chronic problems with sleep would also increase the chance of hallucinatory experiences.

Second, the job falls to men, not to women, of the community to understand and resolve spiritual challenges affecting Hmong families. To fail to do so is an egregious, indeed fatal, error. When Adler's interviewees described the importance of multiple attacks, they emphasized that Hmong men were to seek a shaman who could resolve the matter.

But third, and crucially, the kind of spiritual support provided by shamans was not available to Hmong refugees. Away from communities in Laos, and navigating a new life in the United States, the refugees were unable to access the social and cultural support for uncanny encounters with *dab tsog*. Problems could not be shared; shamans could not be consulted. This would appear to explain the increased instances of sudden death attacks in the United States compared to the lack of such attacks in Laos: back home, if the demon came for you, you at least had some backup.

But even if we can explain why male Hmong refugees in particular were stricken by the experience, we are still left with the gap between mind and body. Could a fear so intense really produce such a vivid experience, one so strong that it could threaten life? Adler describes it as a "nocebo" effect: a negative expectation acting on health in the opposite way that a traditional placebo would. This makes some sense—but placebos rarely have such dramatic impact.

To understand how this could be possible, we first need to understand how paralysis can bring presence. The explanations that have been posited, and the consistency of the experiences that are reported, makes sleep paralysis the ideal testing ground for competing theories of felt presence. It also poses a key challenge—are we going to find an answer that is specific to sleep or one that tells us a wider story?

Hypothesis 1: Unbounded Bodies

The first thing to note about sleep paralysis is the radical change that occurs in how we experience our bodies. Ordinarily, there would be no situation in which we are conscious but cannot move a muscle. Various states of inebriation, or even being anesthetized, might represent some kind of parallel, but even in such cases we aren't usually fully clearheaded or even conscious. The change to our bodies in a state of paralysis is clearly an unsettling one, let alone disempowering, and this can quickly induce a state of panic in a number of people.

If we think back to chapter 5, there is ample evidence that changes to our bodies—or more particularly, our sense of our bodies—can lead to unusual perceptions of foreign presences close by. That is, if we are stripped of the usual cues and feedback about our bodies, our feelings of where we start and end will change and become blurred. When we can't move, our brains can't predict where our bodies should be; the whole process of aligning movement and sensation is disrupted. Just like PH's "family," or the shadow figures of brain stimulation, a transformed body map becomes a projected body map, and a sleeper becomes a sinister intruder.

That is the hypothesis advanced by V. S. Ramachandran, among others, to explain the phenomenon of sleep paralysis presences. In a 2014 article with Baland Jalal, Ramachandran drew on evidence of body mapping disruptions to argue for what might be termed a "body hypothesis" of hypnagogic presence.[18] The strength of such a theory comes from the wider framework it draws upon: we know that presences seem closely linked to such body disruptions, and we have plausible mechanisms for how that might occur. Change the body map, conjure the other. Even if in this case, the other might be a demon.

This account therefore offers an appealingly parsimonious view of paralysis. It takes the broadest theory of presence—the body hypothesis—and applies it to the distinct aspect of these experiences—motor paralysis. Mystery solved—or is it?

Let's consider the plausibility of paralysis necessarily inducing body map projection in this way. There are clearly many cases of motor paralysis where hallucinatory phenomena generally do not occur (think of spinal injuries, for example). In some situations, the physical boundaries of our body will not align with our representation of it. Phantom limb phenomena are perhaps one example of something quasi-hallucinatory happening: a radical change to the body (the removal of a body part) being associated with the continued expectation that the body part is still there.[19]

But people don't tend to experience their phantom limbs as malevolent intruders—far from it. A closer parallel could instead be something like "anarchic hand" syndrome, where people with various kinds of brain injury experience the movements of one of their hands as if under someone else's control, just like Peter Sellers's title character in *Dr. Strangelove*.[20] Again, though, this seems far-flung from the bedroom phantoms of sleep paralysis.

A second discrepancy concerns positioning and shape. Sometimes sleep paralysis presences copy the orientation of the sleeper, but very often they don't. You will almost certainly be lying on your back, but the presence may be upright, or hovering, or creeping toward you. It isn't often in a lying position itself, and it isn't the doppelgänger that we might expect, if we thought this was somehow a "mirror" body. If a presence is being created based on a change to our own body map, that map has changed considerably by the time the other figure comes around.

Finally, we have the question of the presence itself. If a disruption to our bodily sense can create another figure, why is that figure often experienced so intensely as a malevolent other—why isn't it something neutral or familiar? It could be that the experience of paralysis leads to an intense sense of fear, and that fear is somehow directly embodied in the intruder. But it isn't clear that a body hypothesis alone can explain how or why that might happen. Put another way, it seems plausible that a disruption to our usual sense of our bodies in space could be a necessary part of the process. But it isn't clear that it's a sufficient account of the overall experience; it doesn't connect the dots to say why sleep presences happen in such a particular way. For that, we need something more.

Hypothesis 2: Ghost Predators

The Canadian psychologist J. Allan Cheyne is one of the people who can claim to have studied the phenomenon of sleep paralysis—and hypnagogic phenomena generally—more than anyone else. His research since the 1990s has attempted to document and understand all the different uncanny phenomena that occur in liminal spaces and states, including some of the largest studies done on the topic.

In 1999, Cheyne led a study that attempted to establish whether the experiences that occur during sleep paralysis all tend to co-occur.[21] That is, if you had presences, would you have other unusual body-related experiences, like feeling you were outside of your body? If you saw things, would you also hear things? It's a common aim for psychology studies to gather data on a large number of experiences or behaviors and see whether one or more underlying or "latent" variables explains them (such as a general "unusual sleep factor"). Establishing if you are dealing with one or more latent variable is important for indicating whether researchers should be trying to identify a single cause for something, or multiple causes instead—it's a bit like disentangling an overgrown set of plants to find the main trunks and roots.

Cheyne and his team started by running a survey among students at Waterloo University in Canada. Of 1,273 students, about a quarter (360) reported experiencing sleep paralysis. Those who did were asked to report how often they had had any of the following: (1) sensing presence, (2) experiencing fear, (3) floating or feeling out of their body, (4) hearing or seeing hallucinations, (5) experiencing changes to their breathing, (6) experiencing pressure on their chest, and (7) feeling pain. Of these, feelings of fear, floating, and pressure were endorsed the most, followed by the hallucinations: presence, auditory, and visual.

Cheyne's team found that the experiences fell into three groupings. First were the hallucinations and fear: if you had presences, you were also likely to have heard sounds, seen visions, and felt fear during sleep paralysis. Cheyne and his colleagues called this the "intruder" factor. The second grouping related to the body: feelings of floating and out-of-body experiences tended to hang together in the people who had them, and these were labeled "unusual bodily experiences." Finally, breathing changes, pressure, and pain tended to group statistically: this became the "incubus" factor in reference to the nighttime intruders of folklore.

This pattern of three different groupings was evident in a university student sample of 360 people and an online sample of 392 adults from the general population. It was then tested again in a second experiment, this time with 407 adults. In that second study, Cheyne's team were able to formally test different models to see if the data was best explained by one, two, or three factors, and whether those factors also correlated. The results suggested that intruder and incubus experiences were strongly correlated, even if they were technically independent. Unusual body experiences, though, seemed to form a grouping that could occur on their own, even without any intruder or incubus experiences. In other words, if you were the kind of person who often had out-of-body experiences, you weren't necessarily also going to have lots of presences visiting you at night.

Since then, Cheyne has managed to replicate this model in various studies, and he has used those results to argue that a focus on the body may be misdirected when trying to understand the presences of sleep paralysis.[22] Instead he argues that we need to pay more attention to the emotion that occurs with lots of these hallucinations: fear.

Cheyne's model, in brief, goes like this. In the state of sleep paralysis, we have various cues to suggest we are under threat: we are lying prone, often in the dark, and we cannot move. In addition, we may still be experiencing the aftereffects of REM sleep: some research shows that rapid eye movements continue in many cases of sleep paralysis,[23] suggesting that elements of our dreams may be creeping into our experience, even if we don't realize it.

From an evolutionary perspective, all these things could activate our deepest defenses against threat. As animals, we understand that, lying prone and paralyzed, we could be preyed upon at any moment.

Therefore, Cheyne suggests, we go into a mode of hypervigilance—our "threat activated vigilance system" takes hold, giving rise to "a non-specific sense of a threatening presence."[24] But shaping our thoughts and feelings is the afterglow of the dream—these are the ideas and images we were just entertaining in an unreal dreamworld.

From this, everything else follows: the feeling of someone being there; sights and sounds, glimpses out of the corner of your eye, even interpretations of breathing and pressure as being malevolent. We fill in the gaps at this point because to be prone and paralyzed wakes up our evolutionary fear of being preyed upon.

This model has a number of convincing points to it. First, it's an account that picks up a unique quality of the sleep state—the transition from dreaming. If you've ever woken up from a dream about a partner and stayed in a mood with them for the rest of the morning, you will have experienced how easily dreams can spill over into waking life in unexpected ways.[25] This seems like a plausible and important component of the sleep paralysis experience. Indeed, lots of people who have undergone it also report a lack of certainty about whether they were awake at all or whether they thought they were awake.

Cheyne's explanation for the presence emerging also seems plausible—even if sometimes evolutionary theories in psychology can be hard to test. You might wonder, why would a strong feeling of threat and being observed create a person? In fact, many different theories in psychology propose that we have either an innate or very early developing skill to detect other things that act in an intentional way—whether they are faces, voices, or moving bodies. This skill is sometimes referred to as a "hyperactive agent detection device," and it has even been proposed to be the basis of much more complicated things, such as the capacity to believe in invisible gods.[26] Such a device would essentially be biased toward erring on the side of spotting something, because the cost of missing a predator would be far too high. Whether or not such a "device" exists, we see supporting evidence around us: the face of Jesus in toast, Donald Trump in some ham, or the pareidolia Shackleton described in the Antarctic.

We also see this kind of bias in other accounts of presence. In our Durham surveys, many of the "endurance" accounts included situations where people were alone, vulnerable, and either in a very enclosed space or a very open space.[27] We found that a feeling of "being watched" was very common in this group in particular. It's like the old idea of being able to feel as if someone is watching you, like you have eyes in the back of your head.[28]

We have an account, then, of sleep paralysis presences that broadly contrasts with a body hypothesis. Rather than relying on understandings of how our brains map our bodies in space, we have a theory that draws upon agent detection, evolutionary concerns, and dream states to conjure a terrifying prospect: a phantom predator. It might be a different story than those we have heard about for other kinds of presence—but sleep presences are strikingly distinct and may require their own account. Case closed, then?

Hypothesis 3: Social Phantoms

Cheyne's explanation for the presences of sleep paralysis has its strengths, but it also has some loose threads. Recall how Helen described her experiences: she knew that something was present, and the fear followed from that. This wasn't an inference about a threat, nothing was holding her down. The conviction came first that the entity was there, right at that moment, in the room with her. The feelings of anxiety or fear came after.

That minimal sense of being accompanied, that unshakable awareness, brings us back to the presences encountered in so many places already: the feeling of something just being there. It also takes us back to the question of hallucination versus delusion. At its core, are we thinking something when it comes to such a basic awareness, or are we sensing something?

In Cheyne's earlier work, he had described sleep presences as a very basic form of hallucination.[29] But writing in 2007 with Todd Girard, he argued instead that they were more of a delusional phenomenon: the presence is a belief about threat, a bit like a paranoid state. This would seem to account for lots of stories of sleep paralysis— particularly when we think about the sheer terror of the Hmong sleepers, waking up to find *dag tsog*. But does it apply to all people in that state?

This question was posed by another sleep and dream researcher, Tore Nielsen, in a commentary he wrote in response to Cheyne and Girard's paper.[30] Tore is a Dane by birth and has studied dreaming for over thirty years in his adopted home of Montreal. He has designed and run experiments that have explored nightmares, lucid dreaming (when people are aware that they are dreaming and can control their events), and even dream engineering, when the content of dreams can be manipulated by techniques like changing the position of the sleeper. His interest in dreams goes right back to his childhood: for as long as he can remember, he has had nights of the most vivid dreams you can imagine.

Tore and I had previously crossed paths when I ran a short project on dreaming at Durham University. The project was called Threshold Worlds, and it involved working with a colleague of mine from the English studies department, Dr. Marco Bernini, to explore the similarities between dreams, hallucinations, and imaginative story-worlds.[31] We were particularly interested in ideas and sensations that seemed to break across the usual boundaries that divide our experience: things that stepped from reality into dreaming or permeated out from a dreamworld into waking life. Naturally, this included subjects like hypnagogia and sleep paralysis.

I wanted to talk to Tore again because his 2007 commentary made two key observations about the presences of sleep paralysis. First— though many are negative, not all are: some people report positive or neutral experiences, just like in Third Man phenomena or those encountered by people with Parkinson's. As such, trying to explain the presences of sleep paralysis purely in terms of threat wouldn't seem to fit with the range of emotions that can actually occur in the moment. Second, a lot of the experiences seem to relate to what people bring to the situation themselves. People who have preexisting problems with anxiety, for example, seem to have particularly anxious experiences of presence. This is in fact true of many negative sleep experiences— people with preexisting mental health difficulties suffer from more nightmares, more sleep paralysis, and more negative hypnagogia.[32]

And, as it turns out, Tore was one of them. Along with lifelong vivid dreams, he has experienced both sleep paralysis and visiting presences on multiple occasions. "I've had classical sleep paralysis and some nonclassical as well—I mean I've had the range! I've never had the classical demon sitting on my chest and preventing me from breathing, but I have had vivid ones. One was just the devil emerging from hell and wrapping himself around me, in a kind of ethereal form. He just started squeezing and squeezing me, lifting me off the floor, floating and spinning slowly in space, and I couldn't breathe. It got worse and worse, and I thought I was going to die. He's talking in my ear—the voice's depth and resonance (it seemed to be coming through a tunnel from a long way down) made it seem like it was emanating straight from hell. It was terrifying."

Tore is almost chuckling to himself as he describes "just" the devil doing this to him. He is talking to me over Zoom from his home in Montreal. He looks a bit like Bruce Willis, if Bruce Willis was asked to play a session guitarist from a 1970s rock band. Appropriately enough, the walls behind Tore are bedecked not just with the obligatory piles of books and paper that surround many academics but also guitars and other instruments. I wonder if he is going to play me a song. "Highway to Hell," anyone?

During the visit from the devil, Tore managed to break the spell himself. As his chest became more constricted, he realized it was his own panic that was causing the crushing. So he told himself to relax, and before long, the feeling subsided, and the demon disappeared. I ask Tore why he thinks such intense negative feelings are so consistent in sleep paralysis—and why they had happened to him. "The malevolent evil aspect is a mystery to me because it doesn't correspond with any feelings that I have in my waking life. I don't have feelings like that toward other people, and I don't think I've felt that kind of feeling toward me by others."

He goes on: "I don't really understand why that particular constellation of impressions would come in a situation of vulnerability, although I suppose that that would be the argument if you were completely vulnerable. But it still doesn't necessarily make sense, why a person would imagine the absolute worst scenario."[33]

We talk about the chicken-and-egg questions that seem to surround sleep paralysis. Do we feel threatened, so we experience an intruder? Or is it the other way around? Why do such specific and archetypal forms like the devil come to visit? And should we be trying to explain what happens in sleep paralysis, or should we aim to explain something more general about presences? "Of course, every experience has its own specific antecedents and factors influencing it—sleep being an obvious example," says Tore. "You need REM sleep atonia (i.e., muscle paralysis) going into the waking state—or vice versa—and that's not something you see in any other condition for any other presence. But then again—you probably wouldn't have those archetypal forms without a schematic component too."

By "schematic component" Tore means something like a representation of our body, transported as if it were another person. This is similar to the body hypothesis, but he means something more—something like a kind of social imagery that gets projected out, like PH's imaginary family, or the visit of Paul Burgum's grandfather. Not just a mirror of us, but a mirror of those who are on our mind, somehow. If this is the case, then we might still color the experience with all the different emotions we have at the time—including terror—but ultimately the encounter could be positive or negative. It doesn't have to be the devil each time—it depends on *who* is getting projected.

When I think about the distinction between Tore's and Cheyne's approaches, it makes me think of the difference between "lumpers" and "splitters," terms usually attributed to the American paleontologist George Simpson.[34] Scientists often aim for the Occam's razor approach, where the simplest explanation is applied wherever possible. But what counts as a simple explanation depends on the kind of theory you are trying to propose, and the scope of what you are trying to explain. We might select a small group and divide them off from others, focusing on their close similarities, thereby simplifying by splitting, in the same sense as "splitting hairs." Lumping, on the other hand, focuses on generalizing across wider categories—grouping things together—thereby ignoring some differences in an attempt to simplify.

When we approach something like sleep paralysis, it might seem intuitive to try to explain the experience as a kind of nightmare—in other words, to provide an explanation specific to the context of waking from sleep, but one that doesn't extend into other situations. It is therefore a kind of "splitting" explanation, in that it divides sleep paralysis presences from the wider context of illusory or imaginary people, from the varieties of felt presence more broadly.

On the other hand, we might think the most elegant explanation for sleep paralysis would be a general one, one that brings sleep presences back into the fold. This explanation would rely on the same general principles that drive presence in other contexts too. Sleep paralysis might be an extreme example, but the relevant ingredients are all there—a change to the body, and the arrival of an "other," something with a distinct sense of identity, separate from you, existing immaterially and yet clearly in the world around you. By including the phantoms of sleep in the family of presences—linked together as forms of social imagery, in some way—what Nielsen is effectively doing is proposing a "lumping" theory.

I am torn between the two. On the one hand, the consistency of sleep paralysis accounts and the specific conditions in which they occur makes me think we need a sleep-specific explanation, like the one that Cheyne offers. On the other hand, I can't help but feel there must be a general principle at play—something that is driving the sudden perception of another in that environment, with sleep paralysis perhaps acting as a particularly unusual sweet spot for conjuring presence. I think that makes me more of a lumper than a splitter.

What seems clear is that the state of paralysis, and the reactions it prompts, creates another ideal setting for felt presence. Could social imagery be the driver of what is going on? This is a hard question to answer. In my research I have come across many unwanted entities, and even some deceased relatives, but the kind of imagery that occurs doesn't often easily align with predictable factors.

Consider Helen's example. When I asked her about the identity of her entity, she was very clear that it wasn't demonic—it even felt like a category error to compare the experience to anything she believed about the religious and spiritual parts of her life. So even though she had plenty of thoughts and feelings about entities that could plausibly have been "the intruder," that wasn't what was being projected. If it was a kind of social imagery, it wasn't anything Helen recognized.

And what of the deadly *dab tsog*? Could expectation, or fear itself, really scare people to death? It's hard to overlook the social and cultural factors that Shelley Adler identified in her study of Hmong refugees. But we do know now that experiences of the heart, the head, and the senses are even more closely linked than we might expect. It seems that even momentary changes in our arousal levels can shift the confidence—i.e., the power—of our expectations over our perception. In one study led by American researcher Micah Allen, participants were shown very quick images of disgusted faces—too quick to register consciously—while they were attempting a perception task in which they judged whether rotating dot patterns were going in one direction or the other.[35] The direction was difficult to perceive, requiring participants to make a bit of an effort to "see" how the patterns moved. The subjects were also having their hearts monitored. Unbeknownst to them, however, the flashes of disgusted faces briefly raised their heart rate, and their judgments of moving dot patterns shifted during these flashes, making them more, and not less, confident about the way they were seeing the world. It's like the rules of their perception had shifted, causing them to judge the world around them in a different way—perhaps one driven more by effort and expectation.

It's not hard to think how this might apply to other situations when our feelings might shape what we hear and see. Think of how you feel after watching a horror film: Do you think twice before going into a darkened room, or scan the house for sounds before you pass through it? If how we feel inside can subtly shift our perception, we might literally start viewing the world in a different way: catching things out of the corner of our eyes, thinking we hear something when there shouldn't be anything there. Like in many horror films, one world—whether it's Freddy Krueger's or the Babadook's—begins to creep over into the other.

And what happens if we see something? What is it that our minds are producing? If we see a demon, or a grandmother, or nothing much at all, what does that say about us? It could be a kind of social imagery, like Tore Nielsen suggested. Or we could think of it almost as a kind of emotional imagery—a perceptual world fueled and colored by a surge of arousal and feeling.

The phenomenon of sleep paralysis acts as an important testing ground for many of the key questions around felt presence. Whether it is the body hypothesis, the role of threat, or the importance of others, each of these factors could be playing a role in the creation of the experience. They may offer a simple theory of sleep-based presences, or they may have implications for a bigger story. If we can untangle all of that, we might be able to understand a lot more about these invisible visitors.

Unless, of course, they *are* ghosts. I do know some people who think that. It's probably time I talked about them.

10

Spirit

"I speak to humans, animals, trees. Anything with a spirit, really," says Karen, looking out over her garden.

"And when was the last time you did that? Speak to one of them, I mean?" I reply.

"This morning actually—I connected with that tree, over there."

She pauses. A wind blows a flurry of leaves across the lawn in front of us.

"What did it say—if it's OK to ask?" I continue.

Karen responds: "Well, it's quite funny, actually . . . it told me to piss off. . . ."

* * *

IN PSYCHOSIS RESEARCH, there is an idea that is sometimes referred to as the "continuum."[1] The claim is this: For experiences of seeing or hearing things, or having unusual thoughts, we shouldn't think of them as being exclusive to mental health conditions like schizophrenia. Instead, these things are tendencies that we all have, and they cascade out in degrees across the general population. They happen to some people less often, to others a bit more often, and to a certain group they happen all the time. Imagine people spread out on their way up a mountain: some people are at base camp, some are in the foothills or halfway up, and some are really close to the top. We all occupy a space somewhere on this continuum of psychosis, and we could in theory move up and down it.

The idea of a continuum comes from a few different places. An evergreen question in psychiatry asks, should we think about the characteristics of mental health conditions in a categorical way—so you either have a condition or you don't—or should we think about them dimensionally, with mental health more a matter of degree? The messiness and uncertainty of mental health, and the difficulty of keeping things in neat, conceptual boxes, means that a lot of thinking in this area has moved toward the latter. The most recent version of the American Psychiatric Association's diagnostic rulebook—the DSM-5[2]—embraces a dimensional approach for many conditions.

Another argument that people sometimes make is that we should be thinking of distressing experiences as an extension of healthy mechanisms and processes instead of as something completely outlandish and alien to us. Unusual ideas and recurring thoughts are things that happen to us all, the argument goes, but these become too much (in some way) for certain people, and they tip over a threshold, leading them to require specialist support. This might sound similar to thinking about the characteristics of mental health dimensionally, but the two claims come from subtly different places and go in different directions. The idea that mental health conditions exist on dimensions can be understood as extrapolating the features of a mental health condition out into the healthy population. Or, in other words, rolling the concept down the mountain. In contrast, if we think about distressing experiences as being an extension of healthy cognition, we are pushing our way up the mountain. We are saying that the contents and processes of poor mental health are, in essence, normal—while still also being extraordinary.

The distinctions between each claim matter. On the one hand, we could be suggesting that healthy people are "at risk" of a condition to differing degrees, which in some way emphasizes the affinities we all have but also potentially pathologizes everyday experience. Or, on the other hand, we could be saying that distressing situations, occurring in people who are in poor mental health, are simply part of everyone's psychology. That might be a comforting idea for some, but it could also come across as patronizing or dismissive to others.

We can see this happen in discussions about the psychosis continuum, which continues to be a controversial idea. Some people welcome this kind of thinking as a way of normalizing the unusual experiences of psychosis.[3] Hearing voices and seeing visions become things that can and do happen to anyone—they lose the stigma of being unknowable, baffling, and scary things that only happen when you have a "mental disorder." Placing the idea on a continuum can help people feel that they are not on their own—that other people have these experiences too, and that they could happen to any of us.

Others argue that the continuum idea misses the point of how mysterious and unsettling a lot of psychosis is.[4] Thinking you hear your name once or twice a year, or maybe hearing or seeing things around the boundaries of sleep—these aren't the same as a voice that is constantly there, mocking, undermining, and threatening you. To draw that comparison, the argument goes, is to trivialize genuine distress, and this risks mixing up one-off tricks of the mind with chronic, debilitating encounters with the unreal. Normalizing an experience might help some people, but for others it could minimize it.

While debate around the continuum rumbles on, the concept certainly gets used a lot in research on psychosis. Even if some of the comparisons between psychosis and healthy experience may not be perfect, many researchers take a pragmatic view—trying to learn what they can from healthy people who happen to hear or see things that others don't.

What can we learn from this approach? We have already heard about many cases of the uncanny drifting into everyday life: Third

Men, phantom runners, nighttime visitors. But some people do seem to have a genuine affinity for encountering things like these. They are used to living in a world of voices, visions, and presences. They might have heard voices since they were children or reported seeing the spirits of relatives after they had passed away. These people can be hard to find, and even harder to get involved in research, but they are out there.

If we knew how or why these kinds of experiences occur in people who do not find them distressing, we might understand more about how to help people who are in distress. If a hallucination can be normal—healthy, even—then it theoretically opens up a range of possibilities for support. Understanding psychosis becomes a study of tipping points, alternative trajectories, and possible futures—even for those who are struggling the most.

A world of voices

The concept of hearing voices being a normal and healthy thing is one with a long and varied history, but its contemporary origin is often traced back to a televised conversation in 1987 between Dutch psychiatrist Marius Romme and one of his patients, Patsy Hague.[5] Hague frequently heard voices, and Romme was trained to interpret her experiences as a potential symptom of a mental health disorder (which in Hague's case meant a diagnosis of schizophrenia). But Hague challenged Romme on the assumptions behind that interpretation—if people throughout history had heard voices and recognized them as deities and spirits, why couldn't she? Why assume they are a problem?

From this conversation, Romme was inspired to find more people who lived with voices and needed no support. Working with the journalist Sandra Escher, Romme started something that eventually grew into the International Hearing Voices Movement. This movement is constantly changing and includes a diverse group of people with many different opinions, but they are often united behind Hague's original objection: Why think that someone's experiences are pathological, just because you don't share them?

It is perhaps no coincidence then that the largest ever study of "healthy"[6] voice-hearing was conducted in the Netherlands. Led by Iris Sommer at the University of Utrecht, a team of researchers recruited a sample of over one hundred "nonpsychotic" people who hear voices.[7]

In a series of papers they observed the following about this group:

(1) The voice-hearers without psychosis scored high for hallucinations on standard clinical measures—such as scales and interviews— but without showing any distress or any **other signs of psychosis**. For example, their score for unusual thinking (delusions) would be much lower than for someone with psychosis. Along with their voices not being distressing, the lack of delusional thinking was often one of the key reasons why they didn't qualify for a psychiatric diagnosis: their beliefs didn't stop them going about their everyday lives.

(2) When voice-hearers without psychosis underwent an MRI scan, their brains tended to **activate similar regions** to those in people with psychosis when hearing voices. The procedure to test this involved pressing a button when the voices started and stopped (a technique known as "symptom capture"). When hearing voices, people with and without psychosis activated areas of the brain related to hearing and producing speech.[8]

(3) Finally, the voice-hearers without psychosis were **more likely to hear illusory words.** To test this, subjects were given a listening task that involved completing sentences. For example, participants would hear an incomplete sentence like, "The sailor sells his . . ." Instead of the final word, which would be missing, some white noise was played instead. Healthy participants who heard voices were the most likely to say they heard the word at the end of the sentence, followed by people with psychosis, and then control participants who did not hear voices.[9]

Findings 1 and 2 here are important because they suggest that the healthy group was having similar—or similar enough—experiences to people with psychosis, based on interview and brain data. The difference simply seems to be that they were experiencing voices without all the other things that would usually lead to someone receiving a diagnosis of a psychotic disorder. This is significant, because an obvious worry is that those in this group were reporting and describing a kind of experience quite different to hallucinations in psychosis. Instead, based on evidence from standard tools and methods used in research in this area, the groups' results were comparable.

Finding 3, though, pointed to something different: that people in the healthy group seem to perceive ambiguous signals differently than other people do. It was like their brains were quick to fill in the gaps with a meaningful signal, in this case the word that would complete the sentence (even when it wasn't actually there). This is like having a conversation with someone who keeps completing your sentences, their mind racing ahead with the expectation of what comes next. It suggests that these "healthy" voice-hearers listen to the world in a different way than the rest of us do.

We have come across this kind of thing before in chapter 6: it's an example of a "top-down" effect on perception. In 2017, I ran a study with the Portuguese researcher César Lima that found a similar effect, again in a group of (what we called) "nonclinical" voice-hearers.[10] We played something called "sine wave" speech—an ambiguous, artificial speech that usually just sounds like R2D2 to unsuspecting listeners—to our participants while they lay in an MRI scanner. To understand sine wave speech you usually need to know what to listen for: you need to rely on your existing knowledge of speech to decipher the signal, like using a speech template to fit to the sounds.

In our study, the participants were initially asked to listen for other, unrelated sounds; the underlying speech was not mentioned. We expected that voice-hearers wouldn't detect the speech until we told them it was there, but that telling them to listen for speech would prime them to use top-down information—to draw upon their own speech templates. Like in other research where people with psychosis have showed greater use of top-down signals (see chapter 6), we thought their perception might be enhanced with the new information, the extra push to listen for meaning in the noise. We expected that they would then understand the speech, and perhaps do better than control participants—but only once they knew speech was there.

Instead, we found that they didn't even need the push: they could begin to decode the signal spontaneously, even without us telling them to listen for speech. While the rest of us might hear R2D2, the voice-hearers could parse the signal from the noise. We can't know for sure, but we think this result was picking up on something similar to the sentence-completion test given to the Utrecht voice-hearers. It was like they couldn't help but use the templates they already had for making sense of the world. When they were faced with something unusual, participants strove to make meaning of it—even without being prompted to.

A major caveat of our 2017 experiment was that far fewer people participated in it than in the Utrecht study. While Utrecht could recruit over one hundred voice-hearers, no other research group has found so many willing to take part in this kind of study. We found seventeen people in the UK and scanned twelve in London—which is comparable to most other studies in this line of research.[11] It's hard to get people involved, and for good reason. Imagine if you had been hearing voices all your life, but they have never been a problem. Would you tell anyone? Would you tell a researcher, or a clinician? How might they react? No one, after all, wants to be told they are crazy. Remember how the concept of the continuum—the logic that people who have these experiences are on some sort of sliding scale. Some might see this scale as sliding *toward* schizophrenia rather than away from it.

This is how I ended up in Karen's garden, talking about her antisocial trees. Karen had experienced voices and visions of different kinds for most of her life and had worked for many years as a kind of spiritual communicator for people who sought such services. Karen might talk to your dead pet if you asked her to, or even a deceased relative. For her, communication with spirits was a common part of her life, acquiring knowledge from them that she knew was not part of her mind; it had to have come from elsewhere. What she described might sound very unusual to others, but she was content with her experience. Not only that, she was also confident enough in her interpretation to volunteer for our study. She definitely wouldn't call her experiences hallucinations, but she was willing to get involved if her participation helped those who did.

She wasn't the only one who was motivated for that reason, and she wasn't the only one who was making a living based on her experiences. Our study led me to meet spiritual practitioners, diviners, psychics, and mediums, and many, but not all, considered themselves spiritualists. For them, there was no great mystery when it came to presence. It was spirit, pure and simple.

In search of a phantom

The Society for Psychical Research (SPR) was founded in London in 1882. Its first president was Henry Sidgwick, Knightbridge Professor of Moral Philosophy at the University of Cambridge, and its honorary members included Alfred, Lord Tennyson; the critic John Ruskin; the naturalist Alfred Russel Wallace; and the prime minister at the time, William Gladstone.[12] The aim of the SPR was to investigate "that large body of debatable phenomena designated by such terms as mesmeric, psychical and spiritualistic,"[13] although the society was at pains to point out that investigating such matters did not equal endorsement. The society's constitution began by stating:

> To prevent misconception, it is here expressly stated that Membership of this Society does not imply the acceptance of any particular explanation of the phenomena investigated, nor any belief as to the operation, in the physical world, of forces other than those recognised by physical science.[14]

The society's first publication was *Phantasms of the Living*, a collection notionally focused on experiences of telepathy, but including in it a "vast class of cases" of "apparitions"—hallucinatory experiences, connected to others, that could otherwise not be explained. *Phantasms of the Living* surveyed several reported cases of telepathic communications and unusual apparitions, which to the SPR's members seemed abundant at the time in Victorian society. The SPR—set up in response to a wave of such phenomena—actively invited people to send in examples of impossible events.

The writers of *Phantasms of the Living* were very concerned with establishing what kinds of events could be considered hallucinations and what kinds of mental faculties they may involve. Making that distinction included collecting stories of experiences that were apparently hallucinatory but without any sensory content. In some ways these were described as a bit like presences, although they also bore a resemblance to Eugen Bleuler's idea of soundless voices: messages from an other, directly experienced, in a way that couldn't otherwise be described (see chapter 1). Typically, the experiences seemed to play the same role or to function as some of the presences we have met already. The stories that the writers collected were very often of a particular type: the disembodied voice that warns, stepping in and pulling someone back from the brink, just at the right moment.

One reported case came from the Reverend P. H. Newnham, a vicar from Devonport in the UK. He had traveled to New Zealand as a nineteen-year-old in 1858, where he stayed in a hotel in Invercargill on the southernmost tip of South Island. The place, the reverend described, "was as wild as wild could be," with few buildings or other surroundings to speak of at that time. There he ran into a seaman who had worked on the long passage over from Britain. A rough character, the sailor had been put in irons at one point on the voyage for "mutinous language." When his ship reached sight of New Zealand, he led a gang of six men to desert the vessel and steal a whaling boat.

Despite this, the reverend struck up a conversation that night with the sailor and a group of his friends. While sitting around a roaring fire, drinking, smoking, and sharing stories, they explained to the reverend that they had a plan for the next morning. They were going to sail to Ruapuke Island, where there was a mission station, to seek out the missionary there and organize a marriage for one of the men in the group. They had extensive provisions and planned to stay a couple of days on the island to hunt wild boar. They invited the reverend to join them, telling him he would need to be ready at 4 AM, as the best crossing of the sandbar in the bay would be at 5.

The reverend, clearly a brave and inquisitive type himself, was keen to see the mission. As the only visitor at the hotel apart from the men, he could have easily offered his excuses and waved them on their way. But he didn't: he turned in to bed at 11 PM, intending to grab some sleep before joining the men in the morning.

I left them with the fullest intention of going with them I ever had of doing any-thing in my life. . . . I had no candle on the way, but usually struck a match when I reached the bedroom, and lit the candle in the room. When I left the kitchen I walked through a good-sized room, or second kitchen, and into the front part of the inn, and came to the staircase.

I had got up about four or five stairs, when someone or something said, "Don't go with those men."

There was certainly no one on the stairs, and I stood still and said, "Why not?" The voice, which seemed as if some other person spoke audibly inside my chest (not to the ear), said in a low tone, but with commanding emphasis, "You are not to go." "But," said I, "I have promised to go." The answer came again, or rather I should say the warning, "You are not to go." "How can I help it?" I expostulated, "they will call me up."

Then most distinctly and emphatically the same internal voice, which was no part of my own consciousness, said, "You must bolt your door." All this time I had stood still on the staircase. I did not even remember there was a bolt to the door, for I recollect just for a moment thinking I must and would go, and then such a strange feeling of mysterious peril that I wondered how I should secure the door in case there was no lock or bolt. On reaching the room I lit the candle, and felt very queer, as if some supernatural presence was very near me.[15]

The young reverend was relieved to find the door did indeed have a bolt, and he fastened it before climbing into bed. Then, at 3 AM, he was awakened by a hammering on the door, followed by shouting, swearing, and cursing. The reverend lay very still and waited for the men to depart—all the while still wondering if he had made a mistake.

Morning came, and the reverend walked down to breakfast at 9 AM. The dining room was empty, apart from a soldier who was eating alone at a table. As the reverend entered the room, the soldier looked up and asked him if he had heard what happened at Ruapuke that morning. No, the reverend answered. "Their boat has been capsized on the bar, and they are every one of them drowned," came the reply.

Along with the reverend's story, the authors of *Phantasms of the Living* collected multiple examples of a purer kind of presence, many of which are like those we have already heard about. Mr. W. de V. Wade, of the Downs in Dunmow, described waking in the middle of the night convinced that his brother—who lived in America—was right there in the room with him. Joseph Kirk—of the Audit Office, Royal Arsenal, Woolwich—described a niece who experienced a nighttime presence: "An unseen visitant, which lasted some time before it culminated in a clear auditory impression, the words 'I must go now—good night.'"*

Much of *Phantasms of the Living* involves the authors weighing up the possible causes of hallucination within the healthy population—including an extended discussion of whether indigestion, and in particular lobster salad, could be the cause of many unusual experiences.[16] The accounts of potential neurological explanations are arguably ahead of their time, with much consideration of the role of basic

---

* This is perhaps one of the politest presences on record.

sensory processes in causing one-off visual and auditory phenomena. Presences—like so many of the accounts that we have come across already—are referred to as "potential hallucinations" and "delusions." In other words, things that hang on the edge of what can be spoken of, experiences that boil down to a simple, visceral "knowing."

But throughout the book, and at the center of its conclusions, are some experiences that simply *cannot* be explained in a scientific way. In particular, accounts of crucial foresight (like the reverend's story) or communications from distant others are offered by the work's authors as key examples where mechanisms of the mind alone cannot account for the kind of new knowledge imparted. Stories of presences, voices, and visions telling people things they could not possibly have known—these were the true phantasms of the living.

It might seem strange to have a book so dedicated to scientifically explaining so many experiences conclude on a note of endorsing, well, telepathy. But this was the SPR all over: committed to scientific enquiry, but with an uneasy curiosity, bordering on desire, to believe in the truth of at least some of what people were describing.

What followed *Phantasms of the Living* provided an even clearer example of this tendency. The 1894 Census of Hallucinations surveyed seventeen thousand individuals from five different countries. A century before the internet, it remains one of the largest ever research studies on hallucinatory experience—and it could have been larger (they were aiming for fifty thousand accounts). The goal of the census was to establish the prevalence of visitations from absent others, and in particular "how far chance may account for the numerous cases where such hallucinations have coincided with the death."[17] It began in 1885 and rolled on for nearly a decade, with the International Congress of Experimental Psychology taking on the responsibility for running it in 1889 and William James leading recruitment in the United States. By 1890, its aims had widened somewhat to include a whole range of unusual phenomena and establish their prevalence, while it still maintained the original goal of establishing whether "veridical" accounts could really be occurring above chance.

The SPR were keen to screen out experiences that could otherwise be explained as dreams, delirium, or insanity. From the 17,000 respondents, 2,270 answered "yes" to the key census question: Had they ever, when awake, had the impression of seeing or hearing or of being touched by anything that, so far as they could discover, was not due to any external cause? Of these, 1,942 remained after screening—or over 10 percent of the overall sample. Mr. S. Walter-Anderson of Tickhill, Yorkshire, reported:

> "An aunt of mine, who died in England last November 1890, appeared before me in Australia, and I knew before I received the letter of her death that she was dead." On later checks, he claims he had established that the visitation had indeed come on the day of his aunt's death.[18]

The researchers working on the census had a very specific method for establishing the potential truth of such claims—how likely would it have been that an event such as Mr. S. Walter-Anderson's happened by coincidence? They reasoned it would have to depend on the average number of people someone knew, and the chance of any of them dying on a specific day, and then the chance of someone experiencing a hallucination within twelve hours (their predetermined window). Using these calculations, they arrived at a number of one in nineteen thousand—which seems, if anything, an overestimate. The census, on the other hand, reported a different figure: one in forty-three people reported such uncanny encounters.[19]

The conclusion of the census is both flawed and ingenious. Although the authors took great pains to emphasize that false positives— and people deliberately trying to subvert their survey—would only increase the likelihood of unusual experiences in general (i.e., not the ones they were specifically interested in), their recruitment methods could never avoid one fatal flaw: response bias. If you ask people to share their unusual experiences, the only people who are likely to reply are those who have had the experience—why else would someone take part? The number of accounts collected is impressive, but their method of acquisition is akin to people sharing stories in a chat room: the storyteller and the listener are joined in a common aim. People who have something to say will respond to this kind of research; people who don't, won't.

Of course, it is not clear that any scientific study based on these methods could really prove the existence of such phenomena. And yet, the census still stands today as an impressive achievement in psychological research and international collaboration. It sheds much light on the kinds of unusual experiences everyday people were having at that time in Victorian society: experiences of loved ones long lost, sometimes coming around the boundaries of sleep or during times of stress and trauma.

And the work demonstrates how intertwined the origins of experimental psychology and paranormal research were in the late 1800s. The aim of much psychology around the time was to restlessly push the boundaries of what was possible, to use any potential techniques to establish new frontiers of the mind. This tradition would continue, but the subsequent history of psychology and spiritualism became generally more adversarial. Attempts to account for such unusual phenomena mostly became exercises in debunking—although many experimenters would precariously tread a line between rational skepticism and vicarious immersion.

Some investigators would become national celebrities. One, Harry Price, who became known for investigating famous mediums, was called upon to observe the strange case of Gef the Talking Mongoose (a poltergeist that visited a rural family on the Isle of Man for over ten years[20]), and was finally accused of exaggerating accounts of the haunting of Borley Rectory on the basis of scant evidence.[21] People who sought to test the claims of spiritualists seemed to inevitably get caught up in the experiences reported, so that these researchers would eventually end up being doubted by all sides: too skeptical for the believers, too interested in the paranormal for the establishment. And because of this, psychological research grew further and further away from the world of spirits and mediums.

The presences of grief

The concerns of the SPR, and of men like Harry Price, may seem a world away by today's standards. Concerns of mediumship or visits by poltergeists feel very much of their time—and parapsychological research tends to sit at the fringes of experimental psychology today. What, then, is relevant here for understanding felt presence?

The first point is that such accounts perhaps come closest to what many people think of when contemplating something like felt presence. Presences that we cannot see or hear, and yet whose arrival cannot be mistaken; presences that inhabit and haunt certain spaces and times, creating atmospheres of their own. In the popular imagination, presences often *mean* spirits or ghosts. And according to some estimates, belief in ghostly encounters has risen in the postwar period. In the UK, for example, one study reported that approximately 15 percent of adults endorsed such beliefs in the 1950s, compared to over 30 percent in the 1990s. Moreover, such stories still get shared and recounted, and the trope of the ghost story, or after-death encounter, is a familiar one that many people will hear. These might seem like fringe experiences—but that doesn't mean they are uncommon.[22]

In 2020, I was part of an international working group that reviewed the evidence of people reporting experiences of the deceased during bereavement.[23] A lot of the data available is quite piecemeal, and it can be hard to run large-scale, systematic research on the topic. As with many of the experiences that we have heard about so far, people can be reluctant to talk about them. They might be concerned about how the listener will react, worrying that they will be misunderstood or even laughed at. They might not be able to make sense of it themselves, and their experience—like those of sleep paralysis—might clash with what they hold to be possible. And yet, these incidents can have huge significance for people.

In our 2020 review, we referred to these accounts as "sensory experiences of the deceased," or SEDs. Based on the data we do have, there were some things that we could say with some confidence:

(1) **Felt presence is a common (perhaps the most common) kind of SED.** In survey work of bereavement phenomena, the simple feeling of presence (absent of any clear sensory cues) occurs most frequently, followed by auditory experiences, and then visual experiences. The presences reported are sometimes very clear—in taking up a particular position in space, for example—but sometimes are more diffuse and abstract. One of the review authors, Edith Steffen, had conducted a small study in 2011 where people described their experiences. One person said, "It wasn't a physical thing. I didn't feel anything physically. But I felt it so strongly. I felt him." Another was more specific: "You know, it wasn't like a shadow or anything. She was literally there at the bottom of my bed."[24]

(2) **The relationship of SEDs to past experience is . . . complicated.** While for many the feeling might be comforting, SEDs can include the persistence of unpleasant people and relationships. This was a surprise to me, and it's something that one of the other review authors, Jacqueline Hayes, has drawn attention to in her research.[25] It's an important observation because it suggests that the driver of such experiences cannot just be coming from the emotional needs and desires of the subject. If SEDs only ever occurred in people who were grieving for someone who they dearly wished was still around, it would not be very surprising that these kinds of experiences occur. Longing, isolation, and reminiscence can work powerfully upon an individual; a lifelong partner will stay in that chair if you only keep them in your imagination.[26] But for others, complex—and even abusive—relationships may continue, and it might be a focus

of psychotherapy to break the bond with the deceased in some way.[27] These, however, are not representative of the majority of bereavement experiences. In fact. . . .

(3) **The majority of these experiences are benign.** There is a historical concern that persistent experiences of this kind represent a kind of disorder—in other words, a problem in how grief is being processed by a person. There are diagnoses—such as persistent complex bereavement disorder and prolonged grief disorder—that have been studied in relation to SEDs, but the evidence to suggest a strong association with pathology is not there. It would generally be a mistake to think about these experiences as necessarily being problematic—even if, for some people, they can become a problem.

We can't say how common bereavement-based experiences of presence are, and we know from international research that they can vary considerably across different countries and cultures.[28] The point here is to emphasize that these experiences *are still happening*, in twenty-first-century Western societies. The time of the SPR might seem like ancient history, but if we were to run a Census of Hallucinations today, focusing on similar experiences, who knows what kind of response we may receive?

Many people out there might be looking for a kind of connection with the deceased—even if they themselves wouldn't necessarily say that they believe in life after death or the physical reality of spirits. If that kind of connection is sought, and if it doesn't happen spontaneously, they might choose to see a medium. And sensing presence—understood fundamentally as a kind of spirit—is still a key part of the modern practice of mediums.

The presence professionals

Mediums and psychics are often called "clairvoyant." In fact, clairvoyance is only one component of the ways in which spirits are encountered, referring to visual experiences specifically (hence the association with "seeing" the future). In our research at Durham University, we were often most interested in people with a second kind of sensation: "clairaudient" experiences, or experiences of sound and language that indicate the presence of spirit. We chose this focus because our research was mainly geared toward the phenomenon of hearing voices, so clairaudience would in theory be a close parallel. Often occurring in tandem with clairvoyance and clairaudience is "clairsentience," when people experience a basic feeling of spirit and the knowledge that it can bring. Clairsentience is not necessarily reliant on any of the classic five senses but comes from something separate entirely.

You might think that doing research with people encountering these phenomena would be a waste of time. Lots of people think that self-described mediums are "putting it on," that their work depends on offering something to people at a time when they are emotionally vulnerable, i.e., during a period of bereavement. I understand that response—and if I'm honest, I have met some people who have prompted that reaction in me—but it wasn't the view we took among our team at Durham.

We approached the topic with the starting assumption that people were having some kind of unusual experience. The subjects might interpret it as a supernatural encounter or believe in an explanation that didn't fit with ours, but we took it on good faith that they were having experiences that they couldn't easily explain otherwise. And we fundamentally wanted to know what the experience was like—not what caused it necessarily, or how it could be debunked, but how it felt to them in the immediacy of the moment.

Between 2016 and 2019, our team conducted a series of interviews with people who had regular experiences of clairaudience, with voices speaking at least once a month. The subjects couldn't have been diagnosed with any mental health condition that might be associated with hearing voices or similar phenomena. Many respondents were practicing mediums, and some, but not all, were recruited via the Spiritualists' National Union, the largest organization of people with spiritualist beliefs in the UK.

One of the things that quickly became apparent in conducting our interviews was that many of the experiences of spirit were not confined to one sense. Often a sign in one domain would then be followed by another; voice would follow vision, a thought could lead to a tingle or a brush on the shoulder.[29] Some people would not have any experiences in one particular sense—like clairvoyance—but many had a mixture. And all were skilled at detecting a spirit, in any form that it would come—including as a felt presence.

A colleague of mine, Dr. Peter Moseley, led the study. If the subject of presences came up in the interviews, we would typically ask people to define what they meant by that. The response would often include descriptions similar to those we have come across already in the preceding chapters of this book. Some would describe proximity, a kind of bodily awareness that another person was in the immediate vicinity:

I guess it's just like if someone's standing close to you, you don't have to look to see if there's someone there. . . . You just know that there's someone close to you.

I've had some quite distinct experiences like that, where I've felt the presence so close, it's as if it's out, it's here, I could almost touch it.[30]

Sometimes this feeling was more like an energy of some kind, marking that another was there:

Just a feeling that you're accompanied by an essence. Not necessarily the way it would feel with a solid person there.

Often, that feeling of an energy was tied to emotional states associated with the character of the person present.

The very starting point is I'll usually just feel the presence of the communicator and depending on what their personality was like, I'll almost feel that they're really close, they're really far away, if they're a quiet person.

In most cases, the people we spoke to were seeking to connect with the spirit world to receive messages that were for other people—people who had come to see them, exactly to hear such "communication." But in some cases, that sense of presence, and that emotional connection, concerned people the mediums knew themselves, people they felt emotionally close to, and often people they had lost.

I think when it very first started, if I'm honest, was a bereavement like of my partner . . . her uncle passed, and whilst I wasn't particularly close, I almost found it affected us. . . . I just found I was grieving even more than that I even expected. And then after that, within a few weeks, I started feeling presence after that, and that's when I thought there's sommat maybes not quite right.

I know very distinctly one day I felt my father sit, I really felt him sit down beside . . . and it came completely out of the blue, I wasn't expecting him, and I was preparing just quietly for a service, because usually when you're preparing, the medium goes into the back room before the service, if they want to, just to sit quietly and attune as they do. I was sat down, and I suddenly felt his presence and I felt his hand go into mine.

One of the things we were interested in was how spiritualists develop their skills as a medium. One participant in particular was very specific about how she cultivated her skills.

I teach students how to be more focused, rather than just kind of mentally picking up telepathic thoughts, which is what a lot of psychics can do, picking up thoughts, not just from the spirit world but from people around them. How I've started to try and teach students who are very erratic is to imagine that they're in a room with a door behind them, and when they're ready to, to invite the spirit world to link with them, to kind of give permission to open the door and let them in—but it's into a space, by getting them to imagine a room. And so initially, as you feel that presence, what does the presence feel like? Don't worry too much about the communication, get the presence, build the connection, and then allow the communication to start to flow, in whatever way is going to work for them, because it could be very different for everybody. So in my own way, I do that, but I don't have a room and a door, but I have this space that I focus into. And I shift my whole focus from my physical presence and place where I am into being aware of another dimension of life. I'm focusing into that space. I don't quite know how to express it any clearer than that.

In some ways, the presences of mediums are not so different from those in many of the accounts we have heard so far. Presences feel like someone close by, within touching distance even. An energy, an identity, an intent, or a personality. Like a physical person, but not quite. And often someone significant; someone lost, or someone needed.

But at the same time, it is important to acknowledge that something potentially quite different is going on here: these are presences that are cultivated. They are sought for, teased out, sensed before they appear. People must learn to find them in many cases; they must know what to look for, what clues to pay attention to. They often identify an "energy," but what does that mean? Some kind of awareness, a redirection of attention. Like in the final quote above, a turning away from themselves and their own physical space and out into . . . well, the *ether*, as it is sometimes called.

That searching, that need to learn, would set off a whole set of alarm bells for most psychologists. Indeed, many scientific researchers would question the worth of thinking about these experiences at all. Aren't they just an extension of folk beliefs, elaborate displays of wishful thinking, vivid imaginations, and even collective delusions?

If we assume that mediums are having these kinds of experiences, a key chicken-and-egg question arises: What came first, feelings of presence (or other apparent visitations) or the will to believe that such things are possible? In other words, do people become mediums because they have such experiences or because they want to have them?

Two members of our team, Pete Moseley and Adam Powell, further explored this question within the spiritualist community. In a 2020 survey, they found that about two-thirds of a sample of sixty-five spiritualists reported having unusual experiences from a young age, sometimes decades before becoming aware of the spiritualist movement or attending a spiritualist church.[31] Since childhood, they would see and hear things other people could not, like they lived in a different sensory world. The overriding impression of the survey results was that experience was coming before belief: a special connection or skill, an affinity with the spirit world, which led people to develop spiritual beliefs about the world. They didn't go looking for presence; presences came to them.

Of course, there is still a worry about the authenticity of these results, that they rely on what people simply want to tell us—people might recount experiences of having this skill from a young age in order to elevate their own self-perception. What is more powerful, being a natural or being a striver? Will someone believe you if you said it took you ten years to connect with a spirit, but eventually you did?

We don't have to rely solely on what people say, though. We also know from other scientific research that people from these groups can learn about sensory signals in sometimes very unique ways. A study run by Phil Corlett and Al Powers at Yale University in 2017 showed that people with schizophrenia who hear voices are susceptible to a certain kind of conditioning for hallucinations—but so are psychics.[32] The concept of conditioning, as famously demonstrated by the early psychologist Ivan Pavlov, involves forming a strong association between a stimulus and a response. With enough training, many kinds of responses can be conditioned—even the tendency to hear and see things that are not there.

In the Yale study, participants learned to associate a tone with a faint visual signal, then the tone was gradually removed during the experiment. Participants then had to report if they heard the tone when presented with the visual cue, and some people would still hear the tone just based on the visual stimulus appearing (i.e., no sound was actually played). In other words, the illusion of sound had been conditioned. Both the patients who heard voices and the psychics were more likely to hear the tone even when no sound was there. People with schizophrenia who didn't hear voices and healthy control participants were less likely to experience the conditioned hallucination. This pattern of results is key, as it suggests that having a schizophrenia diagnosis isn't the thing driving the results; instead, it's the tendency to hear voices, whether you are a patient or a psychic. Something similar seems to be going on in how perception works for psychics and people with schizophrenia who have frequent hallucinations. Whatever is occurring might set these groups on a different path to the rest of us.

But even so, these kinds of findings only slightly loosen the Gordian knot in front of us. How can we possibly separate the experience of hearing spirits or feeling their presence and the set of beliefs that surround it? When we know that some people are looking for this kind of experience—training themselves even—how can we be confident about what is happening to them? Understanding hallucinatory experiences seems hard enough, but understanding them when people actually *want* them to occur—and separating them from imagination, desire, memory, even dreams—feels dauntingly impossible.

I needed to enlist some help, to talk to someone with experience of this kind of knot—someone with decent scissors (or perhaps even a set of knitting needles). It was time to talk to Tanya.

Learning presence

Tanya Luhrmann is a professor of anthropology at Stanford University and a widely selling author on the topic of spiritual experiences and beliefs. In a long and varied career, Tanya has spent time with witches in London, Vineyard church followers in California, and *okomfo* (shamans) in Ghana, to name just a few. In books like 2012's *When God Talks Back*, she has documented and explored the many ways in which people seek out dialogue and connection with the spiritual realm.

My research has overlapped with Tanya's on more than one occasion. I wanted to talk to her because, more than most, she can claim to have a real overview of these kinds of experiences across many different cultures and contexts. And those experiences aren't just about seeking dialogue with an invisible Other—they include pure presence too. Her most recent book, *How God Becomes Real*, came out in 2020, and we spoke not long after its publication.

We talk over Zoom across an eight-hour time difference between the UK and California. If you imagine the home of an anthropologist in your mind—walls festooned with artwork and artifacts from countries around the world—then you can already picture Tanya's house. While we talk, she is also occasionally beset by two dogs, who have been her sturdy companions since all the COVID lockdowns began.

I start by asking her to define presence—what does it mean to her? "So, I see presence when somebody says there's another person with them. I'm almost always talking to people about 'persons' or 'entities,'" she explains. "And you know, sometimes people talk about God, sometimes spirits, sometimes people talk about energy—almost always they are talking about what I might call a mind."

Tanya has just finished a hugely ambitious project that aimed to understand how people experience hidden spirits across countries and cultures all around the world. The study included sites in California, Ghana, India, Thailand, and Vanuatu, and the results were published in *Proceedings of the National Academy of Sciences* in early 2021.[33] "We tried to ask about it in this big cross-cultural survey—and I am not sure that we asked effectively—but there is just this sense of what I would call localized presence, a bit like the Third Man experiences. I remember talking to a woman who was an evangelical Christian, and she was just casually talking about God. She said she would be sitting in the park, and she knew exactly where God was—sitting on a park bench. She couldn't smell him, she couldn't touch him, but she knew exactly where he was in this space."

This is a pretty typical conversation with Tanya: no small talk, just straight to God on a park bench. Much of her work has involved working with different people within the Christian tradition who ascribe to a very real, very tangible sense of God—a God whom you could converse with, whose presence is as discernible as anything else in the world around you.

"When Christians talk about presence," Tanya explains, "it's often hard to know what on earth they are talking about! Some people will be very clear, but often people will use the term metaphorically. It's not like they are having an experience: they are using the term to *experiment* metaphorically. It's an intellectual commitment, or sometimes it's about warmth. There's often a loose quality of presence. Like with the Hardy project."

The project Tanya refers to is the Alister Hardy archive, a database founded in 1969. A British ecologist at the University of Oxford, Hardy was convinced that it was possible to connect to a higher power of some form, and so he put out a request for accounts of such connections. In it he asked: "Have you ever been aware of or influenced by a presence or power, whether you call it God or not, which is different from your everyday self?"[34]

"So, he gets these three thousand postcards, and someone pulled out all the accounts of presence, hundreds of examples," continues Tanya. "And they are *all over the place*."

This a worry for me, and it has been all along. The ineffable nature of spiritual experience might bring this worry to the fore, but for such a vague idea as presence, couldn't it be an issue *anytime* someone uses a term like that? How do we really know that people referring to presences in psychosis, or Parkinson's, or survival situations are really talking about the same thing at all?

Philosophers have an intuitive name for this kind of problem: loose talk. I might give something the same name as you, and we might think we are talking about the same thing, but underneath it all, behind the word, we are talking about different things entirely. Maybe like the experience itself, the idea of presence is little more than an illusion?

It doesn't seem like Tanya really thinks that, though. When I share my concerns with her, she offers an answer. "My guess is that they all share the sense of the mind—another mind. When we look for presence, we look for agency."

I can see why she thinks that might be the case. The sense of a spiritual entity that you can converse with implies the presence of another mind; another intelligence that has something to communicate to you. And when you think about some of the presences in sleep paralysis, for example, for there to be pure intent, there must be an agent, an entity, something with the capacity of having an intention. In such cases, the sense of another mind would seem impossible to ignore.

But then, what about the phantoms induced in Olaf Blanke's lab or the snowy companions of Third Man accounts? They often had bodies and position . . . but did they have minds? It doesn't quite seem to fit. I put that quandary back to Tanya.

"I honestly think that presence *means* mind, in that if it is just a body, you're not aware of it. If it's a body, it's like a rock. To have presence, it's gotta have some capacity to do something, even if it doesn't interact with you. If you walk into a room and there is a demon in the corner, even if it's not currently aware of you, it could be, and it could come up to you."

How do we make sense of that? A presence that is less a body and more . . . a mind? A mind that we can recognize somehow, something identifiably intentional, and capable of dialogue, capable of interaction. This seems like a different way of interpreting the experience, perhaps one involving imagination, expectation, even emotion.

We can all imagine various unusual things though, and not all of us get ghostly visitors. What makes imagining a mind turn into a felt presence? Tanya has a theory about this—and it is a recipe with three key ingredients.

Ingredient 1: Talent

"I think there's a story of what I call 'proclivity.' Some people are more likely to have these experiences than others," says Tanya. Think back to that survey data collected by Pete Moseley and Adam Powell: some people described having experiences from a young age. A world in which they saw things a different way, where sounds and sights were all that more vivid, and figures stepped out of the night.

I am reminded of a voice-hearer who took part in our 2017 study, where people listened to sine-wave sounds that contained hidden speech. Most people need to be told that there are words hidden in the sounds, while our voice-hearing group began to detect them automatically. Usually this occurred within five to ten minutes of a twenty-minute scan, but I remember one participant who discerned the words much quicker. She was named Elaine and was from the south side of Glasgow. She'd had a rough upbringing, remembers moving a lot when she was young, and there were problems between her parents. But she also remembers her granny visiting her at the seaside, hovering above the sand like an angel and speaking to her. That was the first time she felt she had encountered spirit: a vision, with words.

When we came to ask Elaine if she had noticed anything funny about the sounds we played while she was in the MRI scanner, she laughed. "Oh yes, there were words in there, weren't there?" she replied.

I said that there were and asked if she knew when she had begun to recognize them?

"Oh, from the first one or two." I thought she meant the first one or two blocks: we had divided the experiment into six blocks of sounds, each containing about twenty clips. It would mean she began to understand it between five and ten minutes into the scan. I asked her if that was correct.

"No, the first one or two sentences—right away!" she replied.

I was dumbfounded. I had never met anyone who could do that. When we analyzed the data in the weeks that followed, we could plot which areas of the brain responded the most when people seemed to "tune in" to the sounds early. One area was particularly strong, part of the middle cingulate gyrus, right in center of the cortex. Frustratingly, it is an area associated with lots of different psychological processes, making it hard to work out what it might be doing. But when we looked in that area of Elaine's scan, her signals were completely off the charts. When she said she understood it right away, I believed her.

That's the kind of thing I think Tanya means by "proclivity." A knack, a natural affinity, to find things that others don't. A talent for discerning the signal in the storm, or a spirit in the ether. What that knack really is, what it is based in, is hard to say. It could be bias in our perceptions, like pareidolia, driving us to find meaning and agency even where there are none. It could be expectation or imagination filling in gaps for us when we are faced with ambiguity. Or it could be a kind of flexibility in how we approach the world—always exploring, always wondering, never ruling out the seemingly impossible.

Elaine was a spiritualist, but despite her early experiences, it took her a long while to consistently have spiritual encounters. She openly admitted that she went looking for them. She had to work at them, attending a spiritualist church meeting near her for nearly ten years before spirits would speak to her, when she felt like she had finally "opened herself up" to the world. It took dedication and training to achieve the connection—and what was involved brings us to the next ingredient in Tanya's theory.

Ingredient 2: Practice

"Then there is a story of practice, or an interaction of practice and proclivity," explains Tanya. As she describes in *How God Becomes Real,* she keeps coming back, through her work across various groups and cultures, to the elaborate procedures and rituals that people describe learning and practicing. These practices involve people putting themselves in a state where they not only bring forth spirits but actively control the process.

A medium I once interviewed put it to me like this: "You can't be a dripping tap." What she meant was, anyone might have a spontaneous tendency to experience voices or receive messages, but you need to learn to control it, to do it on your terms. It requires focus and discipline. It might involve turning your attention away from the world and concentrating on the contents of your mind or the sensations in your body. You might need to pay close attention to what feels like your thoughts, and learn to discriminate what feels like other people's thoughts, and other people's ideas. Things you really couldn't otherwise have known. It might require some kind of trance, or a change in your consciousness.

Tanya thinks these practices cultivate two cognitive processes: absorption and "inner sense." The latter is a kind of imagination, an awareness of changes, uncertainties, vividness in one's inner experience. We know that some people have extensive imagery skills, while others have absolutely none (aphantasia).[35] Cultivating one's inner sense is a bit like growing a garden of the imagination, one rich in meaning and significance.

Absorption, on the other hand, is arguably an altogether more unusual process. All of us will have experienced it at some point—being so engrossed in an activity that we lose track of the world around us (we once subjected our team of researchers at Durham to an absorption scale, and most of the academics were off the charts). But some people seem to experience frequent absorption, being drawn into other possibilities and worlds so completely that they could have stepped into an alternate reality. Tanya's work, in countries across the world, seems to show that absorption is a consistent trait in people who report having unusual encounters with spiritual presences.[36] And, according to her observations, it seems like many spiritual groups encourage a kind of deep absorption to achieve such experiences in the first place.

People initially need some skill, but then they have to practice it. But what else might they need?

Ingredient 3: An Open Mind

"The final story, I think, is about the mind," says Tanya. As we are speaking, it is early in the morning for her and late in the afternoon for me. We both need to wrap up soon, but I really want to hear more about this final component.

"I think that you are more likely to allow yourself to have these experiences if you have a model of mind in which a thought is connected to the world, so the mind-world boundaries are permeable."

OK. Let's try that one again.

"Your thoughts can go into the world, and other people's thoughts can come to you. Things can pass over the boundaries of the mind."

There is an experience described in psychosis known as thought insertion, where one feels like the thoughts in your head are not your own.[37] They are implanted here, imposters belonging to someone else. But this isn't what Tanya means. What she is referring to is an idea that people will have different basic conceptions about what is possible for the mind to do, and where our minds stop and the world begins.

"It doesn't matter who is doing the interview, who is doing the data collection or how, what faith the person is, whether they are Christian or non-Christian," says Tanya. "If they commit to having this model of the mind, in which thought can act in the world independently and you can be vulnerable to someone else's thought, people are more likely to experience gods and spirits. They are more likely to have a sense of presence."

Of all Tanya's observations, I think it's this idea that I find really intriguing. Your own model, your own philosophy of mind, could be delineating real and unreal, self and other.

She has data to back it up too. In 2015, she published a study exploring the experiences of people diagnosed with schizophrenia in Ghana, India, and California, hearing distressing voices.[38] The content of what the voices were saying to the American participants was much more self-directed and abusive, including threats of sexual and physical violence. The content of what the voices were saying to Ghanaian and Indian participants, in contrast, didn't have that focus or intensity. They were still distressing, but they spoke more about hexes, spirits, and social issues. When participants in each country were asked about their views on spirits, the mind, and the universe, there were a number of both overlaps and dissimilarities in their responses. But noticeably, the Ghanaian and Indian participants were open to the possibility that a mind could contain spirits, that it could have other entities passing through. Their local cultures and practices contained stories of those things happening—they were already a part of life. The Americans, on the other hand, couldn't think of anything worse, anything that would be more shameful. When a voice that wasn't yours came, it was a kind of abomination. Your mind was your castle—it wasn't open to visitors.

* * *

TANYA MUST GO, and so must I. We could have talked for another hour or so. It felt like we were only just getting started.

Her model made a lot of sense to me. It helped me think through what might be going on for people who seem to have unusual—and potentially spiritual—experiences of presence throughout their lives. But I wasn't sure how I felt about all of Tanya's three ingredients.

It seems quite hard to pin down the relative roles of proclivity and practice in understanding why presences occur. Does that just push the question along, but with different names for the concepts? And do they lead to the same thing—does the person who sees things from the age of five end up with the same kind of presences as someone age thirty-five who must practice to achieve them? What about the experiences that you don't want—where do they fit in? Sometimes I just want to ask more questions about the tap that keeps dripping. What happens if it doesn't stop?

Tanya's idea about the boundaries of the mind is intriguing too. If the tendency to experience things like voices, visions, and presences depended on your own beliefs about the mind, about it being a porous place or not, it would make sense of a lot of things. It could explain cultural differences in how people respond to these kinds of phenomena, and it could plausibly be part of the story of how people train themselves to experience things like presence. But in a way, it also feels too neat. Tanya's data is a start, a proof of principle, but I suspect we need more to hang a theory on, let alone an explanation.

The thing that talking to Tanya helped make more concrete for me, though, was thinking about this other path to presence. We have heard about bodies and the bodily self, and all the ways in which a presence could potentially arise when our bodily signals go awry. But stories of endurance, or accounts of sleep paralysis, don't just involve bodies, they involve minds. Accounts of spiritual presences seem to be all about minds—they rest on recognizing an identity, an agent, a person. They might even involve looking for specific people.

For those kinds of stories, we might need a second route to presence, one that doesn't necessarily involve bodies. It could be something like the expectation hypothesis that we heard about in chapter 6 or it could be something that goes beyond that. The stories of endurance—of the rowers and the runners—took us from expectation into something else. The examples of spiritualism and practicing to feel presences confirmed that shift. My head was swimming with comparable examples, but now I was thinking about presences of the mind, and not the body.

And to think: if Tanya's right, this strange experience that we call felt presence could be shaped by our very own models of what is possible in the mind. We draw the boundaries, we decide who gets in and gets out. We might be the architects of where we stop and the other begins.

Truly a presence of our own.

11

In Two Minds

In 2017, our team at Durham ran a study on reading. Working with the *Guardian* newspaper and the Edinburgh International Book Festival, we invited readers to share with us their particularly vivid experiences of voices and characters. We were interested in testing out an unusual observation that periodically gets made—that reading, in some senses, could be considered almost like a hallucinatory experience.[1] When we plunge into a book, immersing ourselves in a new world, and see, hear, and smell characters that we come to know, it could be said that we are losing a connection with reality, engaging in some kind of simulation, cut off from the world around us.

The comparison can be a little overblown, but I was nevertheless intrigued by some of the parallels between imagination and hallucination. Would people who "hear" characters' voices in books also hear unusual things in everyday life? Can they picture the hills looming around Thornfield Hall in their mind's eye,[2] or see Banquo's ghost at the feast and then experience uncanny visitors in the night? Like Tanya Luhrmann's ideas about absorption, are all these things on the same kind of path—a meandering road to unreality?

I published the results of the survey in 2017 in an article written with two colleagues from Durham, Charles Fernyhough and Marco

Bernini. Charles is a developmental psychologist and lead of the Hearing the Voice project we all worked on in Durham. Marco is a narratologist who studies the intersection of writing and cognition, specializing in how writers use texts to model different mental phenomena.

The survey ended up mostly recruiting people from the United Kingdom and the United States, although it included participants from all over the world, with over fifteen hundred people taking part. Most participants just filled out the bit of the survey containing questionnaires. We asked them to rate the different kinds of experiences they had when reading (for example, the vividness of various sights and sounds they encountered when engaged in a book), plus we included some questions about their tendency to hallucinate. We found that people with vivid reading experiences did indeed seem to be prone to hallucinations elsewhere, and they frequently reported other kinds of elaborate inner experiences as well, such as having a lot of inner speech (or inner monologue).

But that wasn't the surprising bit. About four hundred participants also wrote us short paragraphs, snapshots describing what their reading experience was like. Marco and I tried to come up with codes that could capture what they were describing, picking out not only features like sounds or pictures but also characteristics of the overall process—in other words, the dynamics of the experience. This could include feeling like you are immersed in the situation, or hearing a character's voice that seems to be constructed from the voices of people you know.

Some of this was relatively straightforward: for beloved books, people could describe incredibly vivid experiences of narrators, characters, and places. On more than one occasion subjects referred to Jack Ryan, Harry Potter, or *Twilight*, but also things from unexpected places. The voices of real people in autobiographies. Historical figures. Striking first-person narrators, like Holden Caulfield in *The Catcher in the Rye*.

What surprised us was what happened after people stopped reading.

A sizable minority of those four hundred participants—20 percent of them—described characters staying with them *after* the book had finished. Some were characters that "kept going" between and after books: Harry, Ron, and Hermione, growing old and continuing their adventures. Some were characters that seemed to exert a gravitational pull on the reader, so that they almost started to shape the subject's thoughts and language. For this, we borrowed a term from the study of linguistics—"mind style."[3] This refers to a character literally changing the way you think. One participant described it like this: "If the 'voice' of a good book gets into my head, it can seep into my own experience of the world, and I find myself thinking in that voice, as that character, while carrying out normal activities."[4]

And for some people, characters seemed to fully cross over into the real world. Marco—who has a knack for coining new terms—described the experience as "experiential crossing." In one particularly vivid example, one reader described being accompanied by Clarissa Dalloway from the Virginia Woolf novel:[5]

> Last February and March, when I was reading *Mrs. Dalloway* and writing a paper on it, I was feeling enveloped by Clarissa Dalloway. I heard her voice or imagined her reactions to different situations. I'd walk into a Starbucks and feel her reaction to it based on what I was writing in my essay on the different selves of this character.

I can't really imagine being enveloped by a character, but I know I have been deeply engrossed in books before, almost overdosing on them at times. When I was young, I went through sci-fi and fantasy phases; I remember plowing through *The Lord of the Rings* to the point that I saw text swimming across my closed eyelids. When I first read Frank Herbert's *Dune*, well, I completely freaked out. There is a parallel phenomenon in gaming known as "game transfer phenomena," or sometimes "the *Tetris* effect," where you play a game so much that thoughts and sensations from it jump over into the real world.[6]

That's happened to me before too—my thumb trying to control a
real-life goalkeeper during a particularly strong FIFA phase.*

To return to *Mrs. Dalloway*, what was striking about that reader's
example was the sense of a continuing "life" for the character and the
strong feeling of accompaniment the reader still had. Readers in such
situations continued to wonder and imagine even when they weren't
reading—they were taking an active role in maintaining the sense
of a character—but there's a sense of something bigger happening,
something out of their control. Something almost like inhabitation,
or even possession—an imaginary presence, a ghost in the machine.

When I spoke to Tanya Luhrmann about spiritualists, I wondered
whether these kinds of experiences are actually a more relevant parallel to absorption. When we dive deep down into an imaginative well,
we may come back up to the surface with something—or someone—
else, something of our creation but at the same time not clearly of
us. A build-your-own presence, not in body, but in mind.

It was around the time of doing the reader survey that I had also
come across another kind of case. Something similar, but if anything,
much stranger. And it starts with *My Little Pony*.

Animal magic

In 2014, the magazine website *Vice* ran a piece by Nathan Thompson: "The Internet's Newest Subculture Is All About Creating Imaginary Friends." It referred to a new practice that was believed to have
started by "Bronies"—men who share a deep love of the children's
TV show *My Little Pony* and chat via online forums and message
boards like Reddit. Some had developed a kind of sentient imaginary
friend based on characters from the show—a companion with its
own personality, image, and voice that could apparently talk back to
them. It was literally their own little pony.

The *Vice* article featured a range of people who were accompanied

---

* I better not mention the *Grand Theft Auto* example.

by these companions. One, Nick Kingston—a design student from Plymouth in the UK—had three of them: "They've been with me 20 months; their names are Twi, Dash, and Scoots. They are three anthropomorphic ponies about a foot high."[7] The three animals were his friends, entities he could share things with and be open to in a way that he couldn't otherwise.

What Kingston was doing has a name: "tulpamancy." It consists of a set of practices, similar to meditation, in which the "tulpamancer" focuses their imagination, repeatedly and over many hours and weeks, on the creation of another being: a tulpa. Crucially, this being has to have its own agency. It isn't a puppet, it isn't fully under the creator's control—it is independent, even if it still just resides in one's head.

The name and practice are typically ascribed to Tibetan Buddhism.[8] A tulpa is a kind of emanation of the mind, usually conjured via intense meditation, as a form of spiritual practice. This, though, is not the focus of modern tulpamancy: the very act of creating an apparently sentient agent is the goal. Techniques for how to achieve this goal are shared openly among the online tulpamancer community, and these might involve narrating for the tulpa initially or imagining its body. With focused practice over time, narratives might become gradually more like dialogues, and effortful imagination becomes something more fluid and automatic. And when this occurs, a connection with another mind is reported as being experienced—someone (or something) is truly there. For some people, it might feel like the process created the tulpa; for others, that the tulpa was always there, waiting for them.

There are no in-depth interview studies published at the moment on what this experience is quite like, but the *Reply All* podcast series ran an eighteen-month investigation of the topic that culminated in a 2016 episode. This is the kind of thing they came across: in the following exchange, a reporter asks a young man about his tulpa, called Tamber.

Reporter: Can you tell me a bit about Tamber?

Tulpamancer: I suppose I can tell you a bit about Tamber . . . he's hard to pin down. For the most part he is calm, and tends to be rather direct, I guess.

Reporter: So where is Tamber right now?

Tulpamancer: Erm . . . sort of . . .

Reporter: Like is he hearing this conversation?

Tulpamancer: Yes, I suppose that is kind of important to say, isn't it? Yeah, he is what we would call "present."

Reporter: Is he always present?

Tulpamancer: Not always. Although more often than not, yes. So it's more just that his own presence, looking out through my eyes, I guess.[9]

Various websites are available that provide resources and guidance on tulpa development. They often emphasize that this is an ongoing process: "Like any person, a tulpa is never 'done.'"[10] But tulpamancers report—even when their work is in progress—perhaps some of the strangest feats of the human mind. Multiple characters that talk of their own accord, personalities with biographies, preferences, and values. And entities that feel so real—some would say *are* so real—that to cause them to vanish would be tantamount to a kind of murder.

Once more, we have to ask . . . what on earth is going on?

One of the first people to write about tulpamancy was Dr. Sam Veissière of the University of Montreal. In a survey of 141 tulpamancers in 2014, Veissière reported that 37 percent described that their tulpas felt "as real as a physical person."[11] Over half endorsed that their tulpas were "somewhat real," in that they were distinct from other people but also distinguishable from the subject's own thoughts. Who was reporting these experiences was quite marked: overwhelmingly young men aged between nineteen and twenty-three, with all but a handful coming from white backgrounds, mostly spread across the United States, the United Kingdom, and Russia. The respondents were typically "highly cerebral, imaginative, articulate, upper-middle-class, [and] formally educated" who "consistently pursued interests, talents, and hobbies, but [maintained] limited channels of physical social interaction."[12] On questionnaires, the group also scored highly for loneliness and social anxiety.

At this point, a stereotype might begin to form in your mind: a young man, feeling alone, struggling socially, connecting with others in internet forums, sharing niche interests, and finding the interactions of the mind simpler and easier than the messy work out there, in real life. There is a term that has been used in the past to describe imagined relationships of this kind: *parasocial*. The concept was introduced by two sociologists, Donald Horton and Richard Wohl, who were interested in how people's engagement with mass media sometimes causes them to form intense attachments to particular TV or radio characters. This, they argued, leads to "the illusion of a face-to-face relationship with the performer."[13] In this interaction, the relationship is all happening in the consumer's mind; it cannot be a two-way thing. And the efforts that tulpamancers make to conjure their companions might seem to represent something similar, albeit in an intentional way.

I am not a big fan of the term *parasocial*, as I think it can encourage a certain kind of negative interpretation. It can add undesirable fuel to the fire when we imagine the reasons why someone might invest so heavily in something that *seems* social, but doesn't quite fit the definition. And, as with any stereotype, things aren't as straightforward as they might seem. Veissière assessed empathy skills in his survey, for example. You might think that this kind of group would struggle with understanding and imagining the emotional lives of others if they were cut off from real-world interactions. But the truth was far from it. Veissière found empathy scores, as well as measures of theory of mind (or the ability to represent the mental states of others), to be high in tulpamancers. A factor that also scored highly in this group was one we have heard about before: absorption. Measured on the

Tellegen Absorption Scale,[14] tulpamancers in Veissière's survey reported elevated levels of absorbed and concentrated states.

According to Veissière, tulpamancers always share more or less the same prescription of techniques to try: "Visualise, concentrate, build shape and personality traits and wait until you experience voices and touch from sentient tulpas."[15] In other words, engage your imagination, and have faith. After a while this creates a kind of internal repertoire that is intensely personal but also rewarded when it is shared with others on forums like Reddit. The consequence of this social reward is that it leads to automaticity. Doing this process repeatedly sends the subject deep into an inner world, creating the conditions for involuntary and automatic imagery—so much so that apparent sentience doesn't seem all that extraordinary. This kind of ingrained process, this procedural learning, goes beyond the effortful and becomes second nature. Veissière likens this to the kind of muscle memory we get from a well-practiced skill—one that never leaves us: "Getting rid of a tulpa, for a seasoned tulpamancer, could be analogically situated somewhere between unlearning the piano or correcting one's posture."[16]

What Veissière describes is similar to something our Durham group found in research we did on professional writers, again in collaboration with the Edinburgh International Book Festival. Across two surveys—one conducted in 2014, one in 2018—we asked over 190 writers to describe how they experienced the voices of their characters, if in fact they did.[17] Some writers have specifically said in the past that their characters do come to somehow have a life of their own—saying things for themselves, correcting their authors if they aren't written into the right scenarios, and acting as if they have been there all along, just waiting to be happened upon by the writer. Charles Dickens, for example, described being spoken to spontaneously by some of his characters when he was writing their parts (the character of Mrs. Gamp from *Martin Chuzzlewit* would apparently bother him repeatedly).[18] The author Philip Pullman has often described something similar in his approach to writing. "Once you have got the characters established in your mind you can hear what they say to each other quite easily," wrote Pullman in his 2017 collection of essays, *Daemon Voices*. "And because they give you the words, you can write them down."[19]

In our survey—which was led by writer and literary scholar John Foxwell—we didn't find that all writers were like that. Far from it. While some were adamant that this was the only way you knew a character really worked—until they could talk for themselves, they weren't a proper character or didn't have a full personality—other writers were equally convinced that this was, put simply, utter rubbish, a tale told by a community notoriously loose with the truth to add to their own mystique. And both sides, as you might expect, were convinced of their own truth and experience.

At Durham, we have worked with a wide range of remarkable people, reporting some of the most unusual experiences you could put into words. Voices, visions, presences; psychosis, dissociation, trauma; spirits, telepathy, and demons. But we have never had to try to work with data as slippery as what we got from the Edinburgh writers. Appropriately enough, it wasn't hard to feel like you were being spun a yarn sometimes.

And yet: the process that many writers described was not at all unlike that suggested by Veissière for tulpamancy and proposed as a rule by Tanya Luhrmann and others. The writers described an effortful and deep attention to their imagination, often but not always beginning with dialogue: what would the character say, what would they do, over, and over, and over. After a while—and it almost always was only after a while—the character would begin to "speak," as the routine became the norm, the author having built the pattern for the new character to inhabit.

In psychology there is an idea that we have "personality models" of people that we build and use to predict others' behavior. The philosopher Sam Wilkinson has described them to me as being a bit like counterfactual machines for people, which we are always—or at least much of the time—ready to use to anticipate what someone would do in each situation. It's not hard to think of tulpamancers and writers using something like personality models in their imaginative process: building an incredibly detailed model of how a character would behave, revisiting it, and polishing it again and again until eventually it does behave in that way. Only in this case, the model is of a person that never existed.

Testing tulpamancy

There isn't much research that exists on tulpamancers, and some in that community have already become wary of taking part in academic studies. For many people, the kinds of experiences tulpamancers describe might sound like a kind of pathology, a deliberate splitting from oneself that some people can do, but really just because they are already susceptible to mental ill health.[20] Like spiritualists, tulpamancers don't want their experience misconstrued; they don't want to be treated as if they are sick and need attention.

There is a genuine question to be asked about the process that tulpamancers undergo, and whether it represents an enhancement of certain capabilities, such as imagination, or absorption, or something else. Dr. Emma Palmer-Cooper, a lecturer at the University of Southampton, designed a study to explore some of these issues, comparing people who practiced tulpamancy, people who experienced something called an autonomous sensory meridian response (ASMR), and people who did both.[21]

ASMR is the term for a collection of states that people sometimes generalize as the "chills" or shivers down the back of your neck. Quiet whispering, very specific crunching sounds, and certain textures can all hit a sweet spot for some people, giving them a pleasant sensation of arousal. Like tulpa communities, ASMR groups boomed thanks to the internet, as people could share and engage with different videos that induced the sensation for people.

Emma was interested in exploring tulpamancy alongside ASMR as they are both unusual but sought-after sensory experiences. Compared to most hallucinations, both are overwhelmingly reported as positive phenomena. At the same time, they differ in important ways, not least the effect of practice: while tulpamancers clearly work at their art, ASMR is a more spontaneous phenomenon—you either get that specific feeling or you don't, and you don't necessarily get to choose what it is.

The study assessed various factors that could explain the propensity toward these experiences. First, Emma and her team measured proneness to things like hallucinations and delusions, to explore whether people in both the tulpa and ASMR groups were predisposed to a range of unusual experiences and beliefs—even ones that are undesirable. The scales they used assessed for a range of experiences, including felt presences. Second, they evaluated self-esteem and self-concept: Palmer-Cooper included two measures, the Brief Core Schema Scales and Beck Cognitive Insight Scale, to see if people in both groups were able to engage in these experiences because they have a strong sense of self. Such a sense of self could help, for example, if the process of creating a tulpa was somehow perilous for an individual—if you knew for sure who you were, you might be more comfortable exploring the possibility of an imaginary other. Perhaps in pony form.

The third and final factor they measured was "metacognition"—in other words, how aware one is of their own thoughts and experiences. Metacognition is interesting because in theory it gives us control, and distance. If I have an experience I can't explain, it's possible I could get swept up in it, disturbed by the lack of context and narrative. Metacognition allows us to be aware of what we are doing when we are doing it, to distinguish ourselves from the world, even from the thoughts we experience. It is not unlike what people aim for when they engage in mindfulness.

So, one hypothesis might be that tulpamancers, but maybe not people with ASMR, would have enhanced metacognitive skills. All that practice, all that training, could make them skilled navigators of the mind. Or maybe they were already, even before the practice—

and that is what laid the groundwork for their tulpadom. A counter-hypothesis, however, might suggest that going down the rabbit hole and creating the rabbit might not give you great metacognitive capabilities; it might actually blur the lines between thoughts and feelings, self and other.

What did Emma's team find? First, people with both tulpamancy and ASMR tended to rate highly for hallucinatory experiences. Drilling down, people with tulpas—with or without ASMR—were also more likely to have "felt presence" experiences, as measured on a scale called the Multi-modality Unusual Sensory Experiences Questionnaire (or MUSEQ). The scale measures hallucinatory experiences in general, not tulpas specifically, so it's not clear whether these elevated scores represent tulpa presences or a tendency for tulpamancers to experience felt presences of any kind. But in either case, the data supports a link between presence and the experience of tulpamancy.

On metacognition, the results were also broadly supportive of what Emma hypothesized. People who practiced tulpamancy were generally better in their metacognition than those who didn't have tulpas. So this group was likely to maintain more distance from their experiences (and their metacognitive skills did not erode); rather than being less reliable monitors of self versus other, tulpamancers were leaning in and becoming better at making that distinction. And this wasn't the case for people with ASMR, as their metacognitive scores were very similar to controls. Their experience, being so much more spontaneous and nonreflective, didn't seem to be related to metacognition at all. Taken together, these findings suggest that the art of tulpamancy takes in both practice and social reward—as proposed by Sam Veissière—but it also involves the building of a cognitive muscle, a kind of metacognitive capacity.

A friend for life

The concept that tulpas will recall for most people is probably that of imaginary friends. Having an imaginary friend is a common experience in childhood, although estimates tend to vary wildly between 20 and 65 percent for children under the age of ten.[22] They aren't always friendly either, despite the term, and might not do as they are told (as anyone who can remember the Rik Mayall film *Drop Dead Fred* will know). For these reasons, researchers tend to refer to them as *imaginary companions* (ICs) rather than *imaginary friends*.

Periodically links and parallels are made between having ICs and experiences in mental health conditions such as schizophrenia or dissociation.[23] After all, speaking to and seeing an invisible person doesn't seem, on the face of it, too different from the kinds of experiences reported in episodes of psychosis. Our tendencies to see agents and characters in the inanimate world around us, and our growing skills in representing the minds of others—our theory of mind—all lend themselves to the creation of invisible people around us, capable of action and intention. It doesn't feel like a stretch to go from a cloud looking like a face to every cloud looking that way, or to go from recognizing footsteps outside your door to thinking that those feet are coming for you.

Crucially, the evidence isn't there to link ICs and more adverse experiences. The large majority of these kinds of imaginative childhood experiences are just that—part of a developing imagination. They don't clearly signal anything more, let alone represent a liability to engage in fantasy or to struggle with what might come along as part of that. In fact, there is a range of evidence to suggest that having ICs as a child is good for the development of social and cognitive skills.[24]

Research on adults with ICs is thin on the ground. It has been speculated that activities like writing fiction hold some similarities to the process of creating an imaginary friend, but no studies have demonstrated this to date.[25] In our own work, we have tried to shed some light on the ways in which adults with ICs might differ from other people. In 2019 we reported on two studies involving adults who either had ICs in the past or still had them now.[26]

The first was a reanalysis of data we had collected as part of the Edinburgh survey with readers in 2014. Along with asking people to describe their experiences of reading, we had asked them about imaginary friends, their tendency to have hallucinations, and various qualities of their inner speech (or self-talk). What we found was that people who had an IC in the past, and still had a current IC, were much more likely to have hallucinatory experiences than other people. This group also tended to have vivid experiences of inner speech, like dialogues with other people's voices—presumably including the voices of their companions, like those of tulpamancers. This wasn't necessarily the case for people who only had an IC in the past or people who only had a current IC. If you had an imaginary friend at a young age, it doesn't make you stand out. That sounds about right, given that between a third and two-thirds of all children likely share that kind of experience. If you have an IC only as an adult, that might be judged as quite unusual, but it doesn't mean that your cognitive skills are any different. Having an otherwise normal cognitive profile would make sense if it was something people were potentially *choosing* to do for the first time as an adult and needing to practice. The thing that really makes people stand out here is *persistence*, the continued presence of the other throughout one's imaginative life, a true proclivity.

Our second study was conducted by a postgraduate student of mine, Ashley Watson. For his dissertation, Ashley recruited a sample of fourteen adults who had ICs as children. Asking people retrospectively about this experience can be fraught with difficulty, so researchers have to take steps to improve the reliability of whatever data they collect. In this case, all the participants in the IC group had to ask their parents to fill out a form as well about whether their child had an IC, whether they spoke to it, and whether they interacted with it.

We then compared this group's performance on an auditory signal detection task to a group of thirty-four other adults with no history of an IC. The task involved listening closely to bursts of white noise—like radio static—to see if they could detect traces of mumbled speech in the background. The trace of speech hidden in the noise was intentionally faint and impossible to understand. In some trials we adjust it so it is clearly there, sometimes it is right on the edge of perception (so you would only get the answer right around 50 percent of the time), and sometimes it just isn't there at all. If you report speech being present in the white noise when it isn't there—that's a false alarm. If you show a tendency to do this a lot, reporting speech when it is and isn't there—that's a bias in your perception.

Compared to the group with no history of an IC, our IC group showed a significant bias in their perception, tending to say that speech was present. On questionnaires, they also reported a greater tendency to have hallucinatory experiences—just like the larger sample from the reading study. What was interesting about the bias results, though, was that they were very similar to what we see in two other groups: people with psychosis who hear voices, and people who report experiencing spiritual voices, such as mediums. This kind of perceptual bias is one of the most consistent findings we have to indicate that someone fits the profile for hallucinations.[27]

How can we make sense of this? Does it mean that people with imaginary friends, and people who claim to be psychic, are just on a kind of psychosis spectrum, their brains not being that much different from somebody who might go on to develop a condition like schizophrenia?

In a word: no. The results we found in this study tell us something specific: that perception might be working in a similar way for some of the people in these groups. How their perceptual skills ended up like this might be for different reasons across different people. One person might have a slight bias in their perception, present since they were a child, while someone else might experience a change in how they interpret the world during a significant stage in their life. That kind of change might also lead to different outcomes: a perceptual system that is slightly more likely to indicate "something is there" could lead some people to have a range of unusual but positive and meaningful experiences, while for someone else this could be the trigger that leads to feelings of paranoia and persecution.

What this kind of observation does, though, is give us a hint of what Tanya Luhrmann's idea of "proclivity" might mean. *Proclivity* might refer to an intense imagination, a tendency toward absorption, or maybe just a perceptual system with its dice loaded for a particular outcome. The rest of us might be rolling two 3s, balancing out expectation and sensation, while others might roll a 4 and a 2, where expectation fills in the gaps that sensation leaves open. Over time, if your perception of the world relies on that filling in, repeatedly, then the boundaries between reality and fantasy, between the shared and unshared, the external and internal—between *me* and *you*—could easily blur, shift, wax, and wane. All it might take is some small event in the beginning for someone to end up with a radically different picture of the world as its effects ripple out further and further.

Are you talking to me?

The other notable thing about the people with ICs in our study was how much, and how elaborately, the subjects talked to themselves. This experience is one that will be familiar to many, and we tend to refer to it as "inner speech" in research. How many of us mutter away to ourselves while we search around the house for something or cogitate on a particular problem? How many of us will anticipate and replay a difficult conversation or presentation? This is the kind of inner speech that seems to accompany many people through their everyday lives.

You might notice that I kept using the word "many" in the paragraph above. It has been claimed in the past that having this kind of inner monologue is something that everyone does—it may even be that we must do it as part of how thinking works, that an inner voice is somehow crucial to conscious experience itself.[28] The evidence we have from various studies suggests the contrary, but what we often come across in our work on inner speech is the surprise that people have about the experiences of others.

For instance: in 2020, a tweet from @KylePlantEmoji went viral with the following observation:

> Fun fact: some people have an internal narrative, and some people don't. As in, some people's thoughts are like sentences they "hear", and some people just have abstract non-verbal thoughts, and have to consciously verbalise them. And most people aren't aware of the other type of person.[29]

The truth of the matter, as always, is a little more complicated than what @KylePlantEmoji suggests. But his first and final thoughts are more or less correct; there does seem to be a lot of variation in the use or experience of inner speech, but many people assume that their experience is representative of most other people's. In truth, the differences between them can be radical.[30]

For instance, I am (almost) constantly having a conversation in my head. It might be a replay or reworking of a conversation I had in the past, it might be about what I will say to someone in the future, or it might be a completely imaginary scenario, trying to explain and articulate something to an imagined audience (who might contribute to the dialogue). My partner, on the other hand, does not do this at all, and thinks I am quite odd for having any dialogue in my head whatsoever.

When you ask people about their own inner speech, most do in fact report dialogue, but to varying degrees, and definitely not all of the time. In our research, we have used a scale called the Varieties of Inner Speech Questionnaire, a tool devised by my colleagues Simon McCarthy-Jones and Charles Fernyhough.[31] The scale includes a range of questions about people's experience of their inner speech, concerning things like whether the subject talks to themselves in full sentences, what the speech is about (e.g., if they did the right thing in a given situation or not), whether there is a conversational structure to it, and even whether other people's voices pop up. Roughly 80 percent of people endorse what we call "evaluative" inner speech, which

encompasses thinking about what you should do, motivating yourself, and so on. About 75 percent of people report "dialogic" inner
speech, which means a back-and-forth conversational structure, our
thoughts being a continuing cycle of question and answer. Around
25–30 percent of people report either "condensed" inner (not full
sentences, more like shorthand) or inner speech that involves *other
people* speaking.

You might find some of these results a bit confusing. Surely, if
someone is talking to themselves, in their head, wouldn't it just be
their voice? Why would anyone else be in there, and why would it
be in shorthand? The answer to this lies in the work of Soviet psychologist Lev Vygotsky. Vygotsky, working in the Soviet Union in
the 1920s and 1930s, argued that the way we talk to ourselves, and,
indeed, the way we think, reflects our early interactions with other
people.[32] That is, as children, all the conversations we have with parents or family members, all the times we play with people and have a
chat while we do so, this, for Vygotsky, lays the groundwork for our
ability to talk to ourselves whenever we want to.

Vygotsky's model is usually described as a sociodevelopmental approach to how thought develops. Within his model of child development, parents and caregivers are crucial in providing the scaffolding
on which a child constructs their intellectual capabilities, giving them
nudges and prompts here and there, guiding attention, and sharing
meaning and joy in things like play. This is shown in the language
parents might use around their children as they attempt a task. They
will often provide a running commentary and ask questions even
before a child can answer them themselves. You can then see this reflected back when children can speak for themselves. If you have ever
eavesdropped on a three-year-old focused on building a train track or
arranging a herd of unruly plastic farm animals, you can hear echoes
of past conversations, questions circulating and forming patterns in
the air around the activity.

That self-directed commentary—spoken out loud but for no one
else—is known as "private" speech. Private speech is often seen in

children around three to seven years of age, but after that it seems to recede, and children might only whisper to themselves quietly, if at all, when playing.[33] You sometimes see the same thing when children are doing arithmetic, and it manifests most dramatically in their reading: what was external becomes internal, as the capacity to read becomes a matter for the mind. Thus, private speech becomes inner speech, and an inner narrator emerges.

Hence, when we come to think about inner speech in adults, asking about full sentences, dialogue, and other people becomes quite important—because the source of these things is, in theory, our outward interactions. The scaffold of language is built and maintained by others, and as we go on in life, we add on extra bits: viewpoints, supporting arguments, opinions, castigations. Our inner linguistic world becomes suffused with the words of others, a social space for us alone.

To give you an example, I have a name for myself when I have really mucked something up—"Benj." I don't particularly like it, none of my friends or colleagues would ever use it, but I say it in my head or just under my breath when I make a mistake. I can't stop myself—it jumps out like a reflex reaction. When that happens, it's like I expected better of myself, like if I had just taken a moment to think, I wouldn't have made an error. It took me years to even notice that only two other people would ever call me by that name: my two older brothers. They don't even use it much or even most of the time—but I do remember them using it, particularly when we were younger. And they clearly used it enough for it to have lodged in my brain, unnoticed for years.

Some people seem to have this ongoing vivid inner life. And the idea is, this comes from development, from our experience. A collaborator of mine, Dr. Jacqueline Hayes, calls the voices in our inner linguistic world "pragmatic echoes," which I think sums it up perfectly. At the same time, some people—like my partner—don't experience much inner speech at all, and it doesn't seem to make any crucial difference to their ongoing life. Indeed, we know from other work on mental imagery that some people just don't have that kind of imaginative world going on. People with aphantasia are unable to produce mental imagery, but that doesn't necessarily interfere with their other cognitive skills. You might think that you need mental imagery for memory tasks involving images, for example—but people with aphantasia don't necessarily perform any worse on such tasks.[34] There can be extreme variation in people's conscious experience, and the implications for the mind just are not known yet. We are likely only scratching the surface.

For these reasons, I don't think having conversations in your head is likely to hold the key to big topics like consciousness, or cognition in general. But we are able to see how much variation and complexity there can be in inner speech. And it is notable that people who report having things like imaginary friends tend to endorse a lot of these more complex characteristics for their inner speech. It's like their inner world is turned up a notch; if one thing is particularly vivid, other things are too. What tulpamancers and writers often end up emphasizing is how they use dialogue to initially build their tulpas and characters. You have to have the conversation first to summon the conversational partner; you build it, and they come. Our capacity to engage in this kind of inner dialogue is but one of the skills in representing "others" that all of us probably have. It's just that some people choose to turn that linguistic scaffold into something more like a mannequin, allowing them to clothe a new being with the thoughts, positions, and feelings we all carry with us, all the time. And if that being begins to speak for itself, it will feel like it has a presence of its own—I can believe that. Regardless of how central inner speech is to cognition or consciousness, it seems like an important part of the puzzle when we try to think through how other kinds of presence can emerge.

A second presence

In a swirl of readers, writers, tulpamancers, and imaginary friends, it can be easy to lose sight of the question we began with. What *are* presences? And what do ponies or Clarissa Dalloway have to do with them?

To me, these kinds of experiences represent all the different ways in which our minds—and more specifically, our imaginations— are able to create a different type of presence than those we heard about earlier in the book. Recall the presence robot, created by Olaf Blanke's team. You reach out, press a button, and nothing comes back. But wait a moment, just out of sync, and you feel a touch on your own back. Another body, another person; a phantom right behind you. When I see the Third Man on the horizon, when I hear about the extra dinner guest for the man with Parkinson's, this is the type of presence I think about. This is felt presence as a body, a visceral ghostly mannequin, inextricably linked to the sense we have of our own bodies.

Examples like the presence robot tell us how something so baffling and so empty can feel so real—a hallucination about nothing, a hallucination tethered to our own form. They tell us *how* presence is possible via bodily self-consciousness. But that isn't the only kind of presence. There must be more.

Those earlier examples don't tell us about all the possibilities of presence—all the identities, all the functions, all the needs, emotions, and roles they can play. What they don't tell us is how we personify the body that appears, how we put a face to the shadow, how we recognize that feeling that only certain people can provide. Not just the one who walks beside us but the one who runs beside us, hoists us back to our feet, tells us it will be OK. The one who apparently passed on, but you know they are still there. The one who could never leave you. Not really, not in here.

I think this is what Tanya Luhrmann means when she talks about presence as essentially meaning "mind." We can create other presences, coming not from our bodies but from somewhere and something else. We can call that imagination, absorption, perception, or emotion, but the key thing is that it comes from us. We are the wellspring; we are the source of the other. We are the authors of our own plurality.

A crucial question that the examples in this chapter pose is, how does imagination truly turn into an "other"? Tulpamancers, for example, don't really care for the word *imagination*; they might agree that the beginning of their journey involves various forms of imagery, but once that tulpa talks back, the tulpamancer is not imagining it anymore. The experience, for them, is deeply real; the tulpa is saying things that feel out of their control, in a way that is consistent with the tulpa's character, not the tulpamancer's. A threshold has been crossed.

When we consider what pushes people over that threshold, we have a few plausible factors to consider. The first thing we have to acknowledge is emotion: people are often deeply invested in this experience. That emotion might go into creating the other, such as a tulpa or a character in a novel. It might go into immersing yourself in an imaginative world as a reader. It might go into play and interaction, as in the case of imaginary friends. Investment, connection, and reward—all of these seem to play a key role in imaginative presence.

The role of emotion connects these experiences with some Third Man stories or examples of presence in bereavement. People can experience random visitors—and we have heard of accounts where that happens. When one is in need, or on the brink of disaster, some kind of significant other comes; the figure is rarely neutral.[35] But, if imagination and longing were all there was to this process, it wouldn't be particularly mysterious or surprising. It might bring people to the threshold, getting them through all the miles and hours to reach that point, but it doesn't always go according to plan. Recall the cases of Leven Brown in chapter 7 and Paul Burgum in chapter 8. Leven would have given anything to be joined by the presence of his grandfather, but the voice he heard was familiar and yet anonymous. Paul sought the support of his grandad Fred, and the spirit sent him striding up the hills of Italy, but he also experienced presences of others that he didn't ask for. It's like both engaged a process, inadvertently or not, that could conjure another. They had the capacity to bring forth a presence, but without having full say in who that might be.

We have imagination and emotion, but perhaps we need something else. Something to push us over the edge, and make it feel like the other is *actually* there. I think that answer has to come back to the self, as it does in the case of embodied presences. That is, these imaginative presences, fueled with emotion, are somehow reflections or echoes of ourselves.

This might sound strange, counterintuitive even. Many of us will have a strong sense of ourselves and our own thoughts. We are in charge, we are the solid line throughout our experience, and no one else is. To think otherwise would be madness. People with split or multiple personalities are often seen as unstable, something to be feared; to be multiple in some way is to have lost control, to be lacking somehow.

But how do you know this is true about yourself? Are you the same person that you were ten years ago, one year ago, even one week ago? Do you ever make resolutions, then break them within a month? Do you ever say one thing to someone and then do the complete opposite, not realizing you had contradicted yourself until you are called out on it? Have you ever forgotten that you once loved something, or needed to be reminded of a lost taste, or stepped into a room and had a wave of emotion and experience flood back across you?

All of these occurrences happen every day for many of us, and yet they represent discontinuities in our ongoing experience of self. They are the glitches and kinks that get smoothed over, the factors that get quietly ushered to the door in our attempt to have a consistent and continuous sense of ourselves. The self is defined by our bodies and our minds; but our bodies change, and our minds are fallible. We like to think we have psychological continuity across time and space, but we don't, not all the time. We connect the dots and forget the gaps.

Other people also help us define who we are: significant others, others as points of comparison, others as supporters, or antagonists, or inspiration. Other people can act like buttresses that hold a sense of self in place; one constantly being revised, updated, imperceptibly shifted from moment to moment through time. It is not just our bodily self that is an ensemble piece, arranged together to give us a sense of unity—it is our whole self; a self defined by our relations to others. And, when people create these other presences, these senses of a vivid imaginary other, it is this kind of self that people are playing with. Not the self of the body but the self as defined by others.

The example of inner speech provides us a hint of that. Look to our inner monologue, and we find dialogue (or, at least, many of us do). Our own words, our commentary, is a patchwork created from the words and opinions of others. We say something to ourselves but also for a wider audience; we answer their concerns, their questions, their challenges. We justify, persuade, mull over, defend—a cogitating self constantly shadowboxing the other.

I think it goes further and deeper than language, though. Think of the way Tamber's tulpamancer described his tulpa, as another "looking out" through his eyes. This kind of presence is a kind of awareness that comes before dialogue. It is an expectancy about someone's point of view, even though that other person is a simulacrum, a shadow almost. It's as much about looking as speaking, attending rather than listening. When he and I were working on our study of reading together, Marco Bernini coined another term: *phantasmal intersubjectivity*. By this he means the sharing of attention with something detached from reality; an idea, a fiction—a phantom. Intersubjectivity refers to the sharing of feelings and experiences between more than one person; it is a concept that originally comes from philosophy and psychotherapy. It's what we do when we share a joke with friends, or when two or more people both enjoy the same film; it's what we do when we really recognize and understand something from another's perspective, without even needing to think twice.

If we look to developmental models of the self—that is, ideas of how the self originates, and how children begin to learn about themselves—it isn't hard to see the presence of others, right from the start, through intersubjectivity. An example I like comes from Daniel Stern, a developmental psychologist and psychoanalyst.[36] Stern built on ideas about the mind and self from figures like Vygotsky in his

1985 book *The Interpersonal World of the Infant*. In it, he proposed that around nine months of age, infants start to develop what he originally called a "subjective" self, which he later dubbed an "intersubjective" self.

For Stern, nine months of age is significant because it is when babies really start to become adept at joint attention. They might point to things for parents to look at or follow their parent's gaze to see what is new and interesting. They might share emotions, becoming excited about a new toy and looking to see if their parent is too, or they might share intentions, with parent and baby both focused on the same goal. All of this is happening mostly via nonverbal communication: expressions of concern or delight, smiles and nods, looks of surprise. All these things are blossoming, and they are core parts of the process of learning to see the world through another's eyes.

Within the tradition that Stern was working in, it has often been assumed that infants have to learn that they are separate from others. That is, we all begin undifferentiated from our mothers—or other primary caregivers—and have to learn to distinguish our unique agency in the world. But Stern argued against this, proposing that we do have some basic elements of a sense of self early on. In fact, in Stern's model, the intersubjective self is the third kind of self that develops in children, coming after the "emergent" self (very basic consistencies of bodily signals, present from birth) and the "core" self (the consistency of the self as an agent in the world, performing actions, having feelings, and so on). The intersubjective self depends on these earlier selves; they provide the grounding and consistency of experience to distinguish self and other in joint attention. When this capacity for intersubjectivity arrives, it doesn't displace these other aspects of self, it just becomes another layer of who we are, another aspect of the self. It's just that this one is constantly being shared or attuned in some way by our interactions with others.

There are other ideas and models of the self that describe something similar, such as a relational self, or a dialogic self.[37] There are dangers here of becoming too theoretical or getting lost in terminology.

But I think this is the kind of idea we need in order to understand a second kind of presence—those that aren't out there in the world but in here with us—and feel even more real for it. If we think of the self, or a part of the self, as being defined in relation to others—even *depending* on others—it shouldn't be a surprise that in some cases we can almost activate that "other" in our lives. It may even be a direct parallel to the ways in which disrupting the bodily self can bring forth bodily presences. Perhaps by mixing, churning, and playing with the intersubjective self, we create these relational presences.

To return to writers, in another essay Philip Pullman describes the process like this: "There are probably daemon voices whispering to us all the time, and we have forgotten how to hear them."[38] In a similar way, I think it was a mistake to think that presences came from nowhere, that we didn't carry them with us already. They are other, and yet they are us—echoed, reflected, and transformed. They are what can come forth when times become strange or pressured, when we lose track of where we begin and where the world ends. Their origin gives presences that feeling of significance and familiarity, for they are that scaffold when all is otherwise lost.

They have been beside us all this time.

12

You Never Asked

April 2020. It is the peak of the first wave of COVID in the United Kingdom.

I am in my car at 10:45 PM, sitting outside the city hospital. I am staring at my phone and trying to stay calm, looking at the news but finding it impossible to focus on anything. I am waiting for a call or a text from my partner, waiting for the signal that I can come in. For the past two weeks we had been taking extra care to make sure we didn't catch anything; any sign of a cough or a cold and I wouldn't be allowed in at all, we were told. She would have to go through it all on her own. Finally, the call came, and I headed straight into the birthing center.

The next day we were home with our new daughter; relieved, elated, and exhausted. Like any new parents, we spent the next days and weeks trying to get our heads around what we were supposed to be doing. Despite the pandemic, visits from midwives and health professionals continued, but other services weren't available. Any baby groups we might have gone to in person were all online.

Also online was . . . well, everything, and everyone else. The ban on household mixing affected everybody in different ways and would continue to do so with every new lockdown. For us it meant that our daughter couldn't meet the rest of our family until several months later. We weren't alone in this, with many new families across the country not able to introduce their babies to grandparents, aunties, uncles, and cousins for months or even years.

And so those meetings happened on Zoom. Social contact began to look like a TV panel show, squares stacked upon squares, friends and family looming, pausing, muting and unmuting, talking over each other or not at all.

Everyone was there, and yet no one was present. Not really. Not like they should be.

This far into the pandemic, many of us will be familiar with a kind of Zoom fatigue. For those lucky enough to be able to work from home, the shift to online working has led to wall-to-wall meetings and a feeling of being constantly "on." Various ideas have been put forward as to why this is so tiring: it could be that we can see ourselves onscreen, making us self-conscious of our own appearance, or it could be the result of us feeling that we are being seen, so we must in turn appear to be paying attention and contributing.[1] It could even be the inconsistent rhythm inherent in online communication. When we speak to someone face-to-face, myriad cues tell us when to talk and when to listen, when to nod or smile, and when to look away. There is an ebb and flow that must be relearned when it comes to negotiating the stilted frames of the online world.

Such technology is astounding in its ability to make these interactions possible. Ultimately, we could still talk to people, we could see them. We could share stories and jokes, we could be with other people in a way that just wouldn't have been possible even five years earlier.

It wasn't the same though—it couldn't be. The obvious difference is that you couldn't touch anyone, you couldn't hug them. But it wasn't just that—it was something else. The feeling of being there with someone, sharing a common space, wasn't there. That sensation, that electric reaction when you walk into a room and see a particular person—you, there, *with* them—was missing.

To comprehend how and why digital interactions feel so different, we need to understand how presence works in the virtual world. And it is this virtual space that will bring us back to where we began: the figure at Alex's shoulder.

*   *   *

THERE IS A specific definition that is applied to presence when it comes to virtual reality (VR): the sense of "being there" in a computer-based environment.[2] Closely related to the concept of immersion, it refers to people actually feeling like they are located in the virtual realm rather than simply viewing it onscreen.[3]

Mel Slater is a researcher who has used VR to explore racial bias, paranoia, embodiment, and even the notorious experiments on obedience to authority that were originally run by Stanley Milgram in the early 1960s.[4] Slater has challenged the concept of virtual presence, arguing that it is not about "being there" but being "rooted in activity."

> "Presence" is considered as the propensity of people to respond to virtually generated sensory data as if they were real. . . . If they see an object on the floor below them, and wish to lift it, then they should be able to bend down, grab it, feel it, feel its weight, and lift it.[5]

In other words, presence here isn't a feeling just about where you are but also about what you can *do*. To feel like you are in an actual environment, you have to be in a space in which you can act, where the information you receive matches the actions you make and the consequences of those actions. This is a similar idea to the logic behind the presence robot: that our sense of the other comes about when we don't get the usual signals about our actions.[6] We expect to move and receive a particular kind of sensory feedback—a touch, a sound, or a flash. When we don't get that, we lose track of our bodies. We don't know our own boundaries, and so we start to draw them anew.

These ideas about presence in VR are focused on the individual's sense of being present, but it is not a great leap to consider how they might apply back to the presence of others. When someone is on a screen, the range of things that they can do is much more limited. They are not truly present because they are not part of our space; they don't change our capacity for action at all. If we see someone in the flesh, we see a living, breathing, moving agent who could in theory act very spontaneously in the space that we are both in. We have to be ready to react, ready to move as well; we have to engage in the environment more exactly because someone else is in it too. Just as we need to feel that capacity for action to feel present in VR, others will only feel present to us if they can act also.

Having their own square on Zoom just doesn't cut it.

A voice with a face

The effects of immersion and presence in VR offer a range of therapeutic possibilities. In 1995, a team at Georgia Tech reported on the successful use of a VR environment to treat a fear of heights (or acrophobia).[7] People with specific or simple phobias—such as the fear of flying or spiders—often respond well to desensitization and "graded exposure" techniques.[8] Typically these involve habituating an individual to the things they are scared of by using a combination of imagery techniques and real-world encounters. Sometimes, though, actually putting someone in a real-world situation just isn't possible—it would be far too stressful. VR can act as a safe step toward that goal—if the subject can successfully be convinced that they are truly present in the situation.

In the last fifteen years, techniques of this kind have been developed to help people with psychosis tackle feelings of paranoia and persecution. One example is a VR ride on a busy train—say, the London Underground—where other people in the virtual environment are seated all around you.[9] At times, everyone appears to look at you, while at other times they are all looking away. Simulating this kind of environment—threatening, unusual, intense—becomes a way of exploring powerful thoughts and feelings in a safe way. Simulated scenarios offer opportunities to learn new strategies and tools that might get sufferers through until things start to feel normal again.

My attempts to understand more about presence started when I spoke to Alex about his voices. For him it wasn't so much suspicion and paranoia but the persistence of those four voices—and their hidden, silent presence—that affected him. Various games and simulations have tried to recreate the experience of hearing voices, although few have tried to use VR (at least, at the time of this writing). There are, however, computer-mediated therapies that come close to it.

A particularly prominent one is known as AVATAR therapy. The method—first developed by psychiatrists at Kings College London—is designed to help people with schizophrenia who have a long history of hearing distressing voices.[10] The aim of the therapy is to enable the voice-hearer to enter into a dialogue with their voices in an attempt to empower and defend themselves from their hidden persecutors.

As the name suggests, AVATAR therapy achieves this in quite an unusual way. In the first session, the voice-hearer and therapist work together to create a computer-based avatar of the distressing voice.[11] A mixing board is used to mimic the sound of the voice—capturing characteristics such as timbre and pitch—while a 3D image of the "face" of the voice is also created. The therapist will ask about things like the accent and age of the voice, and for specific examples of what the voice has said in the past.

Once the face and voice are generated, they are used in a therapy session—but what the avatar says comes from the therapist. The therapist goes into another room and speaks through a voice simulator, using a button to alternate the feed with their own voice. That way, they can talk to the voice-hearer throughout the session, preparing them for moments when they will "be" the voice, and then returning to their own voice for debriefing afterward. The aim is to gradually change the nature of the interaction, with the therapist slowly shifting the character of the voice to something that it is more manageable and less damaging.

This technique might sound far-fetched to many, or even counterproductive. There is a stigma attached to talking back to voices—as the cliché goes, talking to yourself is the first sign of madness. Suggesting that people with psychosis talk back to their voices is not often encouraged, as there is a fear of making things worse by somehow making the voices more real.

The interesting thing about AVATAR therapy is how powerful it seems to be for some people. I should disclose that I have been lucky to meet and work with members of the AVATAR team—while not being involved in the research itself—and I have had the chance to talk to many of them about the day-to-day practice of running the therapy. One example that stuck with me was the story of the person who couldn't be in the same room as her avatar after the first session of creating it with the therapist. She couldn't stand to have its face appear on the screen, so it had to be made as small as a postage stamp and was only gradually made larger over the course of therapy. (This, incidentally, is the kind of graded exposure technique that might be used for treating phobia.) The face on the screen is just a best guess, an E-Fit, of a personality that has never been seen in the outside world, and yet it can terrify someone just by the possibility of its appearance. Rather than being something clunky, approximate, and disconnected from people's experience, the effect of joining of voice and avatar is a powerful and startling one for some.

When AVATAR has been tested in big trials, it seems to show reductions in psychosis symptoms in the short term, even if the jury is still out on its long-term impact.[12] But it can be hard to know what the actual experience is like for people doing the therapy, and whether they really felt the presence of the voice in the process of creating the avatar. To find out more about that, I spoke to one of the main people from the AVATAR team who worked on the trial, Dr. Mar Rus-Calafell.

Mar is an associate professor at the University of Bochum in Germany. She originally trained as a clinical psychologist in her native Spain before moving to the United Kingdom to pursue her interest in VR and mental health. It is a cold October night, and we are both speaking quietly in an attempt to keep small children asleep in adjoining rooms.

We get talking about presence, and how it might mean something different to people who know the VR world. I ask how she thinks that concept of presence might apply to her work on AVATAR therapy—especially given that the therapy itself isn't actually in a fully immersive VR environment.

"Any environment mediated by technology can evoke a sense of presence," she explains. "The concept of presence is normally linked to how immersive the system is, but there are several studies that say you don't actually need an immersive environment."

If not immersion, what else can prompt that feeling of being there? The answer involves going back to Mel Slater's idea of presence being in a space that you can act in. For Mar, this specifically means *inter*action. "To feel a sense of presence, you need a way of communicating. Even a 2D or flat screen can evoke this sense of 'I am in a space or an environment doing things, interacting with things or with someone.' It doesn't have to be fully immersive to create this feeling."

When we consider AVATAR therapy then, a key ingredient would seem to be the potential for that kind of communicative interaction. But at the same time, to even achieve that dialogue, all of the moving parts need to work: the voice, the face, the language of an entity that literally no one else has ever heard before must be properly captured. Wasn't Mar skeptical that this was going to work?

"I was a bit skeptical I think, I wasn't sure we could [make it work]." Mar pauses to think. "It wasn't the greatest technology, but at the same time we were creating something that was a totally un-known stimulus to us. I was thinking, how are we going to be sure this is what we need to have, because the experts there are them"—that is, the voice-hearers themselves.

To counter this worry, Mar asked the participants to rate how convincing the computerized voice and face that they created were. Participants were asked to rate how similar the experience was to their normal experience of the voice, whether it felt like the voice talking to them (as opposed to just the computer avatar), and how often they actually felt that way during therapy. When the participants were asked to rate these three questions on scales of 1 (low) to 5 (high), the average score was over 10 out of 15, suggesting a considerable sense of presence throughout the sessions.[13]

This would be an interesting finding itself—and it attests again to the power of the procedure—but importantly, the feeling that the avatar/voice was really present also seemed to make a difference to how well people did in therapy. People who rated the presence of their avatar voices during therapy highly tended to improve after twelve weeks, but only if their levels of anxiety were also reduced during the therapy. That is, people who felt like their voice was present—and who gradually became less anxious as the therapy continued—usually had the best outcomes.

Of course, there are caveats to any findings observed within a new therapy. One thing Mar regrets is not asking participants specifically about where their voice *was* during the therapy—that is, the voice they tend to hear, not the voice of the avatar. If a participant scored high on the presence scale, were they actually just experiencing a felt presence, separate from anything going on with the therapy? Was their voice in the room with them, watching and listening as they conversed with the therapist/avatar? Mar can't say, and we can't know. The AVATAR team is currently running a larger trial, and they will be asking about that possibility.[14]

What the AVATAR team can report is all the nonverbal cues that people show when engaging in the therapy. During the sessions, a webcam is always focused on the participant so the therapist can see if they are struggling. Just as some people cannot bear to be near the avatar's face, others would show signs of fear if their voice was in the room. Some people would ask to stop the session if the presence of the voice was too much to bear. I have been in interviews myself when some voices will literally stop the interview, such is their perceived power. Close and sustained attention to the voice would become unbearable, as if the subject had been asked to stare directly into the sun.

Another concern about AVATAR therapy is how elaborate and technological the treatment is. Some people would argue that its key ingredients—and in particular, the focus on dialogue—mimic other, cheaper techniques. Another NHS approach is Relating Therapy, where a therapist and voice-hearer might use role-playing to practice different kinds of conversations with a dominant voice. No simulation or avatar is deployed, and yet some people find it useful for reconfiguring the kind of interaction they have with their voices. Members of the Hearing Voices Movement and voice-hearers themselves have advocated for the Voice Dialogue approach, a method where a facilitator talks to the voice and the voice-hearer speaks for the latter. Each of these techniques creates the opportunity for dialogue and seeks in some way to change the relationship between voice-hearer and voice, but not all need computer-based bells and whistles.

These concerns have their merits, particularly when you think about how challenging it could be to use the technology behind AVATAR across the health service on a larger scale. I think the technology is important, though, because for some people it helps to bring that voice into the room, to make it an object of therapy. The presence of the computer avatar means that the voice, at least for the moment, isn't just in there with you, it's outside as well (or, possibly, instead). The way some people react to their avatar shows how powerful the therapy can be.

In the end, AVATAR therapy might offer one promising way of managing voices, but it is a technique that depends on dialogue. It needs a voice that will speak enough for someone to approximate that interaction. The voice, in theory, needs to be one that you can converse with.

And as we know, not all voices do. Some are just silent, and some are just there. What then?

Floating away

When I think about my conversations with Alex and other voice-hearers, I often come back to their descriptions of the body. The feeling of a voice being there is something visceral; it is happening to their body and the space around them, even if touch isn't always part of the experience. It is a feeling that involves shivers and goosebumps, it is the sensation of someone "stepping over your grave."

And it is a sensation in space, although what that space *is* remains very unclear. Alex's voices took up positions; Keira's voices thickened the air. The space that was occupied was intruded upon, infiltrated, and subverted somehow. For such experiences, taking up space and time but not words, I wondered whether dialogue would be enough to create the kind of therapeutic change that someone might need. Could an unwanted presence be talked away?

I think part of the problem is that research on and treatment for psychosis have traditionally not looked to the body as being a significant part of the experience. This kind of Cartesian split, rending mind and body,[15] can be seen across different aspects of mental health, but it feels particularly pronounced when it comes to schizophrenia and psychosis. It also contrasts with the kinds of stories you hear from voice-hearers themselves, in which hearing a voice can really be a whole-body experience.

Things are changing though, with a new wave of research emphasizing the close links between bodies, presences, and psychosis. Researchers have begun to try out variations of the "presence robot" procedure with people with psychosis: they have found that when you induce the feeling of presence, people's judgments about other things change too, like whether or not a recording of a voice was of them speaking, or someone else.[16] Another study with healthy participants showed that the presence robot could even change how we perceived the volume of certain sounds. Usually, our experience of sounds that we generate is automatically quietened by our brains, unlike sounds from other people—but feeling a presence interrupted this process too.[17]

From voice to presence and presence to voice. The ground on which we make judgments about self and other might seem solid, but it can shift and leave you in new and interesting places. Our boundaries feel firm, but they are malleable. On one level, this might feel obvious: after all, if you thought someone new and unusual was present, wouldn't you be on your guard, paying attention to things in a different way? But on another level, this is something happening beyond our awareness, under the hood, in our bones. Our senses are making the call: something is there.

One person who is showing the way for a new understanding of the body in psychosis is Dr. Sohee Park, a professor at Vanderbilt University, Nashville. Originally from Korea, Sohee has been working in the United States on psychosis and schizophrenia for over twenty years, with a stop-off in Switzerland that included meeting Peter Brugger. Since the start of her career, Sohee has been exploring the role of space in the cognition of people with schizophrenia, but it has only been in the past few years that her work on the embodied aspects of psychosis has really exploded. It was time for one more conversation.

We get a chance to talk in the middle of the busy autumn semester, with a meeting wedged between classes, supervisions, and bath time, in my daughter's case. We get talking about how Sohee started in this area. It had taken her a few years working on diverse topics in psychology, like mental imagery and how children learn new linguistic concepts, before she found her niche. Her move into clinical research came from a chance conversation over lunch with Philip Holzman, a preeminent figure in the world of psychosis research. She was working on her PhD in a cognitive psychology lab at Harvard but was unsure about her dissertation topic. When Holzman invited her to work on a cognitive study of schizophrenia, it felt like a perfect opportunity. "So that's how I started—at a state psychiatric hospital. Except I had no clinical training. I was in this inpatient ward running eye-tracking experiments."

There are lots of regulations in place and arrangements to be made when doing research with groups who might be deemed "vulnerable." It is not like anyone can walk into a psychiatric ward. Sohee's experience may be less common today, but even now such baptisms of fire happen more than you might think. For her, though, it sounds like she found herself in a useful position. "It was a blessing in a way because I had no preconceived idea about schizophrenia. I hadn't even taken an introductory clinical psychology class before! Without knowing much, I had walked into a world of people whose lives had been completely upended."

Sohee's eyes light up at this memory. "I didn't even know what positive and negative symptoms were when I started." By "positive symptoms," Sohee means the elements added for a person with schizophrenia—hallucinations, delusions, and so on—and "negative symptoms," the things subtracted—social motivation, interaction, and rapport. "I worked with inpatients who were assessed to have high levels of negative symptoms. But surprisingly, they were friendly, chatty, sociable. Meanwhile, the eye-tracking wasn't going well. Constant talking and moving about were ruining all my attempts at eye movement measurements. Too much social engagement!"

This makes us both laugh. For someone who works on some pretty difficult topics, Sohee laughs a lot. Her experience on the wards doesn't surprise me. Knowing that someone "scored high" on a given scale on a given day often isn't the best indicator of what that person is going to be like. Labels like "schizophrenia" or "psychosis" loom large in how we imagine a person to be, and these can get in the way of seeing the actual person for who they are.

It isn't just labels that work like that though. As researchers, over the years, we develop skills and areas of knowledge, adopt theories or create our own, and grow to depend on particular methods. Added together, all of these things become a framework, a lens through which we view what is happening. We might not think in terms of diagnosis all the time, but we can easily become wedded to specific domains of the cognitive landscape. Memory, attention, language, perception—whatever the categories are, they start to dictate how we view and interpret the world.

That was where Sohee went with her research, for many years. Her doctoral thesis focused on spatial working memory—in other words, the ability to hold in mind complex patterns in space (like a sequence of shapes). The people she saw with schizophrenia struggled with this task in a way that people with other diagnoses, such as bipolar disorder, didn't. In other work, she looked at mental imagery skills and found them to be a strength, not a challenge, for her participants with schizophrenia. The promise of the 1990s and 2000s was that if we learned enough about these specific skills and difficulties, we could lay them all out and build a map of conditions like schizophrenia, bipolar disorder, or even autism.

But she wasn't happy. "I felt that what we were doing in current psychiatry or clinical neuroscience was very good for developing empirical methods to measure whatever you're supposed to measure." By this, she means things like working memory. "But we had completely lost the subjective core. What a person experiences, what they are going through."

Her thinking was shaped by a distinction made by the psychiatrist Arthur Kleinman between the concepts of *illness* and *disease*. *Disease* is what someone has; it has biological basis and structure, and it's the underlying thing you seek to measure. *Illness*, on the other hand, is the world of the patient: "the innately human experience of symptoms and suffering."[18] For Sohee, the scales had tipped too far in favor of the former: "We've basically invested so much in the objective model of the disease, but meanwhile we've grown away from looking at the illness and the person enveloped by this illness."

The solution was to talk to people, to understand their experiences better, and not always just focus on the target of the experiment on any given day. And when they did that, surprising things emerged. "We were doing this rubber hand experiment in the lab and one patient—whom we'd known for ten years and would regularly come in to do all our experiments—told us in a matter-of-fact way, 'Oh, I am hovering above you.' He had exited his body, and was floating in the air."

The rubber hand illusion, as we heard about in chapter 5, is a well-worn technique for momentarily tricking our sense of body ownership.[19] Synchronizing feedback on the rubber hand, and obscuring our own, leads us to adopt the fake limb. But it doesn't usually prompt such extreme reactions as this.

"He was having a full-blown out-of-body experience right there, and we're thinking 'Oh my God!' When he 'came back' to his body, he told us that he has had this experience multiple times in his life. Then he told us that every time he had this experience, he ended up in the hospital. We were petrified by this admission. But he asked us for something to read about his condition." The man left the lab that day with an armful of papers from neurological research—research that documented all the unusual ways a body can be transformed.

But this research usually applied only to neurological conditions, not schizophrenia. Sohee's team were worried what the man would make of it, and even more concerned that he might end up in the hospital.

They needn't have worried, though. The man came back relieved, describing his newfound knowledge as just short of wonderful. He finally had a name for the experiences he had been having all of his life, terms for the feelings that had started his career in unreality. "All these years, we had no idea he was having out-of-body experiences because we never asked. We had conducted standard clinical interviews and asked him about hallucinations and delusions numerous times before, but we had never asked him about his sense of self. We had failed to ask him about himself."[20]

It is impossible to say how or why, but after that day, the gentleman's unusual body-based experiences receded. He did allow Sohee's team to elicit them again through using the rubber hand procedure, and this time he was able to give a real-time commentary on the experience. But the effect he had had on their team was much greater—the experience led them to change the direction of their research, to focus on the body.

Now they ask about unusual events like out-of-body experiences and presences as a matter of routine. They find that over half of the participants diagnosed with psychotic conditions have had these kinds of body-based experiences. Along with asking the right questions, the team is seeking to develop new tools to measure how these experiences work and how they really feel from the inside.

In one recent experiment, they used VR to test the boundaries of peripersonal space in people with schizophrenia.[21] Peripersonal space—which we came across in chapter 1—is that immediate zone around us that we can reach and perform actions in. Research has shown that when something enters our peripersonal space, our reaction times speed up and we get quicker at combining different sensory cues (like sight and touch). Sohee's team used a ball-catching task in a VR environment to study where in a subject's peripersonal space that change happens for people with schizophrenia: Is the area bigger or smaller? Is the change in reaction time abrupt or gradual? The answer was that patients in the study had a smaller peripersonal space than people without schizophrenia—a smaller "action zone," in other words—but the boundary of that space was not as clearly defined as it was for control participants. The researchers also compared what happens when a robot throws the ball versus when another human player throws the ball: when another human was involved, the peripersonal space was even less clearly defined for people in the schizophrenia group. In other words, when it became a more social game involving others, the boundaries of personal space became even blurrier for patients.

In another line of research, Sohee's team used computerized body maps to explore how people with schizophrenia experience the feelings of different emotions throughout their bodies. The technique, called emBODY, was originally developed by a Finnish research team to explore how reports of different emotions are distinguished by their body maps.[22] The maps literally look like bodily outlines, but with heat maps highlighting where in the body different emotions felt like they were based for participants: the head, the heart, the gut, etc. Sohee's team observed that participants with schizophrenia reported emotions that were less distinct across different body maps, especially for subtler feelings.[23] If this is the case generally, it represents another way in which experience of the body may be profoundly different in schizophrenia.

Thinking about the embodied nature of emotion provides a bridge between the two kinds of presence in the stories we have heard: the presence of bodies, and the presence of our relation to others, our intersubjectivity. I ask Sohee, what role does she think emotion plays in how we should understand schizophrenia and psychosis? Are changes to the experience of emotion at the core of these conditions, or is it something happening alongside other things, like hallucinations, or changes to the self?

"I believe they are connected," she replies. "But conceptually it's hard to make that link. It must involve awareness of your own body, and the ability to map that to concepts and categories." I think I know what she means, but I ask Sohee for an example.

"Way back I looked at color name acquisition in two-year-olds. Color is this continuous spectrum, but each language draws up borders for color names. As babies we are supposed to learn that from here to here is red, from here to here is orange. Kids can do that, from about the age of three, but before that it is random. It's likely to be similar for bodily sensation or emotion. Consider a word like *angry*. When we feel this emotion, we have all these sensations going on inside, and we're supposed to put a specific word, *angry*, to those internal sensory signals in that particular context."

She goes on. "I think it's a similar problem. We are giving babies these linguistic conceptual boundaries, and they have to map those concepts onto some undefined sensory space. It's miraculous how children actually learn to do this, to put a word to these mushy internal sensations."

For schizophrenia, Sohee thinks it is this connection, this mapping, that is a fundamental challenge. There is a wellspring of feelings and sensations but no names for them, or more accurately, no names that fit well, while the "everyday" emotions become foreign and indistinct. But could language also provide a way through that?

"Putting a name to things is really powerful, like a magical spell. In folklore and myths around the world, the *naming of things* gives you the power of control—once you know the name of a being, a genie or an imp, their power is dispelled."

By naming a feeling, we can take it out of ourselves. We can share it, discuss it, offer it as an object of attention to others. Like the faces of AVATAR therapy, the internal becomes external; something is articulated when before it could not be spoken of.

The limits of language stand like a high coastal cliff, and yet the waves of words will crash and crash again, chipping away, creating cracks and fissures, finding new gaps and gullies that meaning can pass through. Sometimes progress can be made simply by putting a name to something.

Presence unboxed

When I look at the work Sohee's team is doing, exploring bodies and spaces, putting names to experiences and visualizing the hidden, I feel like new avenues are being opened in every direction. Things that we couldn't explore before start to come into view, sometimes because of technology, and sometimes just because we hadn't thought to look properly. The theoretical sands are shifting under our feet, reminding us that body and mind are inextricably linked. The success of that method reflects Sohee's varied experience and curiosity—she didn't approach a topic like psychosis with a predefined view, so she keeps restlessly exploring the terrain.

But I kept coming back to the example she gave about the man with his out-of-body experiences. I wonder, if he hadn't floated above them that day, during that experiment, if they still might not know about the range and depth of his experiences. Something about them seem central and primary to understanding how his reality had changed, and yet they had missed it for years, never quite hitting on the right question.

My conversations with Alex had led me to explore the idea of presence, but that wasn't because of the questions I had asked him—he had volunteered the information. In Daniel's case, he supplied the information without even being prompted, perhaps coming from a sense of exasperation. "You don't *even* have to hear him . . ." he said to us. Like we were missing the point—and perhaps we were.

What if we hadn't been listening that day, if we hadn't been paying attention to Alex? Would the presences have passed by, on to the next situation, waiting for the next encounter with a confused interlocutor? There, just for a moment, in plain view, but gone just as quickly again. Daring us to understand.

The shift to thinking about the body that Sohee described in her lab is something that I think can be seen in the labs of various researchers and teams around the world, to differing degrees. More and more research on embodiment, psychosis, and schizophrenia seems to be coming out every day. But at the same time, there is that nagging feeling that the researchers are still behind the curve, just catching up with what people with lived experience have been trying to get across for a long time.

In some cases, those people have taken matters into their own hands. During the writing of this book, a new initiative was launched: Psychosis Outside the Box,[24] a project focused on collecting accounts of psychosis that don't conform to the expected stereotypes and models that researchers, clinicians, and society have of it. Rather than focusing on voices or paranoia, Psychosis Outside the Box asks people for their descriptions of "visions and visual experiences," "alterations of time and space," and felt presences.

The project was put together by Shannon Pagdon, a researcher and youth advocate who specializes in trauma and psychosis, and Nev Jones, an assistant professor in the school of social work at the University of Pittsburgh. Shannon is a manager at the Mental Health Association of San Francisco, and a voice-hearer herself, who is keen to change how we as a society think and talk about mental health. Nev is well-known as a researcher whose academic training began in philosophy, moved through psychology, and ended up in mental health services and policy research. She has also personally experienced psychosis. I have had the privilege of working with Nev on a couple of research projects in the past, but they are just a small part of her impact on the field.

It is interesting, then, that Psychosis Outside the Box is explicitly labeled as a "non-research" project. The website describes it as a grassroots endeavor to generate knowledge for others in a similar position. People with psychosis are invited to participate to pass on their experiences in an unvarnished, unmediated way, not to simply become a quote in a paper or someone's particularly intriguing case study. It cuts out the intermediaries of researchers, academics, editors, and journals and aims to present lived experience as it is.

Version 1 of the project is now available to read via Rethink Psychosis, a hub for disseminating resources and knowledge about unusual experiences. The examples of presence given in the report are very similar to many that we have already heard, and I would encourage the reader to look them up and spend time with them. One quote in particular struck me:

> Pretty much anything and everything that my clinicians describe as "hallucinations" or "delusions" feel to me like they have invisible presences that I can sense. For example, people who are maybe chasing me, or voices I might be hearing—they're all, in various ways, out there in the world. But not as literal "visible" figures or people I can reach out to and touch. But also very different to just imaging [sic] something in one's head. They have a kind of ephemeral reality.[25]

Other contributors to the project speak of perception beyond the senses, of possession, or of transformations of their own bodies. Encounters just out of sight, or just behind them. One person highlighted a potential tension in the question—that presence is necessarily something separate from the subject or additional to all the things happening to them. All of these experiences, all of the voices and visions—each of them have presence, that's the point that is being missed by doctors, or by researchers. We might need the idea of pure felt presence on its own to understand the concept of what we are missing—it was, after all, the part that Alex didn't even usually bother to describe—but if we just focus on that, on some particular niche of taxonomy, we might miss the central relevance of presence to psychosis itself. It might *all* be about presence.

The other thing the project asks of people is whether they have any strategies that have helped them manage presence when that experience becomes distressing. Some people very clearly say no, but others list things that work for them, and recurring themes emerge. Movement, physicality, exercise; changing your focus, or prayer. Being with others. The sensory and the social, bodies and relations; changing the experiences you can control to accomodate the uncanny "other" by your side.

I wonder how Alex would have felt if they knew this resource was here. To know that it is not just he who was having this experience. There are others who are trying to articulate what is happening and sharing what they can, even if words can never quite capture that feeling. The potential of such resources makes the sharing of presence experiences so important. It is a therapeutic commonplace to seek to normalize the experience someone is having—one of the first things you might say to someone who hears voices is that many people in the population also have the experience. But for something like felt presence, where do you even start? How do you describe the shadow before you can even give it a name, let alone explain how many others have met this visitor before?

In the end, words are not likely to be enough, and sharing

experiences can only go so far. There are big societal reasons why psychosis persists, encompassing social exclusion, persecution, and deep, structural inequality. There is a reason why someone like Nev Jones has ended up in a school of social work: because for psychosis, that is where a lot of the crucial progress is needed.

But sometimes it's a challenge to even understand what the problem is. It feels like we have barely started having a conversation about presence. Despite all the people I have talked to, I still feel like I have a thousand questions, and only clues as to what is actually happening.

A circle of meaning

In trying to understand felt presence, I have heard about the visceral visitors of psychosis, the harbinger of ill health among Parkinson's sufferers, the doppelgänger of an intoxicated playwright, and a robot that can conjure a ghost. I have listened to stories of saviors but also pursuers, a stormy voice that only visited in the calm, and fellow travelers who aren't always expected. I have been told about evil personified, heard of animal confidantes, and even been offered a theory on how to create such presences myself.

I started this by highlighting how difficult it is for people to put this experience into words. We have all encountered this, and yet no one can quite put their finger on why it is so difficult. But despite this, there are things that can be said about presence—and said with confidence.

We started with the puzzle of a perception with no content; something too empty to be a hallucination but too tangible to be a delusion. That seam runs right through stories of felt presence, whether they involve psychosis, neurology, sleep, or survival. But there is a clear and strong argument to say that felt presence can be considered a hallucinatory phenomenon, not reliant on the five senses but caused by disruptions to bodily self-awareness. That model essentially relies on mirrors of our own body and the malleability of our embodied self. And we can use it, seemingly, to even induce the experience in others.

These facts add up to a kind of "body hypothesis," which is joined by another factor: expectation. Our past experiences, our moods and feelings, all might feed into what we might expect from a situation, and we know that a hallucinatory world can be conjured from such powerful influences. There is vast variation in what people experience, each story a complex web of what the individual brings and what the situation allows. If changes to the bodily self set the scene, we can think of the expectation hypothesis coloring in the gaps.

And yet, expectations are complicated. Some people don't have the experiences they are seeking; some nurture and kindle the connection with the other. And not all expectations are the same. There are particular processes and factors, drives and urges, that push people into this new world of the other, whether unwittingly or deliberately. Focus, wonder, dialogue, passion all might provide the fuel for this shift in awareness. We can say that these add up to another path toward presence, one of imagination, emotion, and social experience. It is one that involves a similar disruption to the self, but a self built and maintained by others from our earliest years. We could call it an "intersubjective" account of presence.

We started with a conundrum posed by Alex, Daniel, Keira, and Simon: the silent presences of psychosis. As we have seen in this chapter, ideas, methods, and findings are changing fast in this field, as is the level of conversation about this experience. To understand felt presence in psychosis, we are ultimately going to need to explore both of these paths: of the body and the mind. A voice that stands too close may change your space and may even have its own body, but the relation to that entity, that mind, will always be crucial as well.

And do these paths, these accounts, offer an exhaustive inventory of the phenomenon? Do they cohere into something like an essence of the experience, or perhaps two different overlapping kinds of phenomenon? That is less clear. When I started this process, I thought a single story would ultimately emerge, that despite its elusiveness, an essence of presence would step forward from the gloom.

That aim, though, may have been a quixotic endeavor from the start. To seek an essence is to make an assumption, and a dangerous one at that. We can well understand a term, or at least understand it enough, to follow someone through a conversation—but that doesn't mean we have grasped its essential core. We could have picked a definition from the outset and excluded cases as we went, divining something specific about a particular kind of felt presence experience. But had we done that from the start, what would have been lost? What would we have missed without Helen's story, or Leven's? If we had not considered Luke, how would we read Shackleton? To tackle a topic such as this—so mysterious, so elusive, we can ill afford to discard stories that don't quite fit. We must understand it in the round. And having tried, having looked, what do we see?

A figure, who is somehow tied to us. A mirror, but not quite. Silent, sentinel-like—but not alone. Because now we know. There is not just one presence. There is another.

And another.

And another . . .

At the head of the circle, a silent voice, unwanted and standing too close. It could speak at any moment, but it doesn't need to.

It is shoulder to shoulder with the unexpected dinner guest. This figure visits the old man every night to remind him of what is coming.

The presence of the dinner guest is unsettling, but it is itself somehow empty and colorless—it could be mistaken for the figure to its side.

That figure is the mannequin, the experimental presence. There briefly to pass on a touch, conjured by robotic means, but with no identity, no feeling.

An icy figure stands next in the circle, waiting to tap its leader on the shoulder, prompting him to keep going. When that touch comes, it can make a person jump out of their skin.

Another figure propels a walker up a hill in the Italian countryside; a presence that was asked for, willed into being through force of imagination.

Next, another shadow; a figure created simply for the act of creation itself. This presence isn't human, but is nonetheless full of humanity.

Just like the ghost standing next along the circle. Recognized instantly, and felt with all the heart, it walks through the house, visiting the dreams of loved ones.

But when they wake, another presence is there. A spirit. Something terrible.

The terror is back. Fear personified.

That figure takes its place next to the silent voice, and the circle of presence is complete.

Who is it that walks beside you? Don't think—look!

ACKNOWLEDGMENTS

This book would literally not exist without the presence of others. It depended on several people taking the time to share their experiences and their knowledge in a fulsome and generous way, and I am grateful beyond words to those who did. Thank you to all those who lent their voices to *Presence*, for the interviews and quotes contained in the book: Jennifer Foley, George Lewycky, Luke Robertson, Naomi Lea, Frank Ormsby, Leven Brown, Paul Burgum, Alistair Murray, Helen W., Tore Nielsen, Carol R., Andrea D., Tanya Luhrmann, Mar Rus-Calafell, Sohee Park, and especially Simon, Daniel, Keira, and Alex. When I began, I realized quickly that I wanted this book to be based in dialogue. Beyond the interviews were many conversations that shaped how I was thinking, often helping me to work out what to leave out as much as what to leave in. Thank you to Tehseen Noorani for the lost chapter on psychedelics, Emma Palmer-Cooper for schooling me in tulpamancy, and Rai Waddingham, Greg Shankland, Akiko Hart, Rob McIntosh, Vaughan Bell, Cherise Rosen, Stephanie Allan, Anne Giersch, Edith Steffen, Jacqueline Hayes, Pablo Sabucedo, Joe Barnby, Pavo Orepic, Peter Brugger, and Nev Jones for many and varied conversations about presence over the years. Several people also responded rapidly to late-night puzzles and bizarre, rambling queries from me: thank you to Robert Howard, Abbie Garrington, John-Paul Taylor, Emma Cernis, Andreas Sommer, Angelika Zarkali, Louis Sass, and Dan Farina. Thank you to Scarlett Barclay for her excellent illustrations.

Every writer is lucky to have readers who will spend time with half-finished thoughts and never-ending screeds. Thank you to Lee McLaughlin, Arthur Rose, and Marco Bernini for being some of the earliest readers, Adam Powell for spotting the two books in one, Peter Moseley for his eagle-eyed precision, Angela Woods for getting it off to the right start, and Charles Fernyhough for reading the whole thing (more or less). Tore, Mar, Jennifer, Sohee, Emma, and Tanya also acted as specialist readers—thank you again.

Much of the book is based on my time with *Hearing the Voice* at Durham University. I learned so much from working with the whole team there, but special thanks go to Sam Wilkinson, David Dupuis, Felicity Deamer, Pat Waugh, Peter Garratt, Victoria Patton, and the marvellous Mary Robson (along with many of the readers mentioned above). Four main studies from that period are included in the book. Thanks must go to Guy Dodgson and Steph Common for their calm reassurance, support, and leadership on the Voices in Psychosis project; César Lima, Sam Evans, Saloni Krishnan, and Sophie Scott for their amazing work on the sine-wave speech study (and Emmanuelle Peters for helping us find the right people); Nick Barley and Edinburgh International Book Festival for making the readers study more than just fiction; and Jamie Moffatt, Kaja Mitrenga, and Becci Lee, for their dogged work on the presence surveys. John Foxwell's quest to understand the minds of writers, while not losing his own, was also a lot of fun.

It is one thing to idly think of writing a book, and another task entirely to turn that into a reality. Marco Bernini is thanked again for repeatedly insisting that I should, and for showing me the way through the conceptual forest. Thank you to Dave Smailes for writing the first *Guardian* piece with me, and Jon Sutton for insisting there was a bigger story (and for his wise words on chapter 8). Thank you to my editor, Michael Flamini, whose instincts ensured this didn't become a neuroscience textbook, and all those at St. Martin's Press who have supported the book, including Claire Cheek, Hannah Phillips, Ellis Levine, and the meticulous Ryan Masteller (all errors in the text are definitely my own). Thank you to Rebecca Wearmouth at PFD, and of course my agent, Kirsty McLachlan. Without her patience, persistence, and belief in *Presence*, it would still just be an idea. Instead, it's been an experience.

Like many first books, this one was written over evenings and weekends, during holidays and naptimes, and often in my head if I didn't have my laptop at hand. Thank you to my family for their sheer enthusiasm and support, for the hours of childcare, the odd cover suggestion, and even sending me *The World of the Unknown: Ghosts* Usborne book (which I can recommend).

Thank you to Mum for all your help.

Thank you to Annabelle, for sleeping just long enough.

And thank you to my wife, Helen. Through highs and lows, great expectations and deadening doldrums, you were the one always at my side. Onward we go!

NOTES

PREFACE

1. William James, *The Varieties of Religious Experience* (1904. Reprint Oxford, UK: Oxford University Press, 2012), 51–52, italics original.
2. Ibid., 52.

1: A THICKNESS IN THE AIR

1. A *mackem* refers to someone from Sunderland, in the northeast of England. It comes from the phrase "make'm and take'm," a reference to Wearside's shipbuilding past.
2. Estimates vary considerably for this statistic. For example, one review found a median rate of 13 percent, but included studies with estimates ranging from less than 1 percent to over 80 percent V. Beavan, J. Read, and C. Cartwright, "The Prevalence of Voice-Hearers in the General Population: A Literature Review," *Journal of Mental Health* 20, no. 3 (2011): 281–292. Most studies, however, are in the 5–15 percent range—for a recent example, see M. M. J. Linszen, J. N. de Boer, M. J. L. Schutte, M. J. H. Begemann, J. de Vries, et al., "Occurrence and Phenomenology of Hallucinations in the General Population: A Large Online Survey," *Schizophrenia* 8, no. 1 (2022): 1–11.
3. The survey was first described and reported in Angela Woods, Nev Jones, Ben Alderson-Day, Felicity Callard, and Charles Fernyhough's "Experiences of Hearing Voices: Analysis of a Novel Phenomenological Survey," *The Lancet Psychiatry*, 2, no. 4 (April 1, 2015): 323–31.
4. B. Alderson-Day, A. Woods, P. Moseley, S. Common, F. Deamer, et al., "Voice-Hearing and Personification: Characterizing Social Qualities of

Auditory Verbal Hallucinations in Early Psychosis," *Schizophrenia Bulletin* 47, no. 1 (2021): 228–236.

5. Similarly, Bleuler's concept of schizophrenia deemed hallucinations and delusion to be merely secondary characteristics, or "accessory symptoms." Instead, he emphasized four concepts at the core of the disorder: disturbances of affect, association, ambivalence, and "autism" (understood specifically as a shutting off from the outside world rather than the concept of autism recognized today). Eugen Bleuler, *Dementia Praecox or the Group of Schizophrenias*, trans. J. Zinkin (New York: International Universities Press, 1950).

6. Karl Jaspers, *General Psychopathology*, trans. J. Hoenig and M. W. Hamilton (Chicago: University of Chicago Press, 1963), 577.

7. These included specific kinds of auditory hallucinations, such as voices conversing with each other about the subject; *gedankenlautwerden*, or hearing one's thoughts spoken out loud; and passivity symptoms, or the feeling that someone else is controlling the subject, their body, or their thoughts. Kurt Schneider, *Clinical Psychopathology* (New York: Grune & Stratton, 1959).

8. An example of this is "SloMo" therapy for paranoid delusions; see P. Garety, T. Ward, R. Emsley, K. Greenwood, D. Freeman, et al., "Effects of SlowMo, a Blended Digital Therapy Targeting Reasoning, on Paranoia among People with Psychosis: A Randomized Clinical Trial," *JAMA Psychiatry* 78, no. 7 (2021): 714–725.

9. Bleuler, *Dementia Praecox*, 111.

10. S. Wilkinson and V. Bell, "The Representation of Agents in Auditory Verbal Hallucinations," *Mind & Language* 31, no. 1 (2016): 104–126.

11. For Jaspers, this was distinguished from *gedankliche Bewusstheit*, or an ideational awareness—a thought, rather than a feeling, that someone may be close by.

12. Translation from K. Koehler and H. Sauer, "Jaspers' Sense of Presence in the Light of Huber's Basic Symptoms and DSM-III," *Comprehensive Psychiatry* 25, no. 2 (1984): 186.

13. M. Critchley, "The Idea of a Presence," *Acta Psychiatrica Scandinavica* 30, nos. 1–2 (1955): 155–168.

14. Bleuler's work was not largely translated into English (with *Dementia Praecox* only translated into English in 1950), but some contemporary reviews of his work did appear in English journals at the time of his writing.

15. C. Norman, "Extracampine Hallucinations [Extracampine Hallucinationen]. (Psychiat. Neurolog. Wochensch., Sept. 19th, 1903.) Bleuler," *Journal of Mental Science* 50, no. 210 (1904): 557–557.

16. G. Fénelon, T. Soulas, L. C. De Langavant, I. Trinkler, and A.-C. Bachoud-Lévi, "Feeling of Presence in Parkinson's Disease," *Journal of Neurology, Neurosurgery & Psychiatry* 82, no. 11 (2011): 1219–1224.

17. Koehler and Sauer, "Jaspers' Sense of Presence," 186.

2: "THINGS WHICH SHOULD NEVER BE SPOKEN OF"

1. T. S. Eliot, *The Wasteland and Other Poems* (London: Faber & Faber, 1940), 45.
2. Paul Firth, "The Man Who Wasn't There," *The Guardian*, May 29, 2003, https://www.theguardian.com/education/2003/may/29/research.highereducation3.
3. Shaun Barnett, "The Third Man," *Wilderness*, September 3, 2011, https://www.wildernessmag.co.nz/the-third-man/.
4. Alex Shoumatoff, "Brotherhood of the Mountain," *Vanity Fair*, October 10, 2006, https://www.vanityfair.com/news/2006/09/messner200609.
5. P. Brugger, M. Regard, T. Landis, and O. Oelz, "Hallucinatory Experiences in Extreme-Altitude Climbers," *Neuropsychiatry Neuropsychology and Behavioral Neurology* 12, no. 1 (1999): 67–71.
6. Beck Weathers, *Left for Dead: My Journey Home From Everest* (Boston, MA: Little, Brown & Company 2000), 51.
7. Peter Suedfeld and John Geiger, "The Sensed Presence as a Coping Resource in Extreme Environments," in J. H. Ellens (Ed.), *Miracles: God, Science, and Psychology in the Paranormal: Parapsychological Perspectives* (Westport, CT: Praeger Publishers, 2008), 14.
8. Ernest Shackleton, *South: The Endurance Expedition* (London: Penguin, 2004), xxvi.
9. Ibid., 78.
10. Ibid., 95.
11. Crean had received a medal for saving the life of Edward Evans, which he had managed by walking solo for fifty-six kilometers across the Ross Ice Shelf.
12. Shackleton, *South*, 126.
13. Frank Worsley, *Shackleton's Boat Journey* (Edinburgh, UK: Birlinn, 2000), 119.
14. Ibid., 121.
15. Ibid., 122.
16. Shackleton, *South*, 197.
17. Ibid., 135.
18. Ibid., 200.
19. Worlsey, *Shackleton's Boat Journey*, 137.
20. Ibid., 203.
21. Michael Smith and Annie Brady, *Tom Crean: Ice Man: The Adventures of an Antarctic Hero* (Cork, Ireland: Collins Press, 2006), 278.
22. Earlier that morning they had briefly anchored about five miles from Punta Arenas at a cold storage works in Rio Seco. When Shackleton went ashore, he was reportedly welcomed by the foreman running down the jetty shouting, "Welcome Captain Scott!" The relationship between Shackleton and Scott was notoriously icy during this period. Roland Huntford, *Shackleton* (London: Time Warner Books UK, 1996), 624.
23. Shackleton, *South*, 193.

24. Huntford, *Shackleton*, 585.
25. Shackleton, *South*, 194.
26. Huntford, *Shackleton*, 669.
27. See for example D. Smailes, E. Burdis, C. Gregoriou, B. Fenton, and R. Dudley, "Pareidolia—Proneness, Reality Discrimination Errors, and Visual Hallucination-like Experiences in a Non-clinical Sample," *Cognitive Neuropsychiatry* 25, no. 2 (2020): 113–125.
28. Shackleton, *South*, 126.
29. E.g., C. J. Dalenberg, B. L. Brand, D. H. Gleaves, M. J. Dorahy, R. J. Loewenstein, et al., "Evaluation of the Evidence for the Trauma and Fantasy Models of Dissociation," *Psychological Bulletin* 138, no. 3 (2012): 550–588.
30. Harold Begbie, *Shackleton: A Memory* (London: Mills & Boon, 1922).
31. Shackleton, *South*, 204.

3: THE DOUBLE

1. A. M. Burton and R. Jenkins, "Unfamiliar Face Perception," *Oxford Handbook of Face Perception* 28 (2011): 287–306.
2. A. Grimby, "Bereavement among Elderly People: Grief Reactions, Postbereavement Hallucinations and Quality of Life," *Acta Psychiatrica Scandinavica* 87, no. 1 (1993): 72–80.
3. The condition takes its name from Leopoldo Fregoli, an Italian actor from the 1920s and 1930s who was famous for his quick-change act.
4. John Geiger, *The Third Man Factor: Surviving the Impossible* (London: Canongate, 2009).
5. Wilder Penfield, *The Mysteries of the Mind: A Critical Study of Consciousness and the Human Brain* (Princeton, NJ: Princeton University Press, 1975): 27.
6. P. Gloor, A. Olivier, L. F. Quesney, F. Andermann, and S. Horowitz, "The Role of the Limbic System in Experiential Phenomena of Temporal Lobe Epilepsy," *Annals of Neurology* 12, no. 2 (1982): 129–144.
7. Y. Takeda, Y. Inoue, T. Tottori, and T. Mihara, "Acute Psychosis during Intracranial EEG monitoring: Close Relationship between Psychotic Symptoms and Discharges in Amygdala," *Epilepsia* 42, no. 6 (2001): 720.
8. For an example of this work, see M. Persinger et al., "The Electromagnetic Induction of Mystical and Altered States within the Laboratory," *Journal of Consciousness Exploration & Research* 1, no. 7 (2010): 808–830.
9. A.-M. Landtblom, "The 'Sensed Presence': An Epileptic Aura with Religious Overtones," *Epilepsy & Behavior* 9, no. 1 (2006): 186.
10. Ibid., 187.
11. A.-M. Landtblom, H. Lindehammar, and H. Karlsson, "Insular Cortex Activation in a Patient with 'Sensed Presence'/Ecstatic Seizures," *Epilepsy & Behavior* 20, no. 4 (2011): 714–718.
12. M. Gschwind and F. Picard, "Ecstatic Epileptic Seizures: A Glimpse into the

Multiple Roles of the Insula," *Frontiers in Behavioral Neuroscience* 17 (2016): Article 21.

13. R. Michelucci, P. Riguzzi, G. Rubboli, L. Volpi, E. Pasini, et al., "Postictal Hyperfamiliarity for Unknown Faces," *Epilepsy & Behavior* 19, no. 3 (2010): 518–521.

14. August Strindberg, *The Inferno* (New York: G. P. Putnam's Sons, Knickerbocker Press, 1913), https://www.gutenberg.org/files/44108/44108-h/44108-h.htm.

15. Sue Prideaux, *Strindberg: A Life* (New Haven, CT: Yale University Press, 2013, electronic edition), 382.

16. Karl Jaspers, Strindberg & Van Gogh, trans. O. Grunow & D. Woloshin (Tucson, AZ: University of Arizona Press, 1977).

17. P. Brugger, M. Regard, and T. Landis, "Illusory Reduplication of One's Own Body: Phenomenology and Classification of Autoscopic Phenomena," *Cognitive Neuropsychiatry* 2, no. 1 (1997): 23.

18. P. Brugger, "Hostile Interactions between Body and Self," *Dialogues in Clinical Neuroscience* 9, no. 2 (2007): 210–213.

19. Intriguingly, Fyodor Dostoevsky was also epileptic, although accounts of his auras tend to center around ecstatic experiences rather than felt presences or autoscopic phenomena. See I. Iniesta, "Epilepsy in the Process of Artistic Creation of Dostoevsky," *Neurología* (English Edition) 29, no. 6 (2014): 371–378.

20. E. Bisiach and C. Luzzatti, "Unilateral Neglect of Representational Space," *Cortex* 14, no. 1 (1978): 129–133.

21. P. Brugger, O. Blanke, M. Regard, D. T. Bradford, and T. Landis, "Polyopic Heautoscopy: Case Report and Review of the Literature," *Cortex* 42, no. 5 (2006): 669.

22. F. Picard, "Epileptic Feeling of Multiple Presences in the Frontal Space," *Cortex* 46, no. 8 (2010): 1037–1042.

4: LUKE

1. Rufus & Chaka Khan, "Ain't Nobody," track 14 on *Stompin' at the Savoy—Live*, Warner (1983).

2. Nunataks are peaks of mountains that push through the ice sheet, appearing as small hills on the landscape.

3. Kevin Macdonald, director, *Touching the Void* (Filmfour, 2007), DVD.

4. I. Pollack and J. M. Pickett, "Cocktail Party Effect," *Journal of the Acoustical Society of America* 29, no. 11 (1957): Article 1262.

5. For a review, see F. Waters, V. Chiu, A. Atkinson, and J. D. Blom, "Severe Sleep Deprivation Causes Hallucinations and a Gradual Progression toward Psychosis with Increasing Time Awake," *Frontiers in Psychiatry* 9 (2018): Article 303.

6. Huntford, *Shackleton*, 634.

7. Begbie, *Shackleton*, 11.
8. Ibid., 48.

5: THE PRESENCE ROBOT

1. S. Arzy, M. Seeck, S. Ortigue, L. Spinelli, and O. Blanke, "Induction of an Illusory Shadow Person," *Nature* 443, no. 7109 (2006): 287.
2. D. S. Margulies, S. S. Ghosh, A. Goulas, M. Falkiewicz, J. M. Huntenburg, et al., "Situating the Default-Mode Network Along a Principal Gradient of Macroscale Cortical Organization," *Proceedings of the National Academy of Sciences* 113, no. 44 (2016): 12574–12579.
3. O. Blanke, C. Mohr, C. M. Michel, A. Pascual-Leone, P. Brugger, et al., "Linking Out-of-Body Experience and Self Processing to Mental Own-Body Imagery at the Temporoparietal Junction," *Journal of Neuroscience* 25, no. 3 (2005): 550–557.
4. M. Botvinick and J. Cohen, "Rubber Hands 'Feel' Touch That Eyes See," *Nature* 391, no. 756 (1998).
5. O. Blanke, P. Pozeg, M. Hara, L. Heydrich, A. Serino, et al., "Neurological and Robot-Controlled Induction of an Apparition," *Current Biology* 24, no. 22 (2014): 2681–2686.
6. M. Costantini, "Body Perception, Awareness, and Illusions," *WIREs Cognitive Science* 5, no. 5 (2014): 551–560.
7. The procedure was evaluated across three experiments; the first did not include any direct questions about presence. Blanke and colleagues then added two specific felt presence options to choose: "I felt as if someone else was touching my body" and "I felt as if someone was standing behind my body." Along with the majority of participants reporting presence when the robot touches were delayed, no differences were observed for other suggestible statements that were included as controls (e.g., "I felt as if I had no body"). See Blanke et al., "Neurological and Robot-Controlled," 2014.
8. Blanke and colleagues have explicitly framed felt presence as a kind of passivity experience (i.e., an experience relating to a lack of control over one's own thoughts and actions), which have historically been grouped as part of Kurt Schneider's first-rank symptoms of schizophrenia.

6: "I'LL SET THE TABLE FOR THREE PEOPLE WHEN IT'S JUST ME AND MY WIFE"

1. D. Chan and M. N. Rossor, "'—But Who Is That on the Other Side of You?' Extracampine Hallucinations Revisited," *The Lancet* 360, no. 9350 (2002): 2065.
2. G. Fénelon, F. Mahieux, R. Huon, and M. Ziégler, "Hallucinations in

Parkinson's Disease: Prevalence, Phenomenology and Risk Factors," *Brain* 123, no. 4 (2000): 733–745.

3. Ibid., 735.

4. B. Ravina, K. Marder, H. H. Fernandez, J. H. Friedman, W. McDonald, et al., "Diagnostic Criteria for Psychosis in Parkinson's Disease: Report of an NINDS, NIMH Work Group," *Movement Disorders* 22, no. 8 (2007): 1061–1068.

5. G. Fénelon, T. Soulas, L. C. De Langavant, I. Trinkler, and A.-C. Bachoud-Lévi, "Feeling of Presence in Parkinson's Disease," *Journal of Neurology, Neurosurgery & Psychiatry* 82, no. 11 (2011): 1219–1224.

6. R. A. Wood, S. A. Hopkins, K. K. Moodley, and D. Chan, "Fifty Percent Prevalence of Extracampine Hallucinations in Parkinson's Disease Patients," *Frontiers in Neurology* 6 (2015): Article 263.

7. T. Pringsheim, N. Jette, A. Frolkis, and T. D. L. Steeves, "The Prevalence of Parkinson's Disease: A Systematic Review and Meta-analysis," *Movement Disorders* 29, no. 13 (2014): 1583–1590.

8. A. H. V. Schapira, M. Emre, P. Jenner, and W. J. E. J. O. N. Poewe, "Levodopa in the Treatment of Parkinson's Disease," European *Journal of Neurology* 16, no. 9 (2009): 982–989.

9. G. G. Celesia and A. N. Barr, "Psychosis and Other Psychiatric Manifestations of Levodopa Therapy," *Archives of Neurology* 23, no. 3 (1970): 193–200.

10. "Review: Frank Ormsby—*The Parkinson's Poems*," Lagan Online, October 11, 2016, http://laganonline.co/review-frank-ormsby-the-parkinsons-poems/.

11. Frank Ormsby, *The Parkinson's Poems* (Edinburgh, UK: Mariscat Press, 2016), 13.

12. Ibid., 18.

13. For a discussion of this topic, see D. Fytche, B. Creese, M. Politis, K. Chaudhuri, D. Weintraub, et al., "The Psychosis Spectrum in Parkinson Disease," *Nature Reviews Neurology* 13, no. 2 (2017): 81–95.

14. M. M. J. Linszen, G. A. Van Zanten, R. J. Teunisse, R. M. Brouwer, P. Scheltens, and I. E. Sommer, "Auditory Hallucinations in Adults with Hearing Impairment: A Large Prevalence Study," *Psychological Medicine* 49, no. 1 (2019): 132–139.

15. For a recent example, see K. Maijer, M. J. Begemann, S. J. Palmen, S. Leucht, and I. E. Sommer, "Auditory Hallucinations across the Lifespan: A Systematic Review and Meta-analysis," *Psychological Medicine* 48, no. 6 (2018): 879–888.

16. G. Schultz and R. Melzack, "The Charles Bonnet Syndrome: 'Phantom Visual Images.'" *Perception* 20, no. 6 (1991): 809.

17. This estimate is according to the Macular Society (The Macular Society, "Charles Bonnet Syndrome," accessed August 15, 2022, https://www.macularsociety.org/macular-disease/macular-conditions/charles-bonnet-syndrome/).

18. B. Alderson-Day, A. Woods, P. Moseley, S. Common, F. Deamer, et al.,

"Voice-Hearing and Personification: Characterizing Social Qualities of Auditory Verbal Hallucinations in Early Psychosis," *Schizophrenia Bulletin* 47, no. 1 (2021): 228–236.

19. Wood et al., "Fifty Percent Prevalence."

20. E. Reckner, L. Cipolotti, and J. A. Foley, "Presence Phenomena in Parkinsonian Disorders: Phenomenology and Neuropsychological Correlates," *International Journal of Geriatric Psychiatry* 35, no. 7 (2020): 785–793.

21. Ibid., 798.

22. *Executive function* refers to tricky tests that require you to plan ahead, hold information in mind temporarily, and control impulses.

23. S. Schneider Williams, "The Terrorist Inside My Husband's Brain," *Neurology* 87, no. 13 (2016): 1308–1311.

24. *Lewy body disease* or *Lewy body dementia* are terms used to refer to DLB and Parkinson's disease dementia (PDD) collectively. DLB is used specifically for when symptoms of dementia have a rapid onset prior to signs of Parkinsonism, whereas the order of symptoms is reversed in PDD.

25. Schneider Williams, "The Terrorist," 1310.

26. John Matthias, "Living with a Visionary," *New Yorker*, January 25, 2021, https://www.newyorker.com/magazine/2021/02/01/living-with-a-visionary.

27. H. Y. Meltzer, R. Mills, S. Revell, H. Williams, A. Johnson, et al., "Pimavanserin, a Serotonin2A Receptor Inverse Agonist, for the Treatment of Parkinson's Disease Psychosis," *Neuropsychopharmacology* 35, no. 4 (2010): 881–892.

28. J. Cummings, S. Isaacson, R. Mills, H. Williams, K. Chi-Burris, et al., "Pimavanserin for Patients with Parkinson's Disease Psychosis: A Randomised, Placebo-Controlled Phase 3 Trial," *The Lancet* 383, no. 9916 (2014): 533–540.

29. K. Y. Liu and R. Howard, "Pimavanserin and Dementia-Related Psychosis: Can HARMONY Prevail?" *The Lancet Neurology* 20, no. 10 (2021): 783–784.

30. Parkinson's UK, "Further Evidence on the Benefits of Pimavanserin," September 25, 2017, https://www.parkinsons.org.uk/news/further-evidence -benefits-pimavanserin.

31. For an example of this, see C. G. Goetz, C. L. Vaughan, J. G. Goldman, and G. T. Stebbins, "I Finally See What You See: Parkinson's Disease Visual Hallucinations Captured with Functional Neuroimaging," *Movement Disorders* 29, no. 1 (2014): 115–117.

32. A. Zarkali, R. A. Adams, S. Psarras, L.-A. Leyland, G. Rees, and R. S. Weil, "Increased Weighting on Prior Knowledge in Lewy Body-Associated Visual Hallucinations," *Brain Communications* 1, no. 1 (2019): Article fcz007.

33. https://psychology.fandom.com/wiki/Gestalt_psychology.

34. For overviews of this idea, see Andy Clark, *Surfing uncertainty: Prediction, action, and the embodied mind* (Oxford, UK: Oxford University Press, 2015), or Jakob Hohwy, *The Predictive Mind* (Oxford, UK: Oxford University Press, 2013).

35. Anil Seth. 2017. "Your brain hallucinates your conscious reality." Filmed July 2017. TED video, 17:00. https://www.youtube.com/watch?v=lyu7v7nWzfo.

36. C. Teufel, N. Subramaniam, V. Dobler, J. Perez, J. Finnemann, et al., "Shift toward Prior Knowledge Confers a Perceptual Advantage in Early Psychosis and Psychosis-Prone Healthy Individuals," *Proceedings of the National Academy of Sciences* 112, no. 43 (2015): 13401–13406.

7: THE WALNUT OF REALITY

1. M. Dudoignon, R. Jardri, P. Basset, and R. Hurdiel, "Acute Sleep Deprivation and Hallucinations in Ultra-Endurance Runners: A Descriptive Analysis During the Ultra-Trail du Mont-Blanc," *International Journal of Sports Physiology and Performance* 11 (2016): S1–5.
2. T. Reilly and T. J. Walsh, "Physiological, Psychological and Performance Measures during an Endurance Record for Five-a-Side Soccer," *British Journal of Sports Medicine* 15, no. 2 (1981): 122–128.
3. B. Alderson-Day, P. Moseley, K. Mitrenga, J. Moffatt, R. Lee, et al., "Varieties of Felt Presence? Three Surveys of Presence Phenomena and Their Relations to Psychopathology," *Psych Medicine* (2022): 1–9.
4. This quote was collected as part of the survey reported on in Ben Alderson-Day, Peter Moseley, Kaja Mitrenga, Jamie Moffatt, Rebecca Lee, John Foxwell, Jacqueline Hayes, David Smailes, and Charles Fernyhough's "Varieties of felt presence? Three surveys of presence phenomena and their relations to psychopathology." *Psych Medicine* (2022): 1–9.
5. This type of experience is sometimes referred to as *hallucinosis*, when one is aware that they are hallucinating.
6. Mihaly Csikszentmihalyi, *Beyond Boredom and Anxiety* (San Francisco, CA: Jossey-Bass Publishers, 1975).
7. For a discussion of such experiences see Maria Coffey, *Explorers of the Infinite: The Secret Spiritual Lives of Extreme Athletes—And What They Reveal about Near-Death Experiences, Psychic Communication, and Touching the Beyond* (London: Penguin, 2008).
8. L. Feldman Barrett, *How Emotions Are Made: The Secret Life of the Brain* (New York: Houghton Mifflin Harcourt, 2017).

8: THE MARATHON MONK OF BILLINGHAM

1. The monks reportedly tend not to speak of their experiences during the runs, although an aim of the activity is to become one with Fudo Myo-o, the "Unshakable King of Light," an incarnation of Buddha Dainichi. According to John Stevens, author of *The Marathon Monks of Mount Hiei* (Brattleboro, VT: Echo Point Books and Media, 1988), this is associated with directly perceiving Fudo as a "living force" whose energy can be drawn upon during the run. Only those who have had the experience recognize it in others who

have also run: "You have seen him, haven't you? Now you have the look of a real marathon monk!" (Ibid., 95).

2. M. G. Carbone, G. Pagni, M. Maiello, C. Tagliarini, L. Pratali, et al., "Misperceptions and Hallucinatory Experiences in Ultra-Trailer, High-Altitude Runners," *Rivista di Psichiatria* 55, no. 3 (2020): 186.

3. Paul Burgum, *Jumping the Cliff to Simply Be: A Solo Walk Across Italy* (Stockton, UK: Sixth Element Publishing, 2016), 59.

4. For a discussion of this issue, see P. Lamont, "Spiritualism and a Mid-Victorian Crisis of Evidence," *Historical Journal* 47, no. 4 (2004): 897–920.

5. Ibid., 58.

6. e.g. M. P. Buman, J. W. Omli, P. R. Giacobbi, Jr., and B. W. Brewer, "Experiences and Coping Responses of 'Hitting the Wall' for Recreational Marathon Runners," *Journal of Applied Sport Psychology* 20, no. 3 (2008): 282–300. "Sometimes I focus on a runner near me or ahead of me and hope that that runner can pull me through. I don't think these strategies really get you through the wall—when it's there it's there to stay—but it does help you keep up a faster pace than if you continue to think about how miserable you feel, in which case you will just keep going slower and slower" (ibid., 292).

9: SEEING DARKNESS

1. J. M. Pearce, "Clinical Features of the Exploding Head Syndrome," *Journal of Neurology, Neurosurgery & Psychiatry* 52, no. 7 (1989): 907–910.

2. F. Waters, J. D. Blom, T. T. Dang-Vu, A. J. Cheyne, B. Alderson-Day, et al., "What Is the Link between Hallucinations, Dreams, and Hypnagogic–Hypnopompic Experiences?" *Schizophrenia Bulletin*, 42, no. 5 (2016): 1098–1109.

3. B. A. Sharpless, "Exploding Head Syndrome," *Sleep Medicine Reviews* 18, no. 6 (2014): 489–493.

4. Waters et al., "What Is the Link."

5. B. A. Sharpless and J. P. Barber, "Lifetime Prevalence Rates of Sleep Paralysis: A Systematic Review," *Sleep Medicine Reviews* 15, no. 5 (2011): 311–115.

6. W. Dement and N. Kleitman, "Cyclic Variations in EEG during Sleep and Their Relation to Eye Movements, Body Motility, and Dreaming," *Electroencephalography and Clinical Neurophysiology* 9 (1957): 673–690.

7. F. Siclari, B. Baird, L. Perogamvros, G. Bernardi, J. J. LaRocque, et al., "The Neural Correlates of Dreaming," *Nature Neuroscience* 20, no. 6 (2017): 872–878.

8. Y. Nir and G. Tononi, "Dreaming and the Brain from Phenomenology to Neurophysiology," *Trends in Cognitive Sciences* 14, no. 2 (2010): 88–100.

9. Herman Melville, *Moby-Dick* (London, Penguin: 2003), 29.

10. Alderson-Day et al., "Varieties of Felt Presence?"

11. For reviews of the topic, see J. A. Cheyne, "The Ominous Numinous," *Journal of Consciousness Studies* 8, nos. 5–7 (2001): 133–150, and Shelley R. Adler,

Sleep Paralysis: Night-mares, Nocebos, and the Mind-Body Connection (New Brunswick, NJ: Rutgers University Press, 2011).

12. M. R. Pressman, "Factors That Predispose, Prime and Precipitate NREM Parasomnias in Adults: Clinical and Forensic Implications," *Sleep Medicine Reviews* 11, no. 1 (2007): 5–30.

13. I. Arnulf, "Sleepwalking," *Current Biology* 28, no. 22 (2018): R1288–R1289.

14. O. F. Aina and O. O. Famuyiwa, "Ogun Oru: A Traditional Explanation for Nocturnal Neuropsychiatric Disturbances among the Yoruba of Southwest Nigeria," *Transcultural Psychiatry* 44, no. 1 (2007): 44–54.

15. J. F. R. De Sa and S. A. Mota-Rolim, "Sleep Paralysis in Brazilian Folklore and Other Cultures: A Brief Review," *Frontiers in Psychology* 7 (2016): Article 1294.

16. Adler, *Sleep Paralysis*, 100.

17. Ibid., 101.

18. B. Jalal and V. S. Ramachandran, "Sleep Paralysis and 'the Bedroom Intruder': The Role of the Right Superior Parietal, Phantom Pain and Body Image Projection," *Medical Hypotheses* 83, no. 6 (2014): 755–757.

19. G. D. Shukla, S. C. Sahu, R. P. Tripathi, and D. K. Gupta, "Phantom Limb: A Phenomenological Study," *British Journal of Psychiatry* 141, no. 1 (1982): 54–58.

20. C. Marchetti and S. Della Sala, "Disentangling the Alien and Anarchic Hand," *Cognitive Neuropsychiatry* 3, no. 3 (1998): 191–207.

21. J. A. Cheyne, S. D. Rueffer, and I. R. Newby-Clark, "Hypnagogic and Hypnopompic Hallucinations during Sleep Paralysis: Neurological and Cultural Construction of the Night-mare," *Consciousness and Cognition* 8, no. 3 (1999): 319–337.

22. J. A. Cheyne and T. A. Girard, "Paranoid Delusions and Threatening Hallucinations: A Prospective Study of Sleep Paralysis Experiences," *Consciousness and Cognition* 16, no. 4 (2007): 959–974.

23. D. Denis, "Relationships between Sleep Paralysis and Sleep Quality: Current Insights," *Nature and Science of Sleep* 10 (2018): 355–367.

24. Cheyne and Girard, "Paranoid Delusions," 961.

25. It has even been proposed that intrusions from REM into waking states could explain hallucinations during daytime, although the evidence from phenomenology and brain imaging studies suggests that they probably rely on different underlying processes. See Waters et al., "What Is the Link."

26. See, for example, S. Guthrie, J. Agassi, K. R. Andriolo, D. Buchdahl, H. B. Earhart, et al., "A Cognitive Theory of Religion [and comments and reply]," *Current Anthropology* 21, no. 2 (1980): 181–203; and J. L. Barrett, "Exploring the Natural Foundations of Religion," *Trends in Cognitive Sciences* 4, no. 1 (2000): 29–34.

27. Alderson-Day et al., "Varieties of Felt Presence?"

28. In fact, the idea that presence is about being watched has been one of the hypotheses put forward for presences more generally. A sense of anxiety, a

chill in one's spine, a heightened sense of awareness—being watched often seems to put us in the kind of bodily state that presences proliferate in. The psychologist Rupert Sheldrake has argued that we might have a capacity to tell when people are watching us. It isn't generally accepted that there is empirical evidence for this phenomenon, but it isn't hard to see why some people would seek to link the experience to felt presence. See for example R. Sheldrake, "The Sense of Being Stared At—Part 1: Is It Real or Illusory?" *Journal of Consciousness Studies* 12, no. 6 (2005): 10–31.

29. Cheyne, "The Ominous Numinous."

30. T. Nielsen, "Felt Presence: Paranoid Delusion or Hallucinatory Social Imagery?" *Consciousness and Cognition* 16, no. 4, (2007): 975–983.

31. The project website can be found at www.thresholdworlds.org.

32. For a recent example see S. Reeve, B. Sheaves, and D. Freeman, "Sleep Disorders in Early Psychosis: Incidence, Severity, and Association with Clinical Symptoms," *Schizophrenia Bulletin* 45, no. 2 (2019): 287–295. For a review, see D. Denis, C. C. French, and A. M. Gregory, "A Systematic Review of Variables Associated with Sleep Paralysis," *Sleep Medicine Reviews* 38 (2018): 141–157.

33. About a week later, Tore wrote to me to add a key detail: "I thought that I had mentioned what I always thought the source of this dream was. If not, here it is. This dream occurred a week or so prior to my PhD oral defense exam. I was quite intimidated by (fearful of) the thought of that exam. And I have always thought that the devil in my dream and my subsequent paralysis and fear was a representation of that fear of the upcoming unknown. Note that others have written about 'oral defense dreams.' The fear of public speaking is such a common phobia that it makes sense that it would underlie many nightmares."

34. George Gaylord Simpson, *The Principles of Classification and a Classification of Mammals* (Bulletin of the American Museum of Natural History no. 85, New York: American Museum of Natural History, 1945).

35. M. Allen, D. Frank, D. S. Schwarzkopf, F. Fardo, J. S. Winston, et al., "Unexpected Arousal Modulates the Influence of Sensory Noise on Confidence," *Elife* 5 (2016): Article e18103.

10: SPIRIT

1. J. Van Os, M. Hanssen, R. V. Bijl, and A. Ravelli, "Strauss (1969) Revisited: A Psychosis Continuum in the General Population?" *Schizophrenia Research* 45, nos. 1–2 (2000): 11–20.

2. American Psychiatric Association, *Diagnostic and Statistical Manual of Mental Disorders* (DSM-5; Arlington, VA: American Psychiatric Association, 2013).

3. See, for example, the 2014 report by the British Psychological Society's Division of Clinical Psychology, *Understanding Psychosis and Schizophrenia* (ed. A. Cooke). Available from https://www.bps.org.uk/what-psychology /understanding-psychosis-and-schizophrenia.

4. E.g., A. S. David, "Why We Need More Debate on Whether Psychotic Symptoms Lie on a Continuum with Normality," *Psychological Medicine* 40, no. 12 (2010): 1935–1942, and S. M. Lawrie, J. Hall, A. M. McIntosh, D. G. Owens, and E. C. Johnstone, "The 'Continuum of Psychosis': Scientifically Unproven and Clinically Impractical," *The British Journal of Psychiatry* 197, no. 6 (2010): 423–425.

5. A. Woods, "The Voice-Hearer," *Journal of Mental Health* 22, no. 3 (2013): 263–270.

6. It is a matter of debate how such groups of people are best referred to, with no one term lacking flaws. People who experience voices without needing mental health support have variously been described as "healthy," "nonclinical," "nonpsychotic," and "without need for care."

7. I. E. C. Sommer, K. Daalman, T. Rietkerk, K. M. Diederen, S. Bakker, et al., "Healthy Individuals with Auditory Verbal Hallucinations; Who Are They? Psychiatric Assessments of a Selected Sample of 103 Subjects," *Schizophrenia Bulletin* 36, no. 3 (2010): 633–641.

8. K. M. J. Diederen, K. Daalman, A. D. de Weijer, S. F. W. Neggers, W. van Gastel, et al., "Auditory Hallucinations Elicit Similar Brain Activation in Psychotic and Nonpsychotic Individuals," *Schizophrenia Bulletin* 38, no. 5 (2012): 1074–1082.

9. K. Daalman, S. Verkooijen, E. M. Derks, A. Aleman, and I. E. C. Sommer, "The Influence of Semantic Top-Down Processing in Auditory Verbal Hallucinations," *Schizophrenia Research* 139, no. 1–3 (2012): 82–86.

10. B. Alderson-Day, C. F. Lima, S. Evans, S. Krishnan, and P. Shanmugalingam, "Distinct Processing of Ambiguous Speech in People with Non-clinical Auditory Verbal Hallucinations," *Brain*, 140, no. 9 (2017): 2475–2489.

11. A brain imaging study conducted a few years before our scanned seven people in Bangor, while a group led by Phil Corlett and Al Powers at Yale managed to find nearly twenty to take part in their research. To this day, the Utrecht cohort remains a significant outlier.

12. It also listed a range of notable luminaries and thinkers as its corresponding members, including William James, Pierre Janet, and Hippolyte Taine.

13. Rolleston, Thomas Williams. "Some Recent Results of Psychical Research." *The Irish Church Quarterly* 2, no. 5 (1909): 42. https://doi.org/10.2307/30067577.

14. Edmund Gurney, Frederic William Henry Myers, and Frank Podmore, *Phantasms of the Living* (Cambridge, UK: Cambridge University Press, 1886, reprint 2011), x.

15. Ibid., 483.

16. "Probably the common view of hallucinations of the sane, so far as they are recognised at all, is that they are in all cases due to disease or morbid excitement, or at the very least to indigestion. Ask the first twenty rational men you meet how they would account for a phantasmal visitant if they themselves

saw one: as many as ten perhaps will answer, 'I should conclude that I had dined or supped too well.' 'Lobster-salad' is an explanation which I have personally heard suggested many times. It may be at once noted, then, as a point of interest—one, moreover, in which the casual and the telepathic classes completely agree—that in not a single instance known to me has the hallucinated in person, according to his own account, been suffering at the time from indigestion. Lobster-salad is the parent of nightmares, of massive impressions of discomfort and horror; not, however, as a rule, even in dream-land, of the distinct and minute visualisation, and the clear-cut audition, which constitute the more specific hallucinations of sleep; and certainly not of waking hallucinations." Ibid., 497.

17. E. Gurney, "A Census of Hallucinations," *Science*, 103 (1885): 65.

18. T. R. Dening, "Report on the Census of Hallucinations. Chapter XII: Death Coincidences," *History of Psychiatry* 5, no. 19 (1994): 407.

19. H. Sidgwick, "Report on the Census of Hallucinations," *Proceedings of the Society for Psychical Research* 10 (1894): 411–412.

20. For an extensive account of this story, see Christopher Josiffe, *Gef! The Strange Tale of an Extra-Special Talking Mongoose* (Cambridge, MA: MIT Press, 2017).

21. R. Morris, *Harry Price: Psychic Detective* (Stroud, UK: Sutton Publishing, 2006).

22. R. Gill, C. K. Hadaway, and P. Long Marler, "Is Religious Belief Declining in Britain?" *Journal for the Scientific Study of Religion* 37, no. 3 (1998): 507–516.

23. K. Stengaard Kamp, E. M. Steffen, B. Alderson-Day, P. Allen, A. Austad, et al., "Sensory and Quasi-sensory Experiences of the Deceased in Bereavement: An Interdisciplinary and Integrative Review," *Schizophrenia Bulletin* 46, no. 6 (2020): 1367–1381.

24. E. Steffen and A. Coyle, "Sense of Presence Experiences and Meaning-Making in Bereavement: A Qualitative Analysis," *Death Studies* 35, no. 7 (2011): 587, 588.

25. J. Hayes and I. Leudar, "Experiences of Continued Presence: On the Practical Consequences of 'Hallucinations' in Bereavement," *Psychology and Psychotherapy* 89 no. 2, (2016): 194–210.

26. In response to Chan and Rossor's 2002 *Lancet* essay (see chapter 6), the Israeli doctor Avi Ohry wrote of being visited by his wife and best friend when in jail for five weeks in Egypt, only for his visitors to disappear when the guards arrived (A. Ohry, "Extracampine Hallucinations," *The Lancet* 361 [2002]: 1479–1479).

27. There is a form of therapy practiced by a small minority in the UK known as "spirit release" therapy, in which an unwanted presence is made to move on from visiting a person. See, e.g., A. Powell, "The Contribution of Spirit Release Therapy to Mental Health," *Light* 126 (2006): 10–16.

28. A famous Swedish study reported felt presences in over half of a sample of fifty older adults (Grimby, "Bereavement among Elderly People"). However,

problems of selection bias and reluctance to report such experiences makes estimating their prevalence highly challenging.

29. P. Moseley, A. Powell, A. Woods, C. Fernyhough, and B. Alderson-Day, "Voice-Hearing across the Continuum: A Phenomenology of Spiritual Voices," *Schizophrenia Bulletin* 48, no. 5 (2022): 1066–1074.

30. Hearing the Voice, 2021. *The Hearing the Voice Spiritual Voices Interviews*, Durham University, unpublished.

    i. "I guess it's just like if someone's standing close to you . . ." is from Interview 19: 9.

    ii. "I've had some quite distinct experiences like that . . ." is from Interview 10: 9.

    iii. "Just a feeling that you're accompanied by an essence . . ." is from Interview 16: 9.

    iv. "The very starting point is I'll usually just feel the presence . . ." is from Interview 4: 9.

    v. "I think when it very first started, if I'm honest, was a bereavement . . ." is also from Interview 4; 11.

    vi. "I teach students how to be more focused . . ." is from Interview 25: 21.

31. A. J. Powell and P. Moseley, "When Spirits Speak: Absorption, Attribution, and Identity among Spiritualists Who Report 'Clairaudient' Voice Experiences," *Mental Health, Religion & Culture* 23, no. 10 (2020): 841–856.

32. A. R. Powers, C. Mathys, and P. R. Corlett, "Pavlovian Conditioning–Induced Hallucinations Result from Overweighting of Perceptual Priors," *Science* 357, no. 6351 (2017): 596–600.

33. T. M. Luhrmann, K. Weisman, F. Aulino, J. D. Brahinsky, J. C. Dulin, et al., "Sensing the Presence of Gods and Spirits across Cultures and Faiths," *Proceedings of the National Academy of Sciences* 118, no. 5 (2021): Article e2016649118.

34. Center for Mind and Culture, "Hardy Religious and Spiritual Experience Project," accessed on August 19 2022, https://mindandculture.org /projects/quantifying-identities-and-ideologies/hardy-religious-and-spiritual -experience-project/.

35. A. Zeman, M. Dewar, and S. Della Sala, "Reflections on Aphantasia," *Cortex* 74 (2016): 336–337.

36. Luhrmann et al., "Sensing the Presence."

37. See, for example, C. S. Humpston and M. R. Broome, "The Spectra of Soundless Voices and Audible Thoughts: Towards an Integrative Model of Auditory Verbal Hallucinations and Thought Insertion," *Review of Philosophy and Psychology* 7, no. 3 (2016): 611–629.

38. T. M. Luhrmann, R. Padmavati, H. Tharoor, and A. Osei, "Differences in Voice-Hearing Experiences of People with Psychosis in the USA, India and Ghana: Interview-Based Study," *The British Journal of Psychiatry* 206, no. 1 (2015): 41–44.

11: IN TWO MINDS

1. For an example, see Huffington Post, "Reading Is Just like Looking at a Dead Piece of Wood for Hours and Hallucinating," January 19, 2018, https://www .huffingtonpost.co.uk/entry/reddit-shower-thoughts-january-2018-part-3_n _5a61cdf3e4b074ce7a0743f2.

2. For a fascinating piece on the presence of Bertha Mason in Charlotte Brontë's *Jane Eyre*, see Akiko Hart, "'Then I Open the Door and Walk into Their World': Crossing the Threshold and Hearing the Voice," in *Voices in Psychosis: Interdisciplinary Perspectives*, ed. A. Woods, B. Alderson-Day, and C. Fernyhough (Oxford, UK: Oxford University Press, 2022).

3. E. Semino, "Mind Style 25 Years On," *Style*, 41, no. 2 (2007): 153–173.

4. Ibid., 103.

5. Ibid., 105.

6. A. B. O. de Gortari, K. Aronsson, and M. Griffiths, "Game Transfer Phenomena in Video Game Playing: A Qualitative Interview Study," *International Journal of Cyber Behavior, Psychology and Learning (IJCBPL)* 1, no. 3 (2011): 15–33. For an example of the *Tetris* effect, see R. Stickgold, A. Malia, D. Maguire, D. Roddenberry, and M. O'Connor, "Replaying the Game: Hypnagogic Images in Normals and Amnesics," *Science* 290, no. 5490 (2000): 350–353.

7. Nathan Thompson, "The Internet's Newest Subculture Is All About Creating Imaginary Friends," *Vice*, September 3, 2014, https://www.vice.com/en /article/exmqzz/tulpamancy-internet-subculture-892.

8. See, e.g., N. L. Mikles and J. P. Laycock, "Tracking the Tulpa: Exploring the 'Tibetan' Origins of a Contemporary Paranormal Idea," *Nova Religio: The Journal of Alternative and Emergent Religions* 19, no. 1 (2015): 87–97.

9. "Making Friends," *Reply All*, #74, August 24, 2016, https://gimletmedia.com /shows/reply-all/49hr6k.

10. Tulpa.info, "What is a tulpa?" accessed January 30, 2022, https://www.tulpa .info/what-is-a-tulpa/.

11. Samuel Veissière, "Varieties of Tulpa Experiences: The Hypnotic Nature of Human Sociality, Personhood, and Interphenomenality," in *Hypnosis and meditation: Towards an Integrative Science of Conscious Planes*, ed. A. Raz & M. Lifshitz (Oxford, UK: Oxford University Press, 2016).

12. Ibid., 61.

13. D. Horton and R. R. Wohl, "Mass Communication and Para-social Interaction: Observations on Intimacy at a Distance," *Psychiatry* 19, no. 3 (1956): 215.

14. A. Tellegen and G. Atkinson, "Openness to Absorbing and Self-Altering Experiences ('Absorption'), a Trait Related to Hypnotic Susceptibility," *Journal of Abnormal Psychology* 83, no. 3 (1974): 268–277.

15. Veissière, "Varieties of Tulpa Experiences," 71.

16. Ibid., 68.

17. J. Foxwell, B. Alderson-Day, C. Fernyhough, and A. Woods, "'I've Learned I

Need to Treat My Characters like People': Varieties of Agency and Interaction in Writers' Experiences of Their Characters' Voices," *Consciousness and Cognition* 79 (2020): Article 102901.

18. Peter Garratt, "Hearing Voices Allowed Charles Dickens to Create Extraordinary Fictional Worlds," *The Guardian*, August 22, 2014, https://www.theguardian.com/books/2014/aug/22/charles-dickens-hearing-voices-created-his-novels.

19. Philip Pullman, *Daemon Voices: Essays on Storytelling* (Oxford, UK: David Fickling, 2017), 39.

20. For a discussion of this idea, see J. J. Isler, "Tulpas and Mental Health: A Study of Non-Traumagenic Plural Experiences," *Research in Psychology and Behavioral Sciences* 5, no. 2 (2017): 36–44.

21. E. Palmer-Cooper, N. McGuire, and A. Wright, "Unusual Experiences and Their Association with Metacognition: Investigating ASMR and Tulpamancy," *Cognitive Neuropsychiatry* 27, no. 2–3 (2022): 86–104.

22. For a recent review see A. Armah and M. Landers-Potts, "A Review of Imaginary Companions and Their Implications for Development," *Imagination, Cognition and Personality* 41, no. 1 (2021): 31–53.

23. For reviews that cover this question, see D. Pearson, H. Rouse, S. Doswell, C. Ainsworth, O. Dawson, et al., "Prevalence of Imaginary Companions in a Normal Child Population," *Child: Care, Health and Development* 27, no. 1 (2001): 13–22; and R. Jardri, A. A. Bartels-Velthuis, M. Debbané, J. A. Jenner, I. Kelleher, et al., "From Phenomenology to Neurophysiological Understanding of Hallucinations in Children and Adolescents," *Schizophrenia Bulletin* 40, no. Suppl_4 (2014): S221–S232.

24. Armah and Landers-Potts, "A Review of Imaginary Companions."

25. M. Taylor, S. D. Hodges, and A. Kohányi, "The Illusion of Independent Agency: Do Adult Fiction Writers Experience Their Characters as Having Minds of Their Own?" *Imagination, Cognition and Personality* 22, no. 4 (2003): 361–380.

26. C. Fernyhough, A. Watson, M. Bernini, P. Moseley, and B. Alderson-Day, "Imaginary Companions, Inner Speech, and Auditory Verbal Hallucinations: What Are the Relations?" *Frontiers in Psychology* 10 (2019): Article 1665.

27. Perceptual bias on signal detection tasks for people with hallucinations was first reported by Richard Bentall and Peter D. Slade. ("Reality testing and auditory hallucinations: a signal detection analysis." *British Journal of Clinical Psychology* 24, no. 3 (1985): 159–169) and has since been replicated in a number of studies. We have observed similar patterns in spiritualists who hear voices (P. Moseley, B. Alderson-Day, S. Common, G. Dodgson, R. Lee, et al., "Continuities and Discontinuities in the Cognitive Mechanisms Associated with Clinical and Nonclinical Auditory Verbal Hallucinations," *Clinical Psychological Science* 10, no. 4 (2022): 752–766).

28. For examples of this kind of view, see Bernard Baars's "How Brain Reveals Mind: Neural Studies Support the Fundamental Role of Conscious Experience," *Journal of Consciousness Studies* 10, no. 9–10 (2003): 100–114.

29. Apparently, this tweet was prompted by a 2011 blog post for *Psychology Today* on variations in inner speaking by the Nevada psychologist Russ Hurlburt. Russell T. Hurlburt, "Not Everyone Conducts Inner Speech," *Psychology Today*, October 26, 2011, https://www.psychologytoday.com /gb/blog/pristine-inner-experience/201110/not-everyone-conducts-inner -speech.

30. A. Morin, "Possible Links between Self-awareness and Inner Speech: Theoretical Background, Underlying Mechanisms, and Empirical Evidence," *Journal of Consciousness Studies* 12, no. 4–5 (2005): 115–134.

31. S. McCarthy-Jones and C. Fernyhough, "The Varieties of Inner Speech: Links between Quality of Inner Speech and Psychopathological Variables in a Sample of Young Adults," *Consciousness and Cognition* 20, no. 4 (2011): 1586–1593.

32. Lev S. Vygotsky, *Thought and Language* (1934. Reprint Cambridge, MA: MIT Press, 2012).

33. B. Alderson-Day and C. Fernyhough, "Inner Speech: Development, Cognitive Functions, Phenomenology, and Neurobiology," *Psychological Bulletin* 141, no. 5 (2015): 931–965.

34. R. Keogh, M. Wicken, and J. Pearson, "Visual Working Memory in Aphantasia: Retained Accuracy and Capacity with a Different Strategy," *Cortex* 143 (2021): 237–253.

35. The role of emotion also invites further parallels with intense relationships, including those of the one-sided variety. Many of us have had a time in our lives when we can't get someone out of our head—and sometimes, this might border on something like a constant feeling of their presence. This kind of experience was noted by William James in his own discussion of presence: "A lover has notoriously the sense of the continuous being of his idol, even when his attention is addressed to other matters and he no longer represents her features. He cannot forget her; she uninterruptedly affects him *through and through*" (italics mine). William James, *The Varieties of Religious Experience* (1904. Reprint Oxford, UK: Oxford University Press, 2012), 62.

36. Someone trained to deliver therapy of the kind developed by people like Sigmund Freud, Carl Jung, and Melanie Klein.

37. E.g., S. M. Andersen and S. Chen, "The Relational Self: An Interpersonal Social-Cognitive Theory," *Psychological Review* 109, no. 4 (2002): 619; H. J. Hermans, "The Dialogical Self as a Society of Mind: Introduction," *Theory & psychology* 12, no. 2 (2002): 147–160.

38. Pullman, *Daemon Voices*, 310.

12: YOU NEVER ASKED

1. J. N. Bailenson, "Nonverbal Overload: A Theoretical Argument for the Causes of Zoom Fatigue," *Technology, Mind, and Behavior* 2, no. 1 (2021).
2. In fact, there is a whole journal on it, appropriately called *Presence*.
3. This concept is also used to refer to one's own sense of presence in the context of psychosis. See, for example, B. Nelson, A. Fornito, B. J. Harrison, M. Yücel, L. A. Sass, et al., "A Disturbed Sense of Self in the Psychosis Prodrome: Linking Phenomenology and Neurobiology," *Neuroscience & Biobehavioral Reviews* 33, no. 6 (2009): 807–817.
4. S. Milgram, "Behavioral Study of Obedience," *Journal of Abnormal and Social Psychology* 67, no. 4 (1963): 371–378.
5. Mel Slater, "The Concept of Presence and Its Measurement," PEACH Summer School, Santorini, Greece, July 2007, https://www.cs.upc.edu/~melslater/PEACH/presence-notes-melslater.pdf.
6. Olaf Blanke et al., "Neurological and Robot-Controlled Induction."
7. B. O. Rothbaum, L. F. Hodges, R. Kooper, D. Opdyke, J. S. Williford, and M. North, "Virtual Reality Graded Exposure in the Treatment of Acrophobia: A Case Report," *Behavior Therapy* 26, no. 3 (1995): 547–554.
8. See, for example, J. Böhnlein, L. Altegoer, N. K. Muck, K. Roesmann, R. Redlich, et al., "Factors Influencing the Success of Exposure Therapy for Specific Phobia: A Systematic Review," *Neuroscience & Biobehavioral Reviews* 108 (2020): 796–820.
9. For an example of this method, see D. Freeman, K. Pugh, A. Antley, M. Slater, P. Bebbington, et al., "Virtual Reality Study of Paranoid Thinking in the General Population," *The British Journal of Psychiatry* 192, no. 4 (2008): 258–263.
10. J. Leff, G. Williams, M. A. Huckvale, M. Arbuthnot, and A. P. Leff, "Computer-Assisted Therapy for Medication-Resistant Auditory Hallucinations: Proof-of-Concept Study," *The British Journal of Psychiatry* 202, no. 6 (2013): 428–433.
11. J. Leff, G. Williams, M. Huckvale, M. Arbuthnot, and A. P. Leff, "Avatar Therapy for Persecutory Auditory Hallucinations: What Is It and How Does It Work?" *Psychosis* 6, no. 2 (2014): 166–176.
12. T. K. J. Craig, M. Rus-Calafell, T. Ward, J. P. Leff, M. Huckvale, et al., "AVATAR Therapy for Auditory Verbal Hallucinations in People with Psychosis: A Single-Blind, Randomised Controlled Trial," *The Lancet Psychiatry* 5, no. 1 (2018): 31–40.
13. M. Rus-Calafell, T. Ward, X. C. Zhang, C. J. Edwards, P. Garety, and T. Craig, "The Role of Sense of Voice Presence and Anxiety Reduction in AVATAR Therapy," *Journal of Clinical Medicine* 9, no. 9 (2020): Article 2748.
14. P. Garety, C. J. Edwards, T. Ward, R. Emsley, M. Huckvale, et al., "Optimising AVATAR Therapy for People Who Hear Distressing Voices: Study Proto-

col for the AVATAR2 Multi-centre Randomised Controlled Trial," *Trials* 22, no. 1 (2021): 1–17.

15. The idea that mind and body consist of fundamentally different substances—mind-body dualism—is typically attributed to French philosopher René Descartes.

16. R. Salomon, P. Progin, A. Griffa, G. Rognini, K. Q. Do, et al., "Sensorimotor Induction of Auditory Misattribution in Early Psychosis," *Schizophrenia Bulletin*, 46, no. 4 (2020): 947–954.

17. P. Orepic, G. Rognini, O. A. Kannape, N. Faivre, and O. Blanke, "Sensorimotor Conflicts Induce Somatic Passivity and Louden Quiet Voices in Healthy Listeners," *Schizophrenia Research* 231 (2021): 170–177.

18. Arthur Kleinman, *The Illness Narratives: Suffering, Healing, and the Human Condition* (New York: Basic Books, 1988), 3.

19. Botvinick and Cohen, "Rubber Hands 'Feel' Touch," 756.

20. Ed Yong, "Man with Schizophrenia Has Out-of-Body Experience in Lab, Gains Knowledge, Controls His Psychosis," *Discover*, October 31, 2011, https://www.discovermagazine.com/mind/man-with-schizophrenia-has-out-of-body-experience-in-lab-gains-knowledge-controls-his-psychosis.

21. H.-S. Lee, S.-J. J. Hong, T. Baxter, J. Scott, S. Shenoy, et al., "Altered Peripersonal Space and the Bodily Self in Schizophrenia: A Virtual Reality Study," *Schizophrenia Bulletin* 47, no. 4 (2021): 927–937.

22. L. Nummenmaa, E. Glerean, R. Hari, and J. K. Hietanen, "Bodily Maps of Emotions," *Proceedings of the National Academy of Sciences* 111, no. 2 (2014): 646–651.

23. L. J. Torregrossa, M. A. Snodgress, S. J. Hong, H. S. Nichols, E. Glerean, et al., "Anomalous Bodily Maps of Emotions in Schizophrenia," *Schizophrenia Bulletin* 45, no. 5 (2019): 1060–1067.

24. Shannon Pagdon and Nev Jones, *Psychosis Outside the Box* v1. (2020), https://rethinkpsychosis.weebly.com/uploads/1/1/0/1/110120995/lowerresoutsidetheboxv1.pdf.

25. Ibid., 13.

INDEX